C++: COMPONENTS AND ALGORITHMS

THIRD EDITION

Scott Robert Ladd

C++: COMPONENTS AND ALGORITHMS

THIRD EDITION

Scott Robert Ladd

M&T Books
A Division of MIS:Press, Inc.
A Subsidiary of Henry Holt and Company, Inc.
115 West 18th Street
New York, New York 10011

ISBN 1-55851-466-X

10 9 8 7 6 5 4 3 2 1

Associate Publisher: *Paul Farrell*

Managing Editor: *Cary Sullivan*   **Copy Edit Manager:** *Shari Chappell*
Development Editor: *Michael Sprague*   **Production Editor:** *Stephanie Doyle*

DEDICATION

All editions of this book are dedicated to Maria, my lovely and talented wife, mother of my three daughters, and the best friend I've ever had. She has been a constant source of inspiration, humor, and sanity. Lord knows I need more of the latter.

CONTENTS

Contents

Contents

Chapter 6: Strings   139

Chapter 7: Array Fundamentals   185

Contents

Chapter 9: Sorting Techniques   255

Chapter 10: Statistics 101   297

Chapter 11: Persistent Objects　　　　　　　　　323

Contents

Chapter 15: File Indexes: BTrees   475

Contents

WHY THIS BOOK IS FOR YOU

This book is about implementing algorithms and components in C++. It includes more than 15,000 lines of working production code for the following tools, now updated to support new ANSI C++ features, Microsoft Windows 95, 32-bit programming, and recent compiler releases from Borland and Microsoft. Included are:

- A complete class library for BTree-based file indexing with variable-length records. It supports keys and data of any types, including user-defined types, and includes the ability to delete records by key, a complicated algorithm often ignored in other texts.

- A complete class library for indexing files via hash tables using any types of keys and data.

- A comprehensive discussion of implementing ShellSort and QuickSort for arrays.

- Thorough introductions to templates and exceptions, two new C++ features used in this book.

- A powerful library of classes for handling type-safe, range-checked arrays.

- An introduction to basic statistical calculations on arrays of numbers.

- A comprehensive dynamic string class, including Boyer-Moore searching.

- Many other classes, binary trees, hash tables, rational numbers, and random number generators.

- A presentation of the author's views about object-oriented program design.

If you have the first edition of this book, you'll want this new edition in order to see how templates and exceptions increase the flexibility and scope of this class library. For owners of the second edition, this latest revision includes new types—rational numbers, balanced binary trees, array manipulators, iterators, shell sorts, and new random number generators—along with minor bug fixes and updates to support the latest compiler releases.

To get the most from this book, you should understand the basic mechanics of C++, have written some C++ programs, and be interested in exploring how C++ can be used in practical applications. You need a Borland C++ v5.0 or Microsoft Visual C++ v4.0 compiler to use the code in this book.

INTRODUCTION

Denver, Colorado, is home to the world's sixth-largest book store, The Tattered Cover. The computer books are on the second floor; they span 50 feet of 10-foot-high shelving. At last count, there were more than 100 books on these shelves with "C++" in their titles; several of them carry my byline, covering topics ranging from basic algorithms to evolutionary computing.

I always ask myself several questions when I begin a new book project. How do I create a book that's different from all the others? How do I avoid repeating what I've already said in my own books? What hasn't been covered? Why should someone spend hard-earned money for this book? If I'm revising a book, have I added anything of value to previous editions? And how should the new book relate to my other books?

I buy lots of books; almost 4,000 of them reside on shelves, floors, and tables in my home. The most useful books in my office are the books that contain algorithms, code fragments, and information on techniques for getting the most out of a programming language. Back in 1991, I decided to write a book about using the powerful features of C++ to create program components and implement algorithms. Since then, *C++ Components and Algorithms* has evolved along with the C++ language and my own activities.

The book assumes that you already know the rudiments of C++ programming. This is not a tutorial on C++ programming. Stroustrup and others have provided more than enough tutorial material on C++. For this book, I assume that you know what a virtual function is, what a class definition looks like, and how overloading is done. However, I've included chapters that discuss templates and exceptions, because these new features are often neglected in compiler documentation.

The thrust of this book is, as its title states, components and algorithms, implemented in C++, using the features of C++ to best advantage. Implementing a sorting function or a file library in C++ is (and should be) different from implementing those tools in C (or Pascal, or FORTRAN, or …). I think a book (or two, or three …) specifically about algorithms in C++ is needed, and that's why I wrote one. In this book, I implement classes for error handling, strings, arrays, and file handling. Along the way, I discuss algorithms for random number generation, sorting, basic statistical analysis, tree structures, and file organization.

In updating this book for the second edition, I included completely new versions of all classes. Instead of creating dozens of tediously similar classes, I've used templates to provide type independence. Files can now store any type of data using any type of key; the system is built on flexibility and simplicity. And to improve error handling, I've implemented a complete system of exceptions and handlers.

For the third edition, I was faced with some tough decisions. I began by moving all the code to 32-bit Windows, a task that required far less effort and change than I expected. I replaced the simple `Boolean` type from earlier editions with an implementation of ANSI's new `bool` type. The code underwent a number of small changes related to recent compiler releases from Microsoft and Borland. I also fixed a few bugs, including a nasty one I found in the `String` class.

I wrote a new testing framework and then added new chapters that focus on random number generation and rational numbers. The chapter on sorting changed dramatically as I introduced the concept of *manipulators* that link process to structure. The `ShellSort` routine is now included here, providing a sorting algorithm that is simpler than `QuickSort`. Array and binary tree iterator classes, omitted from the previous editions, are now fully documented. And, perhaps most important, I expanded the explanations and examples in several chapters, filling in holes and weak spots.

C++ Components and Algorithms is a completely stand-alone part of a two-book set. Its companion volume is *C++ Templates and Tools*, a book M&T first published in mid-1995. The two books share only the exception code and my random number generator class; each stands alone, but their code works together. If you own *Templates and Tools*, you may note that I've moved the *Red-Black* tree material into this new edition of *Components and Algorithms*. I did that to better organize my material, placing all the "tree classes" in this book. *Templates and Tools* will, in a future edition, include many new classes related to its core material.

The code herein is not dependent on anything specific to Borland or Microsoft. I've used some of this code with, for example, UNIX compilers. Everything in the book is based on the C++ language definition and not on a specific vendor's product. I've tested all the code with Microsoft Visual C++ 4.0 and a late beta copy of Borland's C++ 5.0.

In the past, I've had trouble when working code ceases to compile when a vendor comes out with a new compiler version. I needed to make several small changes to code in this book because of vendor changes and new ANSI C++ features. C++ is still a growing, evolving language, and it should be treated with caution. I hope that the vendors will keep backward compatibility in mind when working on new versions—and I hope readers will forgive me if I lack the prescience to anticipate future changes in compilers. Nothing bugs an author more than working on a book for months, only to have a vendor invalidate it before it sees publication!

Finally, I hope that this book provides you with food for thought and code for programs. I've appreciated your letters and comments in the past; in some cases, you've found bugs (now fixed) that I missed. And, as always, I wish you all good luck in your work and lives.

Scott Robert Ladd
9,318 feet high in the San Juan Mountains
Silverton, Colorado
December 1995

CHAPTER 1

A C++ PHILOSOPHY

Programming philosophy, like any philosophy, is a tricky blend of experience and psychology. Everyone approaches software design (and life, for that matter) with a set of preconceived notions and preferences. I know that I've developed some strong feelings about C++ that influence how I write my code, and so I'll begin this book by explaining my philosophy of C++ programming. My goal isn't to lay down an absolute set of laws; instead, I want to make you *think* about how you develop C++ programs. Don't take what I'm about to say as gospel; instead, view it as my perspective of how C++ has (and has not) worked for me.

FROM FUNCTIONS TO OBJECTS

Programmers may quibble about the "best" programming language, but the truth is that the function-oriented programming languages are simply variations on a single theme. An `if` statement is an `if` statement and a function is a function regardless of the language you're using. So when I design a function-oriented program, I don't think in terms of a specific language but rather in terms of overall program design.

Object-oriented languages are, for the most part, extended versions of existing function-based languages. For example, most C++ code looks like C code; the semicolons, parentheses, and keywords all follow the same syntax and logic. What's different about C++ is its object-oriented extensions to C, which suggest a new way of designing and organizing programs. I say "suggest" because you can write a function-based C++ program; however, you probably won't want to do that, preferring instead to work with C++'s object-oriented features.

Changing from a function-oriented language to an object-oriented one requires something more than an understanding of a new syntax. When designing a function-based program, programmers tend to think about what a program does; for an object-oriented program, a programmer must think about what a program is manipulating. Sometimes, that change in perspective causes trouble for programmers steeped in a function-oriented approach to programming.

A change in thinking, though, can be disconcerting, and so some people try to sugarcoat object-oriented programming by couching it in terms familiar to function-oriented programmers. "C++ is C with object-oriented extensions," for example, is a common statement that is accurate but misleading. It can be comforting to believe that moving from C to C++ is simply a matter of mastering a new syntax. Even more misleading is the widespread belief that the use of object-oriented techniques will result in programs that are faster, smaller, and easier to maintain.

Comforting platitudes may make C++ sound less threatening, but the truth is that C++ programming is far more than C programming with a few new keywords. The difference between function-oriented and object-oriented programming is that the programmer must change from designing programs based on actions to designing programs around data types and their interactions. Understanding that difference is a must if you are to get the most out of C++.

In the end, one of these three things may happen to the programmer trying to learn C++:

- The programmer gives up, surrendering to frustration caused by the complexities of C++. "What can be done with C++ that can't be done with C?" the programmer will ask. I've seen this syndrome occur in many old-line C advocates who tried C++ before they understood the need to shift their programming philosophy from actions to objects.

- Finding the new C++ features irresistible, the programmer sets forth to create wonderful and incomprehensible programs. Inline functions, operator overloading, templates, and local declarations predominate, but very few practical classes (and benefits) appear.

- After reading a dozen books, fighting with C++, and alienating friends and family, the programmer finds illumination in an understanding of object-oriented programming; this breakthrough results in the creation of encapsulated, reusable components that become reliable programs.

OK, maybe you *don't* have to alienate anyone to understand C++—but the language is not something to be approached casually. Your attitude toward learning C++ will determine which of the three scenarios applies to you. If you expect C++ to automatically hand you the benefits of object orientation , you'll become disillusioned. Thinking of C++ as a set of new toys for the C programmer will result in your using some C++ features without truly understanding their application. But if you're willing to be patient, to open your mind to the possibilities, and to change the way in which you've built programs in the past, you and C++ are on the road to success.

TERMINOLOGY

Object-oriented programming has a language of its own. A unique terminology lends prestige to a new discipline by making it obscure and mystical. Perfectly good words may exist to describe something, but the new philosophy requires new terms to distinguish it from the past. Unfortunately, fancy new terminology can cloud our understanding of what may be simple concepts.

Let's begin by examining a simple code fragment:

```
double a, b, c, s;

b = 1.0;
c = 2.0;
a = b + c;
s = sqrt(a);
```

The `double` data type provides an abstraction representing a floating-point number. A programmer doesn't need to know anything about the format of floating-point data types to use a `double`; the compiler takes care of the details involved in working with `double`s, making the programmer's job easier. And the use of abstractions doesn't end with data types. The `sqrt` function is a functional abstraction; it provides a "black box" for determining the square root of a floating-point value. Most programmers don't know how to obtain the square root of a floating-point value; they rely on `sqrt` to do the task for them.

C++ allows programmers to create new abstractions. A class defines an interface to a set of related program components. Through the interface (in this case, public functions), you can interact with the abstraction without being involved in its internal workings. As with using `double` and `sqrt` to make handling floating-point numbers easier, your classes should be designed to simplify the use of the abstraction.

The keyword `double` identifies an abstraction. When you declare a `double` in your program, you're creating an *object* that has the characteristics associated with being a double. The term *object* is literal; it means "a thing that has identifiable properties." When you create a `double` object, you know from experience exactly what that object can do.

Intrinsic data types such as `double` and `int` are built into C++; they are always available and their properties are predefined and fixed. A programmer uses classes to create new abstractions in C++; the abstractions you create with classes will have the properties you define. Unlike intrinsic types, the types defined by classes can be extended. You can build hierarchies of related types that share common properties.

Don't be locked into thinking of classes and objects only in terms of data types. For example, Pascal allows a programmer to define several related functions within an outer *shell* function. The shell provides a single entry point for a process, and the internal functions carry out that process. Internal functions reference the data items in the enclosing scope, in effect creating a program within a program. In C++, a class can accomplish the same thing by defining private functions for internal use and public functions as entry points. Data shared by the various functions are part of the class definition.

To *encapsulate* is to bind together the different components that form a single concept or entity, hiding the internal structure of a program component. For example, the `complex` class defines the data structure of a complex number; it also defines the functions that can operate on `complex` values and makes those functions part of the definition of a `complex`. You use encapsulation every day outside the world of computers. A car consists of several components that you think of as a single unit. You refer to the "engine" or the "brakes," which are systems of several parts that work together for a single purpose. Combined with abstraction, encapsulation allows a programmer to combine the components of a larger idea into a single, simplified model.

Inheritance allows us to create new classes from existing ones. For example, a `NumericArray` class might inherit the characteristics defined by an `Array` class, which defines the core features of arrays. `NumericArray` would add its own features to support the arrays containing numbers. In turn, an `IntegerArray` class could be *derived* (inheriting from) the `NumericArray` class, creating a numeric array with features such as bitwise operations. The `Array` class defines the common characteristics of all arrays; `NumericArray` adds basic math and comparisons, and `IntegerArray` defines an array specific to integers.

Inheritance also allows for *polymorphism. Poly* is derived from the Greek word for "many"; *morphus* is from the Greek word *morphous*, meaning "to take a form." Combined with *-ism*, the term *polymorphism* means the ability to take on many forms. In the case of object-oriented programming, a polymorphic data type can have several variants, all of which can be treated in a similar manner. For example, the `Array` class is polymorphic; any class derived from it can be treated as a generic `Array`, allowing a program to treat any type of `Array` in a generic fashion.

CAUTIONARY TALES

An old saying claims that the inherent flexibility of C provides the rope with which programmers can hang themselves. Fortunately, good C programmers know how to avoid wrapping the rope around their necks; from experience, they know what should and shouldn't be done in C, and most of them escape with their necks (and careers) intact.

The unprecedented freedom of expression allowed by C++ requires considerable caution and knowledge on your part. C++ doesn't just supply the rope; it ties the noose, places it over your head, and stands you over the trapdoor with your hand on the release lever. Am I exaggerating? I suppose so—but only a little bit. C++ has bitten me often, and the resultant scars remind me how best to use its powerful and complex features. In six years of C++ programming, I've hanged myself so many times I'm surprised that I can still breathe.

But all those new toys in C++ are inviting, aren't they? There are so many nooks and crannies in C++, you could spend years exploring C++ without ever completely understanding it. As a strong point, the complexity of C++ makes it powerful; as a weakness, complexity increases the chance of mistakes. This doesn't mean that there's anything *wrong* with C++; it merely means that you need to be cautious. Don't jump right in, grabbing every feature you see, just because some pundit (including me!) tells you that's what you should do. Weigh and consider; experiment and test; observe and contemplate. That's how you learn C++—or anything else, for that matter.

C programmers learned long ago that certain programming techniques were bad news. Most C++ programmers have been using the language for only a few months or at most a couple of years; they haven't had enough time to have learned right from wrong. Even worse, C++ has yet to settle into a standard form; the language keeps changing (and in some cases, mutating) as new features and ideas find their way into compilers. I hope that, by passing along what I've learned, I can prevent you from having too many pain-in-the-neck experiences.

The Curse of Clever Coding

I've occasionally written programs that are—well—a bit too "creative" for my own good. I've been bitten by code that didn't appear to have teeth. Quite often, it's a bright idea that gets me into trouble; I'll implement what appears to be a brilliant solution, completely missing a noxious side effect.

A case in point: In C++, a program assigns values to simple (non-object) global data when the program starts. This arrangement works fine for simple data types such as integers, but some data types—dynamically allocated pointers, for example—need to be destroyed when the program terminates. One of my programs had a global data item similar to this:

```
int * array = new int [10000];
```

The program dutifully called `new` to allocate 20000 bytes of space. What the program *didn't* do was to call `delete` when the program terminated, leaving the allocated memory in limbo.

My solution was to create a class wrapper similar to this one:

```
class IntPtr
    {
    public:
        IntPtr(size_t n);
        ~IntPtr();
        operator int * ();
    private:
        int * ptr;
    };
```

```
inline IntPtr::IntPtr(size_t n)
    {
    ptr = new int [n];
    }

inline IntPtr::~IntPtr()
    {
    if (ptr != NULL)
        delete [] ptr;
    }

inline IntPtr::operator int *()
    {
    return ptr;
    }
```

Then I changed my global declaration to this:

```
IntPtr array(10000);
```

And that fixed my problem, right? Not quite. For some mysterious reason, my program began exhibiting the random behavior associated with
a wild pointer. I knew the bug had been created by my IntPtr class,
because it was the only change I'd made in the program.

After an hour, I found the problem. Elsewhere in the program, I'd
written a function similar to this:

```
void DoSomething(IntPtr iptr)
    {
    // unimportant code for this discussion
    }
```

Somewhere else in the program, I'd called DoSomething:

```
DoSomething(array);
```

It looked harmless enough. But somehow, when the program returned from
calling DoSomething, the pointer ptr in the array object had been deleted!

After an hour, the answer hit me: DoSomething's iptr parameter was a copy of array. Because I hadn't defined a copy constructor in the IntPtr class, the compiler automatically performed a bitwise copy of array.ptr to iptr.ptr. Then, when DoSomething terminated, the compiler dutifully called the destructor for iptr—and because its ptr equaled array.ipt, my data vanished in a puff of inattentive programming smoke.

After more than a dozen years of writing code, I still make stupid mistakes. The problem should have been obvious; after all, I'm a guy who preaches in books and articles that every class should have a programmer-defined copy constructor. My mistake was implementing something quickly without thinking it through. Cute solutions and nifty hacks tend to produce unreliable programs. A hack is often created when a programmer is faced with a knotty problem and a tight schedule. Hacks are like patches on a boat—if you have too many, something's going to give.

Before you do something clever, ask yourself one question: Do you *really* need to use that trick? Sure, you might impress yourself and others by writing a tricky piece of code, but how understandable will your program be in a month or a year? Programs aren't static; any program written today must be maintained and enhanced tomorrow. Far too often, programmatic legerdemain reflects a programmer's ego over the requirements of a program. If it's a quick and dirty solution, you probably haven't seen all its consequences.

Trendiness

> *It is undesirable to believe a proposition when there is no ground whatever for supposing it true.*
>
> —*Bertrand Russell*
> *Skeptical Essays (1928), p. 1*

Every few years, a new programming technique comes along that promises to make software development easier. Like politicians on the campaign trail, the advocates of "technological breakthrough" eagerly ply us with promises of a better future. The question is, are they (like politicians) promising more than they can deliver?

The champions of object-oriented programming make big promises. They tell us that C++ programs will be easier to build because existing components can be linked quickly and easily. Using objects will make debugging programs easier because problems can be isolated within encapsulated data types. Future changes, they promise, can be implemented merely by deriving new program components from the existing ones.

In theory, that is. As I've worked with C++, I've come to realize that the additional benefits of object-oriented programming require more design and planning on the part of the software developer. It takes time to analyze an application, identify its components, develop the relationships between those components, and create the network of classes.

Many C programmers tend to hack programs together. For whatever reason—be it a lack of design time or a case of *machismo*—C programs tend to be built on-screen, in real time, with a design consisting of a few scribbled notes (in one of my own cases, on napkins from a fast-food restaurant!). To use C++ effectively, however, a programmer needs a clear idea of the data types needed, how they will be used, and their relationships.

C++ was not designed for quick-and-dirty, on-the-fly, seat-of-the-pants programming. To build a useful set of classes, you must know exactly what your program is expected to do. Initial impressions can often be misleading. My first attempts at using C++ ended in redesigns of my original classes. Without thoroughly understanding what my program did, I couldn't plan the required classes.

Of course, we all program in the real world. In 15 years, I have yet to write a program that matched a formal specification. Usually, there isn't any time to create a specification; a user determines the need for a piece of software, and the programmer is expected to produce a working program in short order. When working for the U.S. government, I sometimes wrote program specifications after the program was complete, simply to fulfill an administrative requirement.

Even when specifications exist, they rarely reflect the real-world requirements. I can't count the number of times I've written an application only to have the user say, "Well, can you make it do this?" or "I really need this feature to work differently." In the end, trying to force users to match their original design is virtually impossible.

By now you're probably saying, "Hold it! Didn't Scott just say that C++ programs must be planned? Now he's saying that the plans don't exist or aren't any good! What gives?"

Both facts are true: C++ requires planning, and time for planning is usually limited. So what is a good programmer to do? You design as you program. An often-overlooked feature of object-oriented languages is that they provide a mutable and extensible framework around which a program is built. Thinking flexibly also has advantages after the program is completed. Programs change during their creation and after they begin work. Studies show that programmers spend most of their time updating and modifying existing programs. The same flexible program structure that helps in creating the program will also allow you to easily change the program later.

Inheritance Follies

The most important decision you can make in an object-oriented program is the organization of your classes. Choosing the wrong organization can be fatal later, when you suddenly discover that you need a branch here instead of a limb there. As with a real tree, you can't easily change a branch's position. Unplanned class hierarchies often degenerate into class "thickets" as programmers patch in new classes. Multiple inheritance adds to this problem by creating multiple paths of ancestry.

When you create a new class via multiple inheritance, be aware of the ancestry of the classes that are being combined. For example, Figures 1.1 and 1.2 show portions of class hierarchies from the libraries of two vendors. Vendor A's library provides basic container classes; Vendor B's hierarchy consists of classes that encapsulate numeric data types. Note that the two classes named `Object` are different.

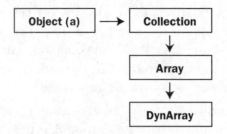

FIGURE **1.1** VENDOR A'S CLASS HIERARCHY.

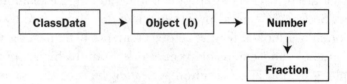

FIGURE **1.2** VENDOR B'S CLASS HIERARCHY.

What happens when you want to create a new class, named FracArray, based on Vendor A's DynArray class and Vendor B's Fraction class? Figure 1.3 shows the ancestry of the FracArray class.

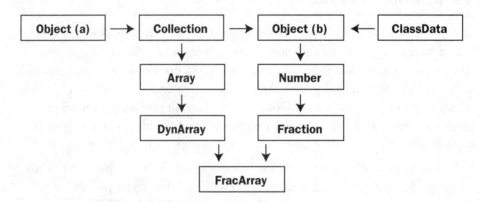

FIGURE **1.3** AN ATTEMPT TO COMBINE BOTH HIERARCHIES.

Everything looks OK until you realize that you have two *different ancestral* classes named Object. Were the Object classes identical, the declaration of

Collection and Number could be modified to declare both Objects as virtual base classes. Unfortunately, because the two Object classes are different, the virtual mechanism won't work. The compiler will complain about ambiguous base classes; the linker will complain that there are two classes with the same name. And let's not think about problems with identically named header, source, and object files!

An obvious solution is to rename one or both of the Object classes, assuming that you have the source code for the vendor's classes. Although it solves the immediate problem, renaming a class requires a substantial amount of work. Object is likely to be the base for every class in a vendor's hierarchy, so you'll have to change every reference to Object. Even with a sophisticated text editor, that's a lot of work! And when the vendor upgrades its class library, you'll have to choose between renaming the class again or not upgrading.

Let's assume that changes have been made so that the two conflicting classes are now named ObjectA and ObjectB. Everything's OK now, isn't it?

Not by a long shot. The purpose of a single-tree hierarchy is to make it easier to manipulate polymorphic objects. Most Object-type classes provide virtual functions for determining an object's class, comparing two objects for equality, obtaining the object's size, and performing I/O on the object. Unfortunately, although the designers of single-tree hierarchies may agree on what the Object class should define, they probably don't agree on how that definition should be implemented.

Something as simple as different naming conventions can cause a huge headache. Vendor A defines the virtual member function PrintOn in ObjectA. Vendor B's ObjectB class, however, defines a PrintTo virtual member. In all likelihood, PrintOn and PrintTo have completely different semantics. Your FracArray class inherits both of these member functions, and you'll need to provide your own implementations of PrintOn and PrintTo specific to FracArray. In addition, the two vendors probably use different names and conventions for class identification, equivalence, and size calculation member functions. What a mess of redundancies! I don't even want to think about inheriting from more than two class hierarchies. The very thought sends shivers down my spine.

Namespaces

The ANSI C++ standardization committee is attempting to solve these problems by adding the concept of *namespaces* to C++. A `namespace` declaration combines a set of declarations under a single group name. For example:

```
namespace Frog
    {
    void EatBug();
    void HopAround();
    };

namespace Toad
    {
    void EatBug();
    void HopAround();
    };
```

A `using` statement determines the default namespace, and the scoping operator `::` declares the explicit use of a given namespace:

```
void Bouncy
    {
    using Toad;
    EatBug();        // calls Toad::EatBug()
    Frog::EatBug();  // calls Frog::EatBug()
    }
```

To avoid conflicts with your identifiers, the ANSI committee created a `namespace` called `std` that encompasses identifiers defined by the standard C++ library. In theory, Vendor A and Vendor B could enclose their class definitions in namespaces to avoid most of the conflicts I discussed in the previous section.

Although I haven't employed namespaces in this book's code, they are relatively simple to implement by enclosing header inclusions in a `namespace` statement. For example, if my `Array` template were to conflict with another `Array` class, I could solve the problem by using the following piece of code to create a "Coyote" namespace:

```
namespace Coyote
    {
    #include "Array.h"
    };
```

I would employ either a `using Coyote` statement or the `Coyote::` qualifier to specify when I am using my classes.

Object Overkill

A large hierarchy is like a piece of string. Drop a short piece of string to the floor, and it's simple to tell which part of the string goes where. As the string gets longer, it becomes harder to determine which part of the string is which. If the string is long enough, trying to follow it from one end to the other will only generate knots. Long, complex class hierarchies act like long string. They'll bite you later, particularly when you're looking at someone else's code or code that you wrote in the past.

How often do you need to have a data item tell you what type it is? Does every object need to support I/O features? Are generic data structures sufficiently robust for your application? What are the costs involved in having layers of virtual functions? Don't assume that a purely object-oriented approach is the only route you can take; the best feature of C++ is that it lets you use plain old C when it's needed and use C++ when you want objects. Don't add stuff to your C++ programs just because you can; add it because it's needed.

I wrote and tested the code in this book under the Windows 95 operating system; however, my application program doesn't use the Microsoft Foundation Classes (MFC) or Borland's Object Windows Library (OWL). Neither of those class libraries provides, in my opinion, any advantage over writing code directly to the Windows API. In fact, having written a few programs with MFC and OWL, I've come to realize that these application frameworks increase the complexity of Windows programming. Yes, I know that's not what conventional wisdom and advertising hype tell you. But experience has taught me that OWL and MFC do little to hide Windows' complexities even while requiring me to learn a massive class hierarchy. And because neither MFC nor OWL is applicable to non-PC environments, they don't lend themselves to portable code.

This doesn't mean that I don't use classes in my Windows programs; I just define classes where I feel they make sense. Look into Appendix A for an example.

SOFTWARE COMPONENTS

Several object-oriented programming pundits propose that programs be constructed from interchangeable software components just as computers are constructed from standard chips and circuit cards. The result, we are told, will be a new age of perfect software, in which programmers simply connect objects to form new applications.

The assumption is that software is like hardware. A given hardware component is designed to be absolute; a machine has this CPU, these I/O ports, and a specific number of expansion slots. Once a piece of hardware is built, it is nearly impossible to change it significantly. Let's say, for example, that you want to add a new expansion card to your PC, only to find that all your expansion slots are full. You can't simply change the design of your motherboard; adding an expansion slot would be more work than it's worth. You either have to remove an existing expansion card or live without your new card. And the problem becomes more complicated when you want to change how your hardware works. The ROM BIOS is fixed; you can change it only for another BIOS that works in a similar way. Once hardware has been built and software has been cast in silicon, making changes is very difficult.

If discrete software functions could be encapsulated into components, we would build programs as we build cars or computers. Programming would consist of developing networks of unchangeable software ICs. The only difference between software and hardware would be that software would be easier to rearrange than hardware.

Worse yet, some industry analysts predict that software ICs will remove the need for programmers. Without the human element, programs will become sterile and lifeless, lacking creativity and ingenuity. Assembly-line software may be for some people, but I don't look forward to using or writing it.

A better design method is to create flexible and extensible objects. A flexible object allows for changes to be made. An extensible object can be used as the basis for different objects. The array and database classes shown later in this book try to use a flexible hierarchy to provide for flexible expansion.

The relationship of two classes can take on one or more of the following forms:

- The *is a* relationship. Class B is defined as a variant of Class A. The major characteristics of Class B are inherited from Class A, and Class B objects are often used polymorphically via pointers to Class A objects. For example, a class defining an array of `int`s may be derived from a class that specifies the common characteristics of all array types.

- The *modifies* relationship. Class B extends or defines the capabilities of Class A. For example, the `SortableArray` class (Chapter 4) adds sorting capabilities to the `Array` class (Chapter 3).

- The *made of* relationship. Class A objects are components of Class B. In this case, Class A defines a traditional data type, such as an integer or a complex number, and class B defines an object type that contains class A objects.

- The *uses* relationship. Class A objects are tools used by Class B objects, such as a file object that's used by another object to store data.

A programmer must know the relationship among information in a program before determining the types and interactions of classes. This means that the often-elusive program specification must be thoroughly researched. If you make a wrong decision about relating your classes, a program can become difficult to understand and maintain.

SPEAKING THE LANGUAGE

Before you can build a house, you must know how read a plan, measure wood, cut materials to shape, and nail all the pieces together. You can't simply start building a house without knowing how your tools work. The same principle holds true for software development. You can't write software without knowing your development tools.

You can't write reliable programs without first having a thorough understanding of the language. Knowledge of the basics can be gleaned from a book; understanding of the subtleties requires using the language. The biggest programming mistake you can make is to begin a large C++ project when you lack experience in using the language. Begin with small projects; rewrite a few utilities or simple applications to get a sense of how a C++ program fits together.

The original C language was created to build operating systems and utilities; because C was flexible and efficient, some programmers began using it for writing large application programs. That's when C began to exhibit inherent weaknesses. In creating C++, Bjarne Stroustrup grafted the new concepts of object-oriented programming onto C. The new language offers low-level access and high-powered abstraction.

I believe that C++ programmers must be better than their C counterparts. C is a typical function-based language; function-based programming is as old as FORTRAN, and good programmers know how to organize programs along functional divisions. We have decades of experience in developing function-oriented programs, so we can do it very well. C++ adds something new: object-oriented programming. An object encapsulates form and function; it defines both the format and the function of a datum and the operations. New objects can be created from existing objects, creating a hierarchy of related and interacting program components.

Object-oriented programming was first introduced in the early 1980s; it wasn't until a few years ago that object-oriented programming languages became commercially available. C++ has changed several times during its short life. The current, stable definition of C++ has been available only for a few years. This means that the programming community doesn't have much experience in writing object-oriented programs.

As of this writing, C++ has not been standardized by the American National Standards Institute (ANSI) or the International Standards Organization (ISO). Both ANSI and ISO have based their upcoming standards on the definition of C++ given by Stroustrup and Margaret Ellis in their book *The Annotated C++ Reference Manual* (known as the "ARM"). Along with the ARM, I strongly suggest that you find a copy of *The C++ Programming Language* by Stroustrup. As the primary inventor of C++, Stroustrup writes the definitive books about C++. The ARM is a reference document; *The C++ Programming Language* provides insight into Stroustrup's views on C++ programming.

Both books have become somewhat obsolete as competition drives vendors to keep pace with emerging standards. As ANSI slowly moves toward a final definition of C++, compilers sprout new features based on preliminary versions of the committee's work. As of this writing, no vendor has produced a compiler that is even remotely ANSI-compliant, for the most part because the standard continues to change. Some new features of ANSI C++, however, can cause problems for existing code. New rules for overload resolution and implicit conversions required me to make minor changes in several pieces of existing code.

AN ANSI BOOL CLASS

One piece of the ANSI standard is `bool`, a new intrinsic type. As you might expect, a `bool` is a Boolean, true or false value. Before the definition of `bool`, C++ used the C model by interpreting logical statements in terms of `int` values. For example, the result of the logical comparison `(a < b)` is an `int` value of zero when false and nonzero when true. ANSI's `bool` type can take one of two values: `true` (1) or `false`(0).

I can hear the old-time C programmers groaning about what they see as the superfluous addition of `bool`—but `bool` is there, its use is built into

the ANSI C++ class libraries, and the language now defines the object of
a conditional statement as being type `bool`. Some compilers support `bool`;
others don't. I created a simple, inline definition of `bool` that supports
most of the features defined by the current working version of the ANSI
standard. Because Borland C++ version 5.0 supports `bool` (whereas
Microsoft Visual C++ 4.0 does not), I included a conditional statement to
remove my `bool` class if an intrinsic version exists.

```cpp
#if __BORLANDC__ <= 0x460

#ifndef COYOTE_BOOL_H
#define COYOTE_BOOL_H

#include "iostream.h"

enum { false, true };

class bool
    {
    public:
        // constructors
        bool(int b = 0) { Val = (b ? true : false); }

        // assignment
        bool operator = (bool b) { return (Val = b.Val); }

        // conversions
        operator int() const { return Val; }

        // comparisons
        bool operator == (bool b) const { return Val == b.Val; }
        bool operator != (bool b) const { return Val != b.Val; }

        // stream output operator
        friend ostream & operator << (ostream & os, bool b);

    private:
        int Val;
    };

inline ostream & operator << (ostream & os, bool b)
```

```
    {
    os << (b ? "true" : "false");
    return os;
    }

#endif // if COYOTE_BOOL_H

#endif // if BORLANDC > 0x460
```

The `bool` class, defined in the file **bool.h**, follows the ANSI C++ draft definition of the `bool` type. In past editions of this book, I used a simple enumerated type to define a Boolean value; ANSI, however, places specific
requirements on `bool`, so I implemented `bool` as a class.

ONWARD

This book relies on templates, a relatively recent addition to the C++ language that allows the creation of parameterized types. I'll look into the
uses of templates in the next chapter before moving to a discussion of
exceptions and error handling.

CHAPTER 2

TEMPLATES

C++ templates provide you with the ability to define a description of how something works without having to define what it's working on. As you'll see in this chapter, templates are among the most useful of C++ features.

FUNCTION TEMPLATES

If you want to create a set of C++ functions for performing an operation on a variety of data types, the obvious solution is to use function overloading. For example, if I wanted functions to calculate the squares of `int` and `float` values, I could define these two functions:

```
int Square(int x)
    {
    return x * x;
    };

float Square(float x)
    {
    return x * x;
    }
```

For each data type that I want to square, I create a new `Square` function. The C++ compiler determines which function to call based on the argument passed to `Square`.

```
int i = 2;
int f = 12.53;

int isq = Square(i); // call Square(int)
int fsq = Square(f); // call Square(float)
```

The similarity of these functions is annoying. The actual code doesn't change; the only difference between the `Square` functions is their header. I could, of course, use a C-type macro function:

```
#define Square(x) (x * x)
```

A macro, however, always generates inline code. For a complex calculation, it may be better to have callable functions for each data type.

Wouldn't it be nice if I could just create one function that says, "Square any type of number" and leave it to the compiler to generate appropriate code for the data types I use? C++ offers just such a facility: function templates.

A *function template* describes a type of function rather than a specific function. Instead of creating a `Square` function for every numeric data type, I can create a function template like this:

```
template <class T>
    inline T Square(T x)
        {
        return x * x;
        };
```

A function template tells the compiler how to construct a set of similar functions. The preceding template tells the compiler, "Here's a template for a function named `Square`. It has a single argument of class `T` and returns a class `T` value. When a statement calling `Square` is encountered, generate a

`Square` function that replaces `T` with the class of the argument."

For the purposes of a template, the intrinsic types (`float`, `int`, etc.) are treated as classes. For example, the code

```
int i1 = 2;
int i2 = Square(i1);
```

would cause the compiler to generate a function like this:

```
int Square(int x)
    {
    return x * x;
    }
```

The compiler generates code only for those data types used in calls to the template function. And if you add a new class—for, say, complex or rational numbers—those types will *automatically* be supported by the template for `Square`. The only stipulation is that the data type used in calling a template function support the operations performed. For example, this code fragment would generate a compile-time error:

```
char * x = "Dance";
char * y = Square(x);
```

Unless you've defined the binary `*` operator for `char *`s, this line of code will not compile.

A template can have more than one generic argument, and it can have arguments with a specific type. For example:

```
template <class A, class B>
    void MyFunc(A arga, B argb, int i)
    {
    // do something
    };
```

The first two arguments in a call to `MyFunc` can have the same type or different types. The third argument is always treated as an `int`. Templates generate inline functions if the function header is prefaced with the `inline` keyword.

A C++ compiler views template functions as a set of overloaded functions. It's also possible to overload a template-generated function with a nontemplate function. The computer resolves overloads first and then looks for an exact match between a function call's arguments and an existing function; if the compiler doesn't find a match, it generates a new function from the template.

CLASS TEMPLATES

A *class template* tells the compiler how to construct a series of similar classes. I view class templates as forms, with the compiler filling in the blanks based on your template arguments.

As a tool for defining containers, class templates excel. Here's an example of a flexible record type that contains both a key value and data:

```
template <class K, class D>
    class Record
        {
        public:
            Record(K kx, D dx) { Key = kx; Data = dx; }
            K GetKey() { return Key; }
            D GetData() { return Data; }
        private:
            K Key;
            D Data;
        };
```

When the compiler encounters a template, it creates a general definition from which it can build specific types as required. The compiler generates type-specific versions of Record only when it needs to; as with inline functions, a template class or function does not produce any code until it is used for a specific type. For example, the declaration

```
Record<int, String> recis;
```

will cause the compiler to generate a `Record<int, String>` class equivalent to this:

```
class Record
    {
    public:
        Record(int kx, String dx) { Key = kx; Data = dx; }
        int GetKey() { return Key; }
        String GetData() { return Data; }
    private:
        int Key;
        String Data;
    };
```

If I also declare a `Record<long,double>` object, the compiler generates another class definition. In other words, I can create a `Record` class for any types `K` and `D`, all based on a single common template.

Note that this power comes with the usual set of caveats. First, each class created from a template has its own static members, functions, and data members; the more classes you create from templates, the larger your programs will become. Most of your templates will be defined in header files to be included into each source module in which you use that class.

Second, templates do not, in and of themselves, generate code that can be stored in a library for later linking. A smart compiler will combine duplicate template types during linking; a less intelligent compiler may, however, leave your program containing several instances of a class. The C++ standard does not define a standard technique for "precompiling" specific template types, but most have this capability.

Members defined outside the template class definition need to be templates themselves; class scope identifiers must contain template arguments:

```
template <class K, class D>
    Record<K,D>::Record(K kx, D dx)
        {
        Key = kx;
        Data = dx;
        }
```

References to the class type inside the template do not need to be qualified with template arguments, because they are implied by the template.

You can derive classes from template classes; in fact, templates can be derived from other templates:

```
template <class D>
    class Object : Record<int, D>
        {
        . . .
        };
```

A `typedef` statement can define an alias for a template type, thus eliminating the need to specify arguments in angle brackets.

```
typedef StdRecord Record<int,int>;
```

It's also possible to define a template type using another template type as an argument:

```
Record< long,Object<String,double> > rec;
```

Note the extra spaces used to keep the compiler from seeing >> as the right shift operator.

Template arguments need not be class names; template parameters may provide values. For example, most buffer implementations look something like this:

```
class Buffer
    {
    public:
        Buffer(size_t len);
        .

        .

        .
    private:
        char * data;
    };
```

```
Buffer::Buffer(size_t len)
    {
    data = new char[len];

    if (data == NULL)
        throw AnException;
    }
```

A template can provide the size of the buffer as part of the class definition, allowing the buffer to be statically allocated rather than requiring a
call to new:

```
template <size_t n>
   class Buffer
       {
       public:
           Buffer();
           .
           .
           .
       private:
           char data[Len];
       };
```

The definition of a specific buffer size might look like this:

```
Buffer<128> buf;
```

Default values for template arguments let you create a default version of
a class:

```
template <size_t n = 128>
    class Buffer
        {
        public:
            Buffer();
            .
            .
            .
        private:
```

```
        char data[Len];
    };
```

```
Buffer buf; // equivalent to: Buffer<128> buf;
```

Templates aren't difficult to use; I've found that converting my standard library to templates has been far simpler than I expected. What follows is a before-and-after example of implementing templates. The rest of the book relies heavily on templates, and these code examples should help you understand how templates work in the real world.

MOVING TO TEMPLATES

If you compare the first and second editions of this book, you can readily see the importance of templates. The first edition contained several chapters showing implementations of type-specific classes based on generic bases. It made for tedious coding and reading. There was little difference, for example, between an `IntArray` and a `LongArray`.

I'll show you two ways of implementing a basic container class, giving you a before-and-after look at how templates have changed C++ program design. The container I'm using is a double-ended, doubly linked list that can simultaneously act as both a queue and a stack.

In a *queue*, you retrieve items in the order in which they were stored—first in, first out—whereas in a *stack*, you retrieve items in the reverse order of their storage—last in, first out. I've found that a combined queue-stack structure (or a "quack," in my mind) is useful, because I can store and retrieve items from either end of the list.

Implementing a Quack without Templates

My first C++ implementation of a quack was based on my previous C version, wherein I used `void` pointers in storing anonymous data. The class definition looked like this:

```
struct QuackNode
    {
    QuackNode * Above;
    QuackNode * Below;
    void * Data;
    };

class QuackBase
    {
    protected:
        QuackBase(size_t len);
        QuackBase(const QuackBase & qb);

        ~QuackBase();

        QuackBase & operator = (const QuackBase & qb);

        size_t GetCount() { return Count; }

        void PushTop(const void * ptr);
        void PopTop(void * ptr);

        void PushBottom(const void * ptr);
        void PopBottom(void * ptr);

        void IterateUp(void (* func)(const void * ptr));
        void IterateDown(void (* func)(const void * ptr));

    private:
        void Copy(const QuackBase & qb);
        void Kill();

        size_t Count;
        size_t DataLen;

        QuackNode * Top;
        QuackNode * Bottom;
    };
```

QuackNode is a simple structure used internally by QuackBase. It defines a pair of linking pointers to other QuackNodes, and it holds a pointer to data.

QuackBase defines its members as either private or protected, thus preventing any QuackBase objects from being created outside the scope of a derived class. QuackBase works with void pointers, allocating buffers and copying data without any understanding of what it is allocating or storing. Type-specific classes are defined as needed.

As with most of my container-type classes, I created a pair of utility functions to reduce redundant coding. Copy duplicates the members of one QuackBase into another, and Kill removes all entries from a QuackBase list:

```
void QuackBase::Copy(const QuackBase & qb)
    {
    DataLen = qb.DataLen;
    Count   = qb.Count;

    if (qb.Top == NULL)
        {
        Top      = NULL;
        Bottom   = NULL;
        }
    else
        {
        QuackNode * src = qb.Top;
        QuackNode * dest = NULL;
        QuackNode * prev;

        while (src != NULL)
            {
            prev = dest;

            dest = new QuackNode;

            if (dest == NULL)
                throw QuackEx(QE_ALLOC);

            if (prev != NULL)
                {
                prev->Below = dest;
                dest->Above = prev;
                }
            else
                {
                Top = dest;
```

```
                    dest->Above = NULL;
                    }

            dest->Below = NULL;

            dest->Data  = new char [DataLen];

            if (dest->Data == NULL)
                throw QuackEx(QE_ALLOC);

            memcpy(dest->Data,src->Data,DataLen);

            src = src->Below;
            }

        Bottom = dest;
        }
    }

void QuackBase::Kill()
    {
    QuackNode * temp = Top;
    QuackNode * next;

    while (temp != NULL)
        {
        next = temp->Below;
        delete [] temp->Data;
        delete temp;
        temp = next;
        }

    Count = 0;
    }
```

The primary QuackBase constructor simply assigns "empty" values to the data members. The len argument specifies the length of the data stored in void pointers of QuackNode structures:

```
QuackBase::QuackBase(size_t len)
    {
    if (len == 0)
```

```
      throw QuackEx(QE_ZEROLEN);

   DataLen = len;
   Count   = 0;
   Top     = NULL;
   Bottom  = NULL;
   }
```

The copy constructor, destructor, and assignment operator make appropriate inline calls to the Copy and Kill functions:

```
QuackBase::QuackBase(const QuackBase & qb)
   {
   Copy(qb);
   }

QuackBase::~QuackBase()
   {
   Kill();
   }

QuackBase & QuackBase::operator = (const QuackBase & qb)
   {
   Kill();
   Copy(qb);
   return *this;
   }
```

I defined functions that append items to either the top or bottom of the list. I view a Quack, by the way, as a literal stack of information, like a pile of plates; PushTop places a new item on top of the stack, and PushBottom adds a new item to the bottom of the list:

```
void QuackBase::PushTop(const void * ptr)
   {
   if (ptr == NULL)
       throw QuackEx(QE_NULLPTR);

   QuackNode * newnode = new QuackNode;

   if (newnode == NULL)
```

```
        throw QuackEx(QE_ALLOC);

    newnode->Data = new char[DataLen];

    if (newnode->Data == NULL)
        throw QuackEx(QE_ALLOC);

    memcpy(newnode->Data,ptr,DataLen);

    newnode->Above = NULL;
    newnode->Below = Top;

    if (Top != NULL)
        Top->Above = newnode;

    Top = newnode;

    if (Bottom == NULL)
        Bottom = Top;

    ++Count;
    }

void QuackBase::PushBottom(const void * ptr)
    {
    if (ptr == NULL)
        throw QuackEx(QE_NULLPTR);

    QuackNode * newnode = new QuackNode;

    if (newnode == NULL)
        throw QuackEx(QE_ALLOC);

    newnode->Data = new char[DataLen];

    if (newnode->Data == NULL)
        throw QuackEx(QE_ALLOC);

    memcpy(newnode->Data,ptr,DataLen);

    newnode->Above = Bottom;
    newnode->Below = NULL;
```

```
if (Bottom != NULL)
    Bottom->Below  = newnode;


Bottom = newnode;


if (Top == NULL)
    Top = Bottom;


++Count;
}
```

Note that these functions (and `Copy`, too) have no idea what is being stored via the `void` pointers; the functions simply use `memcpy` to copy raw bytes from one place to another. For basic types—`int`s, `double`s, and so on—a raw copy works well. But what happens when I want to store complex objects in a `Quack`? Obviously, a `memcpy` won't be able to correctly store complex objects, and that limitation prevents a `Quack` from being useful in many situations.

The `PopTop` and `PopBottom` functions correspond to the push functions, removing an item from the top or bottom of the list and copying its data into a supplied buffer. Note that many assumptions need to be made here; for example, the destination buffer must be large enough to store the source data. Because `QuackBase` is used only by derived classes, this assumption shouldn't be a problem.

```
void QuackBase::PopTop(void * ptr)
    {
    if (Top == NULL)
        throw QuackEx(QE_EMPTY);


    memcpy(ptr,Top->Data,DataLen);


    QuackNode * temp = Top->Below;


    delete Top;


    Top = temp;


    if (Top == NULL)
```

```
        Bottom = NULL;
    else
        Top->Above = NULL;

    —Count;
    }


void QuackBase::PopBottom(void * ptr)
    {
    if (Bottom == NULL)
        throw QuackEx(QE_EMPTY);

    memcpy(ptr,Bottom->Data,DataLen);

    QuackNode * temp = Bottom->Above;

    delete Bottom;

    Bottom = temp;

    if (Bottom == NULL)
        Top = NULL;
    else
        Bottom->Below = NULL;

    —Count;
    }
```

Finally, I created a pair of functions to iterate through a Quack's entries, calling an external function for each piece of data stored therein:

```
void QuackBase::IterateUp(void (* func)(const void * ptr))
    {
    if (Bottom == NULL)
        throw QuackEx(QE_EMPTY);

    QuackNode * temp = Bottom;

    while (temp != NULL)
        {
        func(temp->Data);
        temp = temp->Above;
```

```
            }
        }


void QuackBase::IterateDown(void (* func)(const void * ptr))
    {
    if (Top == NULL)
        throw QuackEx(QE_EMPTY);

    QuackNode * temp = Top;

    while (temp != NULL)
        {
        func(temp->Data);
        temp = temp->Below;
        }
    }
```

QuackBase is, by itself, useless. In my original system, I created several different classes on QuackBase, each for a different data type. I have Quacks defined specifically for various record types, strings, and simple types; for each one, I had to write a new class. For the purposes of this book, I'll show you a QuackInt class, which (surprise, surprise) works with int values:

```
class QuackInt : private QuackBase
    {
    public:
        QuackInt();
        QuackInt(const QuackInt & qb);

        QuackInt & operator = (const QuackInt & qb);

        size_t GetCount() { return QuackBase::GetCount(); }

        void PushTop(int value);
        int PopTop();

        void PushBottom(int value);
        int PopBottom();

        void IterateUp(void (* func)(const int * n));
        void IterateDown(void (* func)(const int * n));
    };
```

For the most part, QuackInt's functions implement calls to inherited QuackBase member functions:

```
QuackInt::QuackInt()
    : QuackBase(sizeof(int))
    {
    }


QuackInt::QuackInt(const QuackInt & qb)
    : QuackBase(qb)
    {
    }


QuackInt & QuackInt::operator = (const QuackInt & qb)
    {
    QuackBase::operator = (qb);
    return *this;
    }


void QuackInt::PushTop(int value)
    {
    QuackBase::PushTop(&value);
    }


int  QuackInt::PopTop()
    {
    int result;
    QuackBase::PopTop(&result);
    return result;
    }


void QuackInt::PushBottom(int value)
    {
    QuackBase::PushBottom(&value);
    }


int  QuackInt::PopBottom()
    {
    int result;
    QuackBase::PopBottom(&result);
    return result;
    }


void QuackInt::IterateUp(void (* func)(const int * n))
```

```
    {
    QuackBase::IterateUp((void (*)(const void *))func);
    }

void QuackInt::IterateDown(void (* func)(const int * n))
    {
    QuackBase::IterateDown((void (*)(const void *))func);
    }
```

Note how I made a type-specific class by using kludgy type casts. It works, but it isn't very efficient or type-safe.

The following function uses a QuackInt to hold a few numbers:

```
void Test()
    {
    QuackInt qi;

    for (int x = 0; x < 20; ++x)
        {
        if (x & 1)
            {
            qi.PushTop(x);
            cout << "pushed " << x << " at top" << endl;
            }
        else
            {
            qi.PushBottom(x);
            cout << "pushed " << x << " at bottom" << endl;
            }
        }

    cout << "count   " << qi.GetCount() << endl;

    qi.IterateUp(IterInts);

    int n;

    for (;;)
        {
        try    {
            n = qi.PopTop();
            cout << "popped " << n << " from top" << endl;
            }
```

```
        catch (QuackEx ex)
            {
            if (ex.WhatsWrong() == QE_EMPTY)
                break;
            else
                throw;
            }
        }

    cout << "count   " << qi.GetCount() << endl;
    }

void IterInts(const int * n)
    {
    cout << "iterup " << *n << endl;
    }
```

If I want to have a Quack for unsigned ints, doubles, or a structure type, I
must create a new class definition—a task that's tedious and error-prone.
Fortunately, templates provide a tool whereby I can create a single Quack
definition that works for any data type.

Implementing a Quack with Templates

A few quick changes to QuackBase—creating a template class named
Quack—eliminate the need for type-specific derived classes such as
QuackInt:

```
template <class T>
    struct QuackNode
        {
        QuackNode<T> * Above;
        QuackNode<T> * Below;
        T Data;
        };

template <class T>
    class Quack
        {
        public:
            Quack();
```

```
        Quack(const Quack<T> & qb);

        ~Quack();

        Quack & operator = (const Quack<T> & qb);

        size_t GetCount() { return Count; }

        void PushTop(T item);
        T PopTop();

        void PushBottom(T item);
        T PopBottom();

        void IterateUp(void (* func)(T item));
        void IterateDown(void (* func)(T item));

    protected:
        void Copy(const Quack<T> & qb);
        void Kill();

        size_t Count;

        QuackNode<T> * Top;
        QuackNode<T> * Bottom;
    };
```

QuackNode now stores an object of type T, and the Quack functions return
or store type T values. There's no need to keep a length of data values,
because a T object intrinsically knows how big it is. Using templates simplifies the PushTop and PopTop functions:

```
template <class T>
    void Quack<T>::PushTop(T item)
        {
        QuackNode<T> * newnode = new QuackNode<T>;

        if (newnode == NULL)
            throw QuackEx(QE_ALLOC);

        newnode->Data  = item;
```

```
        newnode->Above = NULL;
        newnode->Below = Top;

        if (Top != NULL)
            Top->Above = newnode;

        Top = newnode;

        if (Bottom == NULL)
            Bottom = Top;

        ++Count;
        }


template <class T>
    T Quack<T>::PopTop()
        {
        if (Top == NULL)
            throw QuackEx(QE_EMPTY);

        T result = Top->Data;

        QuackNode<T> * temp = Top->Below;

        delete Top;

        Top = temp;

        if (Top == NULL)
            Bottom = NULL;
        else
            Top->Above = NULL;

        —Count;

        return result;
        }
```

A great deal of error checking goes by the wayside when templates replace "generic" void pointers. If nothing else, a call to the new operator is eliminated. And a simple assignment copies information from one T to another. This technique puts the burden of object duplication on the type T instead of leaving QuackBase to make possibly bogus assumptions.

To keep this text complete, here are the other functions. In every case, using a template simplifies member functions.

```
template <class T>
    void Quack<T>::Copy(const Quack<T> & qb)
        {
        Count    = qb.Count;

        if (qb.Top == NULL)
            {
            Top      = NULL;
            Bottom   = NULL;
            }
        else
            {
            QuackNode<T> * src = qb.Top;
            QuackNode<T> * dest = NULL;
            QuackNode<T> * prev;

            while (src != NULL)
                {
                prev = dest;

                dest = new QuackNode<T>;

                if (dest == NULL)
                    throw QuackEx(QE_ALLOC);

                if (prev != NULL)
                    {
                    prev->Below = dest;
                    dest->Above = prev;
                    }
                else
                    {
                    Top = dest;
                    dest->Above = NULL;
                    }

                dest->Below = NULL;
                dest->Data  = src->Data;
```

```
                    src = src->Below;
                    }

            Bottom = dest;
            }
        }

template <class T>
    void Quack<T>::Kill()
        {
        QuackNode<T> * temp = Top;
        QuackNode<T> * next;

        while (temp != NULL)
            {
            next = temp->Below;
            delete temp;
            temp = next;
            }

        Count = 0;
        }

template <class T>
    inline Quack<T>::Quack()
        {
        Count   = 0;
        Top     = NULL;
        Bottom  = NULL;
        }

template <class T>
    inline Quack<T>::Quack(const Quack<T> & qb)
        {
        Copy(qb);
        }

template <class T>
    inline Quack<T>::~Quack()
        {
        Kill();
        }

template <class T>
```

```
    inline Quack<T> & Quack<T>::operator = (const Quack<T> & qb)
        {
        Kill();
        Copy(qb);
        return *this;
        }

template <class T>
    void Quack<T>::PushBottom(T item)
        {
        QuackNode<T> * newnode = new QuackNode<T>;

        if (newnode == NULL)
            throw QuackEx(QE_ALLOC);

        newnode->Data  = item;
        newnode->Above = Bottom;
        newnode->Below = NULL;

        if (Bottom != NULL)
            Bottom->Below  = newnode;

        Bottom = newnode;

        if (Top == NULL)
            Top = Bottom;

        ++Count;
        }

template <class T>
    T Quack<T>::PopBottom()
        {
        if (Bottom == NULL)
            throw QuackEx(QE_EMPTY);

        T result = Bottom->Data;

        QuackNode<T> * temp = Bottom->Above;

        delete Bottom;

        Bottom = temp;
```

```
            if (Bottom == NULL)
                Top = NULL;
            else
                Bottom->Below = NULL;


            --Count;


            return result;
            }


template <class T>
    void Quack<T>::IterateUp(void (* func)(T item))
        {
        if (Bottom == NULL)
            throw QuackEx(QE_EMPTY);


        QuackNode<T> * temp = Bottom;


        while (temp != NULL)
            {
            func(temp->Data);
            temp = temp->Above;
            }
        }


template <class T>
    void Quack<T>::IterateDown(void (* func)(T item))
        {
        if (Top == NULL)
            throw QuackEx(QE_EMPTY);


        QuackNode<T> * temp = Top;


        while (temp != NULL)
            {
            func(temp->Data);
            temp = temp->Below;
            }
        }
```

The Test function, given with the nontemplate version of Quack, requires only one simple change to make it compatible with the Quack template: Change the line

```
QuackInt qi;
```

to be

```
Quack<int> qi;
```

Now I've created one template that works as is with any data type. No coding a special version; no type casts; no `void` pointers and raw byte-level copies.

Aren't templates wonderful?

You'll find the template-based version of `Quack` on the accompanying source diskette in the files **quack.h** and **quack.cpp**.

ONWARD

Error handling in C has always been a haphazard affair. A C++ program uses exceptions to define types of errors and the handling they require. The next chapter introduces exceptions and their uses.

CHAPTER 3

EXCEPTIONS

Assuming that a function encounters a problem, it has several choices about how it reacts:

- Terminate the program.
- Return after setting a global error value.
- Return with an error value to indicate failure.
- Return after correcting the problem as best it can.
- Return and ignore the problem.
- Call another function to handle the error.
- Ask for user input before doing any of the above.

Most programming languages lack a robust method for handling exceptions. The programmer figures out what technique is best for handling each problem. This leads to a hodgepodge approach to error handling.

The standard C function library provides an excellent example of how error handling can become confusing and disorganized. Some functions set `errno`; others do not. Many functions return special values to indicate exceptions, but the program must test those return values diligently to catch errors. In C++, the `new` operator calls a user-defined `new_handler` function if a problem occurs. Nothing is consistent, and programmers must remember dozens of differing handling options.

BASIC BUG TRAPS

I classify exceptions as follows:

- Failure to acquire a resource (new failed, file couldn't be opened)
- Attempts to do something impossible (divide by zero, index out of range)
- Invalid conditions (lookup in empty list, buffer overflow)

I do not consider input errors to be exceptions. Validating data as it is entered is a part of data entry, and entered data should always be validated before it is stored or used by a program.

An Example Class

To illustrate exception-handling techniques, I created a small String class. Here is the class definition:

```
const char NULCHAR = '\0';

class String
    {
    public:
        String(const char * init = NULL);
        String(const String & str);
        ~String();

        operator const char *()
            {
            return (const char *)Text;
            }
```

```
        void operator = (const String & str);
        void operator = (const char * str);

        char operator [] (size_t index);

        size_t LengthOf()
            {
            return Len;
            }

private:
    char * Text;
    size_t Len;
};
```

Here is the implementation of String's member functions:

```
String::String(const char * init)
    {
    if (init == NULL)
        {
        Text = NULL;
        Len  = 0;
        }
    else
        {
        Len = strlen(init);

        Text = new char [Len + 1];

        if (Text != NULL)
            strcpy(Text,init);
        }
    }

String::String(const String & str)
    {
    if (str.Text == NULL)
        {
        Text = NULL;
        Len  = 0;
        }
```

```
    else
        {
        Len  = str.Len;
        Text = new char [Len + 1];

        if (Text != NULL)
            strcpy(Text,str.Text);
        }
    }

String::~String()
    {
    if (Text != NULL)
        delete [] Text;
    }

void String::operator = (const String & str)
    {
    if (Text != NULL)
        delete [] Text;

    if (str.Text == NULL)
        {
        Text = NULL;
        Len  = 0;
        }
    else
        {
        Len  = str.Len;
      Text = new char [Len + 1];

        if (Text != NULL)
            strcpy(Text,str.Text);
        }
    }

void String::operator = (const char * str)
    {
    if (Text != NULL)
        delete [] Text;

    if (str == NULL)
        {
        Text = NULL;
        Len  = 0;
```

```
        }
    else
        {
        Len  = strlen(str);
        Text = new char [Len + 1];

        strcpy(Text,str);
        }
    }

char String::operator [] (size_t index)
    {
    if ((Text != NULL) && (index < Len))
        return Text[index];
    else
        return NULCHAR;
    }
```

String provides controlled access to an array of characters, and its capabilities are limited. It isn't the type of string class you (or I) would want for most real-world applications; however, it works quite well for showing C++'s exception-handling mechanism.

As implemented above, String does not use exception handlers. If a memory allocation fails, the program creates a NULL string. If an index is out of- , the [] operator returns NULCHAR. Throughout the implementation, I check for a NULL Text pointer before performing operations.

This method works, but it isn't very robust. All sorts of problems could occur; for example, what happens if the program attempts to construct a String using a NULL or invalid char *? And three conditions—a NULL Text pointer, indexing outside the text, or reading the end of the text—can cause the [] operator to return a NULCHAR. My program won't be able to tell what has gone wrong.

Global Error Flags

I could define a global error value:

```
enum { Okay, NullText, OutOfBounds } StringErr = Okay;
```

The [] operator could then set the value of StringErr:

```
char String::operator [] (size_t index)
    {
    char result;

    if (Text == NULL)
        {
        result == NULCHAR;
        StringErr = NullText;
        }
    else
        {
        if (index < Len)
            {
            result = Text[index];
            StringErr = Okay;
            }
        else
            {
            result = NULCHAR;
            StringErr = OutOfRange;
            }
        }

    return result;
    }
```

Then, every time I get a NULCHAR while indexing a String, I'll need to check StringErr to see what happened:

```
function Klunky(String & str)
    {
    char ch = str[5];

    if (ch == NULCHAR)
        {
        switch (StringErr)
            {
            case NullText:
                // do something about error
                break;

            case OutOfBounds:
                // do something about error
```

```
            break;
        }
    }

    // work with ch
    }
```

C uses a similar concept with its `errno` global variable.

Using a global variable works, but the program suddenly becomes longer and more complicated. This design requires me to write specific code to check `StringError` every time I call operator []. And global variables are notoriously unreliable; the value of `StringError` could be changed anywhere in the program.

Error Functions

What about using an error-trapping function? I could create a type that identifies errors:

```
enum StrErrType { NullText, OutOfBounds };
```

And then I could add functions and pointers to the `String` class:

```
typedef void (StrErrFunc *)(StrErrType err);

class String
    {
    public:
        static void SetErrorFunc(StrErrFunc func)
            {
            CallOnError = func;
            }

    private:
        static StrErrFunc CallOnError;
    };

StrErrFunc String::CallOnError = NULL;
```

Then I would implement the [] operator like this:

```
char String::operator [] (size_t index)
    {
    char result;

    if (Text == NULL)
        {
        result == NULCHAR;

        if (CallOnError != NULL)
            CallOnError(NullText);
        }
    else
        {
        if (index < Len)
            {
            result = Text[index];
            }
        else
            {
            result = NULCHAR;

            if (CallOnError != NULL)
                CallOnError(OutOfBounds);
            }

    return result;
    }
```

This solution works, but it doesn't work well. The `CallOnError` function is a black box that must be installed by the program before it works. A typical error-handling function might look like this:

```
void MyStringError(StrErrType err)
    {
    switch (err)
        {
        case NullText:
            cout << "Text not allocated" << endl;
            break;

        case OutOfBounds:
```

```
        cout << "index out of range" << endl;
        abort();
    }
}
```

I would then assign my error-handling function to the `String` class using this statement:

```
String::SetErrFunc(MyStringError);
```

This technique allows me to define exactly how my program handles each error. The `String` class calls the error function, ensuring that problems are always trapped by my function. However, a function that calls operator [] still won't know whether the `NULCHAR` was from the text or from an error. `MyStringError` could set a global flag, but that would put me right back where I started from, with global values that need manual checking. Ugh.

Fancier versions of this method might use objects to encapsulate error-handling routines. But those solutions simply put a fancier face on the same old problems. Fortunately, C++ offers an elegant and powerful solution: exception handlers.

C++ EXCEPTION HANDLING

An *exception handler* is a block of code that processes specific error conditions. By using exception handlers, a programmer can create a central piece of code for managing program problems. This practice leads to consistent and readable code.

To define exception handlers, you must tell the compiler that you're trapping exceptions, and your program must provide code to handle the exceptions that arise. To do those things, you use the keywords `try` and `catch`:

```
class BlewUp { };
class Kaboom { };
```

```
void HardWork()
    {
    try
        {
        if (something_wrong())
            throw BlewUp();

        if (uhoh())
            throw Kaboom();

        twang();
        }

    catch (BlewUp)
        {
        // handle a BlewUp exception
        }

    catch (Kaboom)
        {
        // handle a Kaboom exception
        }

    catch (...)
        {
        // handle any other exceptions
        }
    }
```

The keyword `try` specifies a block of statements that could generate exceptions. A `try`_block is followed by one or more `catch` *blocks*; each `catch` block defines the code to be executed when a specific exception occurs within the `try` block. The `try` and `catch` keywords go together; you can't have `try` without at least one `catch`, and `catch` blocks cannot exist without a `try` block.

A `catch` block is also known as an exception handler. Each `catch` block declares the type of exception it will handle. When a problem occurs, the program throws an object, which is caught by the exception handler corresponding to the type of the object thrown. For example, if the call to `uhoh` returns a nonzero value, the `throw Kaboom()` statement will cause the `catch (Kaboom)` code block to execute.

A `catch` `(...)` block will handle any exception not processed by other exception handlers. If you don't define a `catch` `(...)` block, unhandled exceptions result in calls to a `terminate` function. I'll talk about `terminate()` later in this chapter.

If a `try` block does not generate any exception, program execution continues with the statement immediately following the `try` block's associated list of `catch` blocks. Also, if a `catch` block does not transfer control elsewhere, program execution will continue immediately after the last `catch` block.

Nested Exception Handlers

If a function is called from within a `try` block, any exceptions it throws will be caught by the `try` block's exception handlers. For example:

```
class Problem {};

void Level1
    {
    try
        {
        Level2();
        }

    catch (Problem)
        {
        // do something with a Problem
        }
    }

void Level2()
    {
    Level3();

    if (SomethingBad())
        throw Problem;
    }

void Level3()
```

```
     {
   if (WentWrong())
       throw Problem;
   }
```

When an exception is thrown, the compiler looks back through the chain of function calls for a handler. If the compiler doesn't find a handler or if no `try` or `catch` blocks are active, the `terminate` function is called. In the preceding example, the `throw` statements in `Level2` and `Level3` will result in executing the `catch (Problem)` block in `Level1`.

The search for a handler stops at the first appropriate exception handler to be found. For example:

```
class Bomb { };
class Crash { };

void Level1()
    {
    try
        {
        Level2()
        }

    catch (Bomb)
        {
        // do something about a Bomb
        }

    catch (Crash)
        {
        // do something about a Crash
        }
    }

void Level2()
    {
    try
        {
        Level3();
        }

    catch (Crash)
```

```
        {
        // do something about a Crash
        }
    }

void Level3()
    {
    if (GoingToFast())
        throw Crash;

    if (FuseIsLit())
        throw Bomb;
    }
```

When `Level3` throws a `Crash`, the problem is handled by the `catch (Crash)` block in `Level2`. Because `Level2` does not define a handler for `Bomb`s, `Level3`'s `throw Bomb` statement sends control to `Level1`'s `catch (Bomb)` block.

Automatic Destructor Calls

A `throw` statement moves back up the call chain until it finds the first exception handler for an exception type. Along the way, the program "unwinds" the call chain, destroying objects created in higher-level functions and freeing stack space. For example:

```
class DataRecord
    {
    public:
        DataRecord();
        ~DataRecord();

        // assume a complex class definition
    };

// exception class
class Trouble { };

void StartHere()
    {
    try
```

```
        {
        WorkHere();
        }

    catch (Trouble)
        {
        // handle Trouble
        }
    }

void WorkHere()
    {
    DataRecord dRec;
    DataRecord * pRec = new DataRecord;

    if (some_problem)
        throw Trouble;
    }
```

If the `throw Trouble` statement is executed in `WorkHere`, the program will call the `DataRecord` destructor for `dRec`. However, it won't automatically call a destructor for `pRec`, because `pRec` is a dynamic object.

You can use classes to force the destruction of dynamically allocated objects. If you want to ensure the automatic destruction of `pRec`, the program could be rewritten:

```
class DataRecord
    {
    public:
        DataRecord();
        ~DataRecord();

        // assume a complex class definition
    };

// define a pointer to a DataRecord
class DataRecPtr
    {
    public:
        DataRecord * ptr;

    private:
        DataRecPtr();
```

```
        ~DataRecPtr();
            { delete ptr; }

        operator DataRecord * ()
            { return ptr; }
    };

DataRecPtr::DataRecPtr()
    {
    ptr = new DataRecord;

    if (ptr == NULL)
        throw xalloc("DataRecPtr not allocated",n);
    }

// exception classes
class Trouble { };

void StartHere()
    {
    try
        {
        WorkHere();
        }

    catch (Trouble)
        {
        // do something about Trouble
        }
    }

void WorkHere()
    {
    DataRecord dRec;
    DataRecPtr pRec;

    if (some_problem)
        throw Trouble;
    }
```

Now that pRec is an object, any exit from the WorkHere function—including a thrown exception—will automatically delete (and subsequently destroy) pRec's dynamic DataRecord object.

Using objects to control resource allocations is an important technique. By encapsulating resource allocations (whether requests are for dynamic memory or for the use of a file), you guarantee that those resources will be properly handled on function exit or program termination. It's easy to forget to explicitly close files or delete dynamic objects, and the chance of overlooking this kind of cleanup increases as a program becomes more complex. Objects can make your life easier by making your program remember things for you.

One more point about automatic destructor calls: The compiler will not call destructors for incomplete objects. An object is considered complete when its constructor successfully returns. If you throw an exception inside a constructor, the compiler will not perform any cleanup on the incomplete object. This makes sense, because the compiler has no way of telling a destructor how to destroy an incomplete object.

It's a matter of good program design: Before an exception is thrown, an incomplete object should always return the system to its preconstructor state.

The Terminate Function

Let's look further at something I mentioned in the previous section. If you haven't defined a `catch` (…) (catch all) block and if a type-specific exception handler can't be found, the exception will be handled by a global function named `terminate`. By default, `terminate` is implemented as a call to the standard library function `abort`. A program also calls `terminate` if an exception is thrown and no enclosing try block is found.

Simple termination is too draconian for many applications; before a program terminates, you may want to write to files or release system resources. The `set_terminate` function allows you to define a `terminate` function of your own design:

```
#include "except.h"

void MyTerminate()
```

```
    {
    // cleanup program

    abort();
    }

int main()
    {
    oldterm = set_terminate(My_Terminate);

    // do program stuff

    // restore old handler
    set_terminate(oldterm);

    return 0;
    }
```

The header file **except.h** contains a prototype for `set_terminate` and a definition for the `terminate_function` type:

```
typedef void (* terminate_function)();

terminate_function set_terminate(terminate_function);
```

Some compilers may limit the actions that can be performed inside a `terminate` function, so check your compiler documentation for specifics.

Exceptions as Objects

An exception is identified by a data type. You could, for example, have an exception like this:

```
try
    {
    // do something
    throw 1;
    }
```

```
catch (int i)
    {
    handle an int error
    }
```

However, you couldn't use:

```
throw int;
```

An exception is an object and not a type. To access the data in a thrown object, a catch block can provide an identifier for that object:

```
catch (int i)
    {
    cout << "int exception " << i << endl;
    }
```

A catch block can specify an argument of type T, references to T, and const versions of either. It cannot specify default arguments, though, because a catch block will be called only for an existing object.

You can use an enumerated type to identify exceptions:

```
enum Problem { BadInput, LowMemory, StupidUser };

void SomeFunk()
    {
    try
        {
        // code that throws exceptions
        throw Problem(StupidUser);
        }

    catch (Problem p)
        {
        switch (p)
            {
            case BadInput:
                break;
            case LowMemory:
                break;
```

```
        case StupidUser:
            break;
        }
    }
}
```

Note that a `typedef` merely creates an alias for an existing type. For example:

```
typedef int ExInt;

ExInt ei = 1;
throw ei;
```

The `throw` statement would look for a `catch (int)` block. The compiler should reject any attempt to create both `catch (int)` and `catch (ExInt)` blocks in the same `try` or `catch` statement, because `ExInt` is merely another name for `int`.

Exception Classes

In most cases, your exception types will be defined by classes. Simple types, such as `int`, can pass only simple information. An exception class can provide clear information on the problem and its causes.

Let's go back to my `String` class for a moment and rewrite it to use exceptions. First, I'd create an exception class that defines an indexing error:

```
struct ErrorRange
    {
    size_t index;

    ErrorRange(size_t i)
        {
        index = i;
        }
    };
```

Then, in my implementation of the String class, I would change the []
operator function to throw an ErrorRange exception:

```
char String::operator [] (size_t n)
    {
    if (n > Len)
        throw ErrorRange(n);
    else
        return Text[n];
    }
```

In my program, wherever I index Strings, I can now catch out-of-range
indexes this way:

```
char GetUpperChar(String & str, size_t n)
    {
    try
        {
        return (char)toupper(str[n]);
        }

    catch (ErrorRange er)
        {
        cout << "bad string index: " << er.index << endl;
        abort();
        }
    }
```

Or I can have the operator [] function catch exceptions internally:

```
char String::operator [] (size_t n)
    {
    try
        {
        if (n > Len)
            throw ErrorRange(n);
        else
            return Text[n];
        }

    catch (ErrorRange er)
```

```
        {
        cout << "bad string index: " << er.index << endl;
        return NULL;
        }
    }
```

Catching the error within the `String` class allows me to keep the program running by returning a `NULCHAR`. This method may not be desirable; handling the exception outside the `String` class gives me more flexibility. For example, I could have the `GetUpperChar` function work this way:

```
char GetUpperChar(String & str, size_t n)
    {
    try
        {
        return (char)toupper(str[n]);
        }

    catch (ErrorRange er)
        {
        return NULL;
        }
    }
```

Rethrowing an Exception

You can cascade the handling of an exception by having a lower level rethrow an exception to a higher level.

```
catch (ErrorRange er)
    {
    cout << "String index bad: " << er.index << endl;
    throw;
    }
```

A `throw` statement without an argument rethrows the last exception to the next highest level of exception handler. If no previous exception exists, the program calls `terminate()`.

Exception Class Hierarchies

Using a common base class allows the use of one handler for many related exceptions. For example, a set of exception objects for memory-allocation problems could be derived from a base `MemoryException` class: `OutOfMemory`, `ZeroAlloc`, etc. A single `catch (MemoryException)` handler would catch all memory exceptions, including new ones. This technique makes code more robust and prevents the need to find every set of exception handlers to add new `catch` statements.

Virtual functions allow derived exception classes to use their internal information, which doesn't exist in the base class. For example:

```
class MemoryException
    {
    public:
        virtual void DisplayMessage() = 0;
    };


class OutOfMemory : public MemoryException
    {
    public:
        virtual void DisplayMessage();
    };


void OutOfMemory::DisplayMessage()
    {
    cout << "Out of memory!\n";
    }


class BadPointer : public MemoryException
    {
    public:
        BadPointer(void * p)
            {
            ptr = p;
            }

        virtual void DisplayMessage();
```

```
    private:
        void * p;
    };

void BadPointer::DisplayMessage()
    {
    cout << "Invalid pointer: " << ptr << endl;
    }
```

A generic `catch` block could use the virtual `DisplayMessage` function to display any `MemoryProblem` object:

```
catch (MemoryProblem memprob)
    {
    memprob.DisplayMessage();
    abort();
    }
```

As in the preceding example, you can use pure virtual functions to stop creation of base exception objects.

Using class hierarchies allows you to organize and group related exceptions. Some experts, including Stroustrup, suggest the creation of a universal exception base class:

```
class Exception
    {
    // your common exception mechanisms
    };
```

Having a common base class improves program consistency and simplifies `catch` blocks. A program that contains long lists of `catch` blocks probably has defined too many separate exception types. Using exception hierarchies can vastly simplify your programs.

You might consider having a virtual destructor in an exception base class so that any exception objects will properly clean up any internal resource allocations.

Standard Exception Classes

The proposed ANSI C++ standard defines xalloc, an exception handler for memory allocation problems. The header file **except.h** contains the xalloc class definition. An xalloc object is thrown when a memory allocation fails; you create an xalloc from a string and the number of bytes you requested:

```
size_t array_size = 100;

int * array = new int [array_size];

if (array == NULL)
    throw xalloc("Allocation failure",n);
```

The xalloc exception supersedes the new_handler function mechanism.

Exceptions Throwing Exceptions

Upon entry to a handler, an exception is considered to be handled. If a handler rethrows its exception, the previous handler is invoked, thus preventing an endless loop. If the higher level doesn't have a handler, the program calls terminate.

You can convert one exception type to another using code such as this:

```
catch (ThisException)
    {
    throw ThatException;
    }
```

Templates and Exceptions

Exceptions defined within a template class can be specific to each generated class:

```
template <class T> class List
    {
    public:
        class EmptyList {  }; // exception class
        // ...
    };
```

Then a `catch` block would need to specify the type of `List` that it is handling:

```
catch (List<int>::EmptyList)
    {
    // do something
    }
```

You would need to define handlers for each expected type of `List`; otherwise, those `List` types not listed will have their exceptions handled by the `terminate` function. Or you can define an `EmptyList` exception outside the `List` class, making it global to all list types.

Exceptions defined within a class follow the standard access rules. If a class handles an exception only internally, the exception class should be private or protected. If you want the exception to be handled externally, make it public or define it outside the error-producing class.

Function Declarations

A function declaration may include a `throw` statement. For example,

```
void Boing() throw (Stuck, OutOfBounds)
    {
    // do whatever Boing does
    }
is equivalent to
void Boing()
    {
    try
        {
        // do whatever Boing does
        }
```

```
    catch (Stuck)
        {
        throw;
        }

    catch (OutOfBounds)
        {
        throw;
        }

    catch (...)
        {
        unexpected();
        }
    }
```

Without a `throw` declaration, a function can throw any exception. The `throw()` declaration states that a function does not throw any exceptions.

If a function throws an exception that is not in that function's `throw` declaration, the `unexpected` function is called. By default, `unexpected` calls `terminate`, which in turn calls `abort`. The `set_unexpected` function allows you to define the handling of unexpected exceptions:

```
#include "except.h"

void MyUnexpected()
    {
    // clean-up program

    abort();
    }

int main()
    {
    oldunexp = set_unexpected(MyUnexpected);

    // do program stuff

    // restore old handler
    set_unexpected(oldunexp);
```

```
    return 0;
    }
```

The header file **except.h** defines the `unexpected_function` type and the `set_unexpected` function:

```
typedef void (* unexpected_function)();

unexpected_function set_unexpected(unexpected_function);
```

Unexpected exceptions don't pass beyond the calling function. A `catch` (...) handler won't catch unexpected exceptions from functions that have `throw` declarations.

A function containing a `throw` declaration will probably not be inlined by most compilers. In fact, a compiler is highly unlikely to inline any function containing exception handlers or `throw` statements.

Miscellaneous Technicalities

Each `try` and `catch` block is a separate scope. A `catch` block cannot access objects declared within its `try` block or in other `catch` blocks.

You cannot use a `goto` statement to enter a `catch` block or to skip from one `catch` block to another. A `goto` can jump out of a `catch` or `try` block, though:

```
void BusyWork()
    {
    try
        {
        // do something
        }

    catch (Hell h)
        {
        if (h.HasSnowball())
            goto ColdDay;
```

```
    // handle hell problem
    abort();
    }

ColdDay:
    cout << "A cold day in hell!\n";
}
```

Further Explorations

At the time of this writing, only a few C++ compilers support exception handling. I used Borland C++ 4.0 for the examples I've discussed, and for those in this book as a whole, because the Borland compiler supports the version of exceptions that has been accepted by the ANSI C++ standards committee. Compiler vendors have been reluctant to implement exceptions for a variety of reasons, both political (they don't like ANSI's definition) and technical.

Some compilers provide incomplete or substitute exception-handling mechanisms. Microsoft's Visual C++ version 1.00, for example, uses a set of classes to simulate some features of exception handlers. I avoid these proprietary systems, because their use would lock me into a specific vendor's compiler product; every time I've let that happen, I've learned to regret it. Experience has taught me to keep my programs as compiler-independent and platform-independent as possible.

RESUMPTION

The C++ standard does not support resumption from an exception handler. This issue has generated debate at the ANSI standards committee meetings. Some operating systems internally support resumption from errors, but most do not. Strong arguments exist for both sides, and only time will tell how ANSI handles resumption.

Resumption would be handy for handling nonfatal problems, but you can creatively use exception handlers to get around that limitation. For example, a failure to allocate memory might be solved by compacting memory and trying the allocation request again:

```
CharArray::CharArray(size_t n)
    {
    try
        {
        // allocate memory
        ptr = new char [n];

        // if it didn't work, throw exception
        if (ptr == NULL)
            throw(xalloc("CharArray memory error",n));
        }

    catch (xalloc)
        {
        // try to get more memory
        CompactMemory();

        // attempt allocation again
        ptr = new char [n];

        // if it still doesn't work, pass the exception
        if (ptr == NULL)
            throw;
        }

    // work with ptr
    }
```

This solution isn't quite perfect. For example, the call to new must be duplicated in two places. You'll always have to remember to make both identical changes to both new calls.

Fault-Tolerant Design

One of the buzzphrases in programming is *fault-tolerant design*, which means that software should be self-correcting and reliable. This is how we've always wanted programs to be. A fault-tolerant system is robust in handling exceptions, and it tries to correct problems when they occur.

If you want to catch and handle every possible exception, bracket your statements in main with a try and catch block:

```
int main()
    {
    try
        {
        // program code goes here
        }

    catch (Bomb) { }

    catch (Blast) { }

    catch (...)
        {
        return EXIT_FAILURE;
        }

    return 0;
    }
```

In my programs, I've used main to catch all program exceptions. I base all my exceptions on a single base class called Exception:

```
class Exception
    {
    public:
        virtual ~Exception();

        virtual String TextAbout() = 0;
    };

Exception::~Exception() { } // does nothing
```

My main paragraph then contains a try block like this one:

```
int main()
```

```
{
try
    {
    // do everything
    }

catch (Exception & ex)
    {
    cout << ex.TextAbout << endl;
    abort();
    }

catch (...)
    {
    cout << "Unknown exception caught in main\n";
    abort();
    }

return 0;
}
```

This program catches all exceptions based on Exception and prints a message about the exception using the virtual TextAbout function. To be especially thorough, I would also want to define an unexpected function of my own. Also, if I define a terminate function to perform program cleanup, I might want to change the calls to abort into throw statements, thereby causing automatic calls to terminate.

Cleaning up after yourself is an important part of fault-tolerant design. Here's another example of fault-tolerant design:

```
void DoIt();
    {
    const size_t mem_need = 64;

    char * carray = new char[mem_need];

    if (carray == NULL)
        throw(xalloc("DoIt memory error",mem_need));

    try    {
        // code that may throw an exception
```

```
        }

    catch (...)
        {
        // take care of local business
        delete [] carray;

        // pass the buck
        throw;
        }

    delete [] carray;
    }
```

Better yet, `carray` should be declared an object, using a class that automatically deletes allocated memory with a destructor.

Nonfatal Exceptions

You can use an exception to handle a non-error condition. For example:

```
class Info {};

class TextTable
    {
    public:
        Info Lookup(char * key);

        class LookupFailure { };
    };

Info TextTable::Lookup(char * key)
    {
    // if key is not found
        throw(LookupFailure);
    }

void FindIt(TextTable & table, char * key)
    {
    try
        {
```

```
        Info data = table.Lookup(key);
        }

catch (LookupFailure)
    {
    // handle lack of information
    }
}
```

This code uses an exception to trap a lookup failure in a table. You can use this technique in many situations in which the failure of an operation is not fatal.

I've used exceptions for non-error conditions; Stroustrup even mentions this technique in his own books. However, although exceptions are a powerful tool, using them to control non-error conditions can lead to sloppy programming. As I mentioned earlier in this chapter, exceptions provide a structured mechanism for handling unusual program conditions. Straying too far from that philosophy undermines the concept of layering and organizing your program's code.

Exceptions should not be used for every problem. Exceptions were designed for control of complicated errors. In basic programs, it may be overkill to use exceptions. Stroustrup provides excellent advice when he suggests that exceptions should not be used when other error-trapping techniques can be effectively employed.

A DIAGNOSTIC EXAMPLE

An intelligent data structure knows enough about itself to know when something has gone wrong. To show how to include diagnostic and debugging information in a class, I've created an example based on a singly linked list type. A list is a container, so I implemented a template that describes a family of list classes. My goal is to show you a simple but realistic example of diagnostics, using a piece of code that's been included in live applications.

The DiagOutput Classes

I want my classes to be platform-independent. Any useful diagnostics must be displayed somewhere, either on the screen or in a file. Programs require different output mechanisms for various environments, such as command-line DOS, windowed DOS, and Microsoft Windows. So I created a simple base class that defines the output of text and an error level:

```
enum DiagLevel
    {
    DIAG_MSG,
    DIAG_WARNING,
    DIAG_ERROR,
    DIAG_FATAL
    };

class DiagOutput
    {
    public:
        virtual void DisplayMsg
            (
            const char * msg,
            DiagLevel level = DIAG_MSG
            ) = 0;
    };
```

DiagOutput is a virtual base class from which I derive specific classes for various environments. For MS-DOS command-line programs, for example, I created this class:

```
class DiagOutDOS : public DiagOutput
    {
    public:
        DiagOutDOS
            (
            ostream & strm
            );

        virtual void DisplayMsg
            (
            const char * msg,
```

```
            DiagLevel level = DIAG_MSG
            );

    private:
        ostream & outstrm;
    };

inline DiagOutDOS::DiagOutDOS
    (
    ostream & strm
    )
    : outstrm(strm)
    {
     // otherwise empty
    }
```

You provide a stream object when creating a DiagOutDOS object; usually, I use the standard streams cerr or cout. I implemented the DisplayMsg function as follows:

```
void DiagOutDOS::DisplayMsg
    (
    const char * msg,
    DiagLevel level
    )
    {
    switch (level)
        {
        // note that DIAG_MSG does not display a header!
        case DIAG_WARNING:
            outstrm << "Warning: ";
            break;
        case DIAG_ERROR:
            outstrm << "ERROR: ";
            break;
        case DIAG_FATAL:
            outstrm << "FATAL ERROR: ";
        }

    outstrm << msg;

    if (level != DIAG_MSG)
        {
        outstrm << endl << "Press any key to ";
```

```
        if (level == DIAG_WARNING)
            outstrm << "continue.";
        else
            outstrm << "TERMINATE this program.";

        while (!kbhit());         // wait for keypress
        if (!getch()) getch(); // clear input character
        }

    outstrm << endl;

    if (level >= DIAG_ERROR)
        exit(EXIT_FAILURE);
    }
```

If the error level is DIAG_MSG (the default), DisplayMsg simply displays the string and returns. For a DIAG_WARNING message, DisplayMsg also stops and waits for the user to press a key before it returns. DIAG_ERROR and DIAG_FATAL messages cause DisplayMsg to terminate the program. Several variations on this theme exist; this is how I usually handle problems in command-line programs.

For Microsoft Windows, my DiagOutWin class displays messages in message boxes. Here's its definition:

```
class DiagOutWin : public DiagOutput
    {
    public:
        DiagOutWin
            (
            const char * t
            );

        ~DiagOutWin();

        virtual void DisplayMsg
            (
            const char * msg,
            DiagLevel level = DIAG_MSG
            );

    public:
```

```
        char * Title;
    };
```

`DiagOutWin` reflects the added features of the Windows environment. When creating a `DiagOutWin` object, a constructor parameter specifies the title of any message boxes. Usually, the title will be the name of the program. Because the `Title` data member is dynamically allocated, `DiagOutWin` requires a destructor to free that memory.

```
inline DiagOutWin::DiagOutWin
    (
    const char * t
    )
    {
    Title = strdup(t);
    }

inline DiagOutWin::~DiagOutWin()
    {
    if (Title != NULL)
        delete Title;
    }
```

Following is the default implementation of `DiagOutWin`'s `DisplayMessage` function:

```
void DiagOutWin::DisplayMsg
    (
    const char * msg,
    DiagLevel level
    )
    {
    UINT style;
    UINT sound;
    int response;
    char text[256];

    // copy message to output buffer
    strncpy(text,msg,128);

    // set values specific to error severity
    switch (level)
```

```
     {
case DIAG_FATAL:
    sound = MB_ICONSTOP;
    style = MB_OK;
    strcat(text,"\nPROGRAM WILL TERMINATE!");
    break;
case DIAG_ERROR:
    sound = MB_ICONEXCLAMATION;
    style = MB_YESNO;
    strcat(text,"\nClick 'Yes' to terminate program, "
                "or 'No' to continue");
    break;
case DIAG_WARNING:
case DIAG_MSG:
    sound = MB_ICONASTERISK;
    style = MB_OK;
}

// match icon to sound
style |= sound;

// sound off and display message
MessageBeep(sound);
response = MessageBox(NULL,text,Title,style);

// check for termination
switch (level)
    {
    case DIAG_ERROR:
        if (response == IDNO)
            break;
    case DIAG_FATAL:
        PostQuitMessage(1); // boom-boom
        // program should never reach this point!
    }
}
```

Again, the Windows-based class is more complicated than the DOS equivalent. For Windows, I create different message box attributes based on
the severity of the message. For DIAG_ERROR messages, I include **Yes** and
No buttons in the message box that let the user choose to terminate or
continue the program. DIAG_FATAL messages always cause the application
the stop.

The ExceptionBase Class

All my exception types are based on this class:

```
class ExceptionBase
    {
    public:
        virtual ~ExceptionBase();
        virtual void Explain(DiagOutput & out) = 0;
    };


ExceptionBase::~ExceptionBase()
    {
    // does nothing
    }
```

The virtual destructor is a piece of good programming style that ensures that the proper destructor call is made for any object type derived from ExceptionBase. Most ExceptionBase objects don't need a destructor, and that's why ExceptionBase's destructor is not pure. For those exception objects that need destruction, the virtual designation is vital.

The virtual Explain function displays a text description of the problem through a DiagOutput object. Classes derived from ExceptionBase should implement a problem-specific version of Explain.

The DiagnosticBase Class

Another basic class defines the common features I use when debugging data structures and complex classes:

```
class DiagnosticBase
    {
    public:
        virtual void Dump(DiagOutput & out) = 0;
        virtual void ShowInternals(DiagOutput & out) = 0;
        virtual Boolean CheckIntegrity() = 0;
    };
```

DiagnosticBase is an abstract base class that defines the functions I use for analyzing an object. Dump displays the contents of an object; for example, to debug an array class, Dump would output the elements of the array. ShowInternals outputs control information, such as the number of elements in an array and pointers to the array elements.

CheckIntegrity is a self-diagnostic that returns BOOL_TRUE if everything with the object is OK, and BOOL_FALSE if it finds something wrong. Implementing this function can be tricky, because you must be sure that you've implemented your checks correctly. It's been proven that software can never verify software, because any software—including verification software—can have bugs. I suggest that CheckIntegrity be implemented to look for blatant faults; trying to be too thorough only makes opportunities for errors in verification.

I didn't combine ExceptionBase and DiagnosticBase, because most exceptions will be simple. DiagnosticBase is designed to provide detailed information on the internal structure of a complex object. Combining the two classes would be overkill for most exceptions.

The source code for my diagnostic classes is in the files **diagnose.h**, **diagnose.cpp**, **diagdos.h**, and **diagdos.cpp** on the accompanying source diskette.

The SList Design

SList is a simple list type. Each node in the list contains a data item and a pointer to the next item in the list. Each SList object maintains pointers to the first and last nodes in the list; when a data item is added, its node is appended to the list as the new tail. The list can only be traversed forward, and I provide functions for that purpose. An internal node pointer keeps track of the currently selected node, and another function recalls the data stored in that node. Possible errors include a failure to allocate dynamic memory and an attempt to read data from an empty list.

During testing, performance is secondary to reliability. In many cases, you can create a set of *wrappers* to contain your diagnostic code; once the program is completely tested, you can eliminate the debugging shells and exceptions to improve your program's performance.

I decided to implement two templates. The first template, SList, defines the basic SList class template. The second template, DebugSList, is derived from SList, ExceptionBase, and DiagnosticBase. When an error occurs in an SList, it throws a DebugSList object. Because a DebugSList is created from an SList, it contains the complete information on the original class.

For DebugSList to be useful, it must exactly duplicate the object that it is reporting on. Therefore, a DebugSList contains a shallow copy of the original SList. This arrangement also prevents problems when a memory-allocation error is being reported; obviously, the last thing we want to do is to allocate more memory when a memory allocation has just failed!

Implementing SList

Here is the template definition for SList:

```
template <class T>
    class SList
        {
        public:
            // constructors
            SList();

            SList
                (
                const SList & slst,
                Boolean shallow = BOOL_FALSE
                );

            // destructors
            ~SList();

            // assignment operator
            void operator =
                (
                const SList & slst
                );

            // append a new item to the
```

```
Boolean Append
    (
    const T & item
    );

// get current item
T GetItem();

// TRUE if current item is last item
Boolean AtEnd();

// set current item to head of list
void GoToHead()
    {
    Work = Head;
    }

// move to next item in list
virtual void GoToNext()
    {
    if (Work != Tail) Work = Work->Next;
    }

// obtain # of items in list
size_t GetCount()
    {
    return Count;
    }

protected:
// type defining a node in the list
struct Node
    {
    T Data;
    Node * Next;
    };

size_t Count; // # of items in list
Node * Head;  // first item
Node * Tail;  // last item
Node * Work;  // current item

Boolean IsShallow; // Is this a shallow copy?
```

```
        // internal utility functions
        void DeepCopy
            (
            const SList & slst
            );

        void ShallowCopy
            (
            const SList & slst
            );

        void Kill();

        void SetNull()
            {
            Head  = NULL;
            Tail  = NULL;
            Work  = NULL;
            Count = 0;
            }
    };
```

Note the copy constructor, which has an extra Boolean value to indicate a shallow or deep copy. The safest assumption is a deep copy, so the default value of shallow is FALSE.

Defining DebugSList

The debugging class looks like this:

```
template <class T>
    class DebugSList
        : public SList<T>,
          public ExceptionBase,
          public DiagnosticBase
        {
    public:
        // constructor
        DebugSList(const SList<T> & slst,
                   SListBugType bug);
```

```
          DebugSList(const DebugSList<T> & deblist);

          void operator = (const DebugSList<T> & deblist);

          // virtual exception functions
          virtual void Explain(DiagOutput & out);

          // virtual diagnostic functions
          virtual void Dump(DiagOutput & out);

          virtual void ShowInternals(DiagOutput & out);

          virtual Boolean CheckIntegrity();

      private:
          SListBugType Problem;
      };
```

Implementing SList

For the most part, SList is a basic singly linked list class; I assume that
anyone buying this book is familiar with this kind of basic data structures,
and I won't go into great detail here about links, nodes, and other technical details. Here's the implementation of SList's member functions.

```
template <class T>
    void SList<T>::DeepCopy
        (
        const SList & slst
        )
        {
        if (slst.Count == 0)
            return;

        Node * n = slst.Head;

        do    {
            Append(n->Data);
            n = n->Next;
            }
```

```
        while (n != NULL);

        Work = Head;
        IsShallow = BOOL_FALSE;
        }

template <class T>
    void SList<T>::ShallowCopy
        (
        const SList & slst
        )
        {
        Head  = slst.Head;
        Tail  = slst.Tail;
        Work  = slst.Work;
        Count = slst.Count;
        IsShallow = BOOL_TRUE;
        }

template <class T>
    void SList<T>::Kill()
        {
        if (!IsShallow)
            {
            Work = Head;

            while (Work != NULL)
                {
                Head = Work->Next;
                delete Work;
                Work = Head;
                }
            }

        SetNull();
        IsShallow = BOOL_FALSE;
        }

template <class T>
    SList<T>::SList()
        {
        SetNull();
        IsShallow = BOOL_FALSE;
        }
```

```
template <class T>
    SList<T>::SList
    (
    const SList & slst,
    Boolean shallow
    )
    {
    if (shallow)
        ShallowCopy(slst);
    else
        {
        SetNull();
        DeepCopy(slst);
        }
    }


template <class T>
    SList<T>::~SList()
        {
        Kill();
        }


template <class T>
    void SList<T>::operator =
        (
        const SList & slst
        )
        {
        Kill();
        DeepCopy(slst);
        }


template <class T>
    Boolean SList<T>::Append
        (
        const T & item
        )
        {
        Node * n = new Node;

        if (n == NULL)
            throw DebugSList<T>(*this,AllocFailed);

        n->Data = item;
        n->Next = NULL;

        if (Tail == NULL)
```

```
        {
        Head = n;
        Tail = n;
        Work = n;
        }
    else
        {
        Tail->Next = n;
        Tail = n;
        }

    ++Count;

    return BOOL_TRUE;
    }

template <class T>
    T SList<T>::GetItem()
        {
        if (Work != NULL)
            return Work->Data;
        else
            throw DebugSList<T>(*this,EmptyList);
        }

template <class T>
    Boolean SList<T>::AtEnd()
        {
        if (Work == Tail)
            return BOOL_TRUE;
        else
            return BOOL_FALSE;
        }
```

Note that the assignment operator and the default copy constructor create deep copies of source SList objects. The DebugSList class creates shallow copies.

Implementing DebugSList

The goal of my debugging wrapper is to provide information about what is happening inside my SList objects. This is how I implemented the DebugSList functions:

```
template <class T>
    DebugSList<T>::DebugSList
        (
        const SList<T> & slst,
        SListBugType bug
        )
        : SList<T>(slst,BOOL_TRUE)
        {
        Problem = bug;
        }

template <class T>
    DebugSList<T>::DebugSList
        (
        const DebugSList<T> & deblist
        )
        : SList<T>(deblist,BOOL_TRUE)
        {
        Problem = deblist.Problem;
        IsShallow = deblist.IsShallow;
        }

template <class T>
    void DebugSList<T>::operator =
        (
        const DebugSList<T> & deblist
        )
        {
        Kill();
        ShallowCopy(deblist);
        Problem = deblist.Problem;
        IsShallow = deblist.IsShallow;
        }

template <class T>
    void DebugSList<T>::Explain
        (
        DiagOutput & out
        )
        {
        out.DisplayMsg("SList error! ");

        switch (Problem)
            {
            case AllocFailed:
```

```
                out.DisplayMsg("memory alloc failure\n",
                                DIAG_ERROR);
                break;

            case EmptyList:
                out.DisplayMsg("read from empty list\n",
                                DIAG_WARNING);
                break;
            }
        }


template <class T>
    void DebugSList<T>::Dump
        (
        DiagOutput & out
        )
        {
        size_t c = 0;
        Node * n = Head;

        if (n == NULL)
            out.DisplayMsg("empty list\n");
        else
            {
            while (n != NULL)
                {
                strstream strm;

                strm << "node " << c
                    << " (ptr = " << n
                    << ") is linked to  " << n->Next
                    << ends;

                out.DisplayMsg(strm.str());

                n = n->Next;
                ++c;
                }
            }

        strstream strm;
        strm << "Node count: " << Count << ends;
        out.DisplayMsg(strm.str());
        }
```

```cpp
template <class T>
    void DebugSList<T>::ShowInternals
        (
        DiagOutput & out
        )
        {
        strstream strm;

        strm << "Head node:  " << Head << endl
             << "Tail node:  " << Tail << endl
             << "Work node:  " << Work << endl
             << "Node count: " << Count << endl
             << "Data size:  " << sizeof(T) << endl
             << "Is Shallow? "
             << (IsShallow ? "Yes" : "No") << ends;

        out.DisplayMsg(strm.str());
        }


template <class T>
    Boolean DebugSList<T>::CheckIntegrity()
        {
        // make sure that both Tail and Head
        // are NULL or non-NULL
        if (((Head == NULL) && (Tail != NULL))
        ||  ((Head != NULL) && (Tail == NULL)))
                return BOOL_FALSE;

        // follow linkage to tail (I hope!)
        if (Head != NULL)
            {
            Node * n = Head;

            while (n->Next != NULL)
                n = n->Next;

            if (n != Tail)
                return BOOL_FALSE;
            }

        return BOOL_TRUE;
        }
```

A program can create a DebugSList only from another DebugSList or an
SList. The constructor always makes a shallow copy of the original,

because the `DebugSList` object exists only as a "snapshot" of the `SList` object being examined. The `Append` and `Kill` functions defined by `SList` have checks to ensure that they make no changes to a shallow copy. `Kill` merely sets the control values of a shallow copy to `null`, thus removing any connection to the source `SList`. When called for a shallow copy, `Append` generates an exception.

Using SList Exceptions

Now my programs can contain exception handlers for problems that occur within `SList` objects:

```
SList<int> sl1;

DiagOutDOS dbgout(cerr);

try
    {
    int x = sl1.GetItem();
    }

catch (ExceptionBase & ex)
    {
    ex.Explain(dbgout);
    abort();
    }
```

My generic `ExceptionBase` handler will catch any `DebugSList` exceptions, because they are derived from `ExceptionBase`. The virtual `Explain` function will, if nothing else, let me know what type of error I'm dealing with, even if I haven't created an explicit handler for a derived type. I could also create an explicit conversion handler for `DebugSLists`:

```
catch (DebugSList<int> & debList)
    {
    dbgout.DisplayMsg("\nDebugging info for list #3:\n\n");
    dbgList.Explain(dbgout);

    dbgout.DisplayMsg("\nDumping contents:\n");
```

```
    dbgList.Dump(dbgout);

    dbgout.DisplayMsg("\nDisplay internal data:\n");
    dbgList.ShowInternals(dbgout);
    }
```

Because I'm using a template, I must specify the type of `DebugSList` being caught by an exception handler. For example:

```
SList<double> dbllist;

try
    {
    double d = dbllist.GetItem();

    cout << "found: " << d << endl;
    }

catch (DebugSList<int> & debList)
    {
    debList.Explain(dbgout);
    abort();
    }
```

An exception thrown by `dbllist` would generate a call to `terminate`, because the exception handler will capture only exceptions thrown by an `SList<int>` object.

Using a global base class would allow the generic handling of exceptions thrown by any `SList` type:

```
class SListException : public ExceptionBase { };

template <class T>
    class DebugSList<T>
    :     public SList<T>,
        public SListException, // only change to definition
        public DiagnosticBase
    {
    // keep the same class definition
    }
```

Making this minor modification would allow a program to define `catch (SListException)` blocks that would handle any exception thrown by an `SList` object.

ONWARD

Now it's time to build some classes that put C++ to work. I'll begin in the next chapter with something simple: a class defining rational numbers, or fractions.

CHAPTER 4

RATIONAL NUMBERS

C++, like most programming languages, supports integer and floating-point numbers. One type of value, however, is noticeably absent: the *rational number*, or fraction.

With floating-point numbers, why do we need fractions? Floats and doubles are more than adequate for most computational tasks, but in some cases a fractional representation can be invaluable. For example, the fraction 1/3 cannot be represented by a floating-point number, because it is an infinite sequence beginning 0.3333333.... And many calculations, such as those involving the English measurement system, use fractions.

Most kids hate fractions in school, because working with them seems arcane. Try adding 7/32 and 1/3; it takes a few moments to remember how to create a common denominator before adding the numerators and reducing the resulting fraction. Some calculators, including mine, can handle fractional math—and if a calculator can do it, so can a C++ program.

Rational Class

A rational number class provides a good example for object-oriented programming. My Rational class is a template, defined as follows:

```
template
    <
    class T
    >
    class Rational
        {
        public:
            // constructors
            Rational();

            Rational
                (
                const Rational<T> & r
                );

            Rational
                (
                T num,
                T den = 1
                );

            // assignment operator
            Rational<T> & operator =
                (
                const Rational<T> & r
                );

            // conversion operators
            operator float() const;
            operator double() const;

            // assignment of numerator and denominator
            Rational<T> & operator ()
                (
                T num,
                T den = 1
                );
```

```
// negate
Rational<T> operator - () const;

// basic four operators
friend Rational<T> operator +
    (
    const Rational<T> & r1,
    const Rational<T> & r2
    );

friend Rational<T> operator -
    (
    const Rational<T> & r1,
    const Rational<T> & r2
    );

friend Rational<T> operator *
    (
    const Rational<T> & r1,
    const Rational<T> & r2
    );

friend Rational<T> operator /
    (
    const Rational<T> & r1,
    const Rational<T> & r2
    );

// shorthand operators
Rational<T> operator +=
    (
    const Rational<T> & r
    );

Rational<T> operator -=
    (
    const Rational<T> & r
    );

Rational<T> operator *=
    (
    const Rational<T> & r
    );
```

```
            Rational<T> operator /=
                (
                const Rational<T> & r
                );

            // interrogation functions
            T GetNum() const;
            T GetDen() const;

        // stream input/output
        friend istream & operator >>
            (
            istream & strm,
            Rational<T> & r
            );

        friend ostream & operator <<
            (
            ostream & strm,
            const Rational<T> & r
            );

    protected:
        T Numer;
        T Denom;

    private:
        // reduce fraction & adjust sign
        void Reduce();

        // greatest common divisor
        static T GCD(T x, T y);

        // least common multiple
        static T LCM(T x, T y);
    };
```

I created `Rational` as a template to allow its numerator and denominator to have any signed integer type. There's no sense in creating `float` or `double` Rationals, although you can do such things if you want to.

I created two type definitions to declare Rational types for `long`s and `int`s:

```
typedef Rational<long>  LongRational;
typedef Rational<short> ShortRational;
```

Utility Functions

The LCM function calculates the least common multiple of two T values:

```
template
    <
    class T
    >
    T Rational<T>::LCM(T x, T y)
        {
        x = labs(x);
        y = labs(y);

        if (x == y)
            return x;
        else
            {
            if (x < y)
                return (y / GCD(x,y)) * x;
            else
                return (x / GCD(y,x)) * y;
            }
        }
```

The GCD function calculates the greatest common denominator of two T values:

```
template
    <
    class T
    >
    T Rational<T>::GCD(T x, T y)
        {
        x = labs(x);
        y = labs(y);

        T temp;
```

```
    while (y != 0)
        {
        temp = x % y;
        x = y;
        y = temp;
        }

    return x;
    }
```

Reduce performs fractional reduction by removing common factors from the numerator and denominator of a Rational:

```
template
    <
    class T
    >
    void Rational<T>::Reduce()
        {
        // check for zero numerator
        if (Numer == 0)
            {
            Denom = 0;
            return;
            }
        else
            if (Denom == 0)
                {
                Numer = 0;
                return;
                }

        if ((Numer > 0) && (Denom < 0))
            {
            Numer = -Numer;
            Denom = -Denom;
            }
        else
            {
            if ((Numer < 0) && (Denom < 0))
                {
                Numer = -Numer;
                Denom = -Denom;
                }
            }
```

```
T div = GCD(Numer,Denom);

Numer /= div;
Denom /= div;
}
```

Constructors and Assignment

The primary constructor creates a new `Rational<T>` from a supplied numerator and optional denominator. If you don't supply a denominator, a 1 is automatically supplied to make the value equal its numerator:

```
template
    <
    class T
    >
    inline Rational<T>::Rational()
        {
        Numer = 0;
        Denom = 0;
        }

template
    <
    class T
    >
    inline Rational<T>::Rational
        (
        const Rational<T> & r
        )
        {
        Numer = r.Numer;
        Denom = r.Denom;
        }

template
    <
    class T
    >
    inline Rational<T> & Rational<T>::operator =
        (
        const Rational<T> & r
```

```
    )
    {
    Numer = r.Numer;
    Denom = r.Denom;
    return *this;
    }
```

The copy constructor and assignment operator simply duplicate an existing Rational<T>'s numerator and denominator.

Unary Operators

I defined a unary operator - to negate a Rational's value. Note that the sign of the Rational is kept in the numerator:

```
template
    <
    class T
    >
    inline Rational<T> Rational<T>::operator - () const
        {
        Rational<T> result = *this;
        result.Numer = -result.Numer;
        return result;
        }
```

Assignment

C++ doesn't allow you to change the language syntax; without using strings, I have no way of creating an assignment operator that would accept a fraction such as 1/2 without its first performing a divide and then assigning zero to my Rational number. So I overloaded the function call operator to take two parameters that have the same syntax as the constructor:

```
template
    <
    class T
```

```
>
Rational<T> & Rational<T>::operator ()
    (
    T num,
    T den
    )
    {
    if (den == 0)
        num = 0;

    Numer = num;
    Denom = den;

    Reduce();

    return *this;
    }
```

Binary Operators

Four friend functions implement the basic operations of addition, subtraction, multiplication, and division:

```
template
    <
    class T
    >
    Rational<T> operator + (const Rational<T> & r1,
                            const Rational<T> & r2)
        {
    Rational<T> result;

    result.Denom = Rational<T>::LCM(r1.Denom,r2.Denom);

    result.Numer = r1.Numer * (result.Denom / r1.Denom)
                + r2.Numer * (result.Denom / r2.Denom);

    result.Reduce();
    return result;
    }
```

```
template
    <
    class T
    >
    Rational<T> operator - (const Rational<T> & r1,
                            const Rational<T> & r2)
        {
        Rational<T> result;

        result.Denom = Rational<T>::LCM(r1.Denom,r2.Denom);

        result.Numer = r1.Numer * (result.Denom / r1.Denom)
                    - r2.Numer * (result.Denom / r2.Denom);

        result.Reduce();
        return result;
        }

template
    <
    class T
    >
    Rational<T> operator * (const Rational<T> & r1,
                            const Rational<T> & r2)
        {
        Rational<T> result;
        result.Numer = r1.Numer * r2.Numer;
        result.Denom = r1.Denom * r2.Denom;
        result.Reduce();
        return result;
        }

template
    <
    class T
    >
    Rational<T> operator / (const Rational<T> & r1,
                            const Rational<T> & r2)
        {
        Rational<T> result;
        result.Numer = r1.Numer * r2.Denom;
        result.Denom = r1.Denom * r2.Numer;
        result.Reduce();
        return result;
        }
```

Shorthand Operators

The shorthand operators are inline functions that use the binary operators to perform calculations:

```
template
    <
    class T
    >
    Rational<T> Rational<T>::operator += (const Rational<T> & r)
        {
        *this = *this + r;
        return *this;
        }

template
    <
    class T
    >
    Rational<T> Rational<T>::operator -= (const Rational<T> & r)
        {
        *this = *this - r;
        return *this;
        }

template
    <
    class T
    >
    Rational<T> Rational<T>::operator *= (const Rational<T> & r)
        {
        *this = *this * r;
        return *this;
        }

template
    <
    class T
    >
    Rational<T> Rational<T>::operator /= (const Rational<T> & r)
        {
        *this = *this / r;
        return *this;
        }
```

Conversion

I defined conversion functions to change any Rational<T> into either a float or a double. I don't throw an exception for division by zero; instead, I use the value HUGE_VAL to represent infinity. A Rational is considered zero if its numerator is zero.

```
template
    <
    class T
    >
    Rational<T>::operator float() const
        {
        float result;

        if (Denom == 0)
            {
            if (Numer == 0)
                result = 0.0F;
            else
                result = (float)HUGE_VAL;
            }
        else
            result = (float)Numer / (float)Denom;

        return result;
        }

template
    <
    class T
    >
    Rational<T>::operator double() const
        {
        double result;

        if (Denom == 0)
            {
            if (Numer == 0)
                result = 0.0;
            else
                result = HUGE_VAL;
            }
```

```
    else
        result = (double)Numer / (double)Denom;

    return result;
    }
```

Input and Output

Two stream I/O functions provide for the input and output of Rational<T>
values.

```
template
    <
    class T
    >
    istream & operator >> (istream & strm, Rational<T> & r)
        {
        T n, d;
        char c;

        strm >> n >> c;

        if (c == '/')
            strm >> d;
        else
            {
            strm.putback(c);
            d = 1;
            }

        r = Rational(n,d);

        return strm;
        }

template
    <
    class T
    >
    ostream & operator << (ostream & strm, const Rational<T> & r)
        {
        strm << r.Numer << "/" << r.Denom;
```

```
    return strm;
    }
```

Interrogation Functions

Two functions retrieve the numerator and denominator, respectively, from a Rational number:

```
template
    <
    class T
    >
    inline T Rational<T>::GetNum() const
        {
        return Numer;
        }

template
    <
    class T
    >
    inline T Rational<T>::GetDen() const
        {
        return Denom;
        }
```

Using Rational Numbers

Here is a segment of code from the Testbed application in which I work with Rational<long> values:

```
void TestRational
    (
    strstream & buffer
    )
    {
    LongRational r1, r2, r3;

    r1(11,21);
    r2(21,31);
```

```
r3 = r1 + r2;
buffer << r1 << " + " << r2 << " = " << r3 << "\r\n";

r3 = r1 - r2;
buffer << r1 << " - " << r2 << " = " << r3 << "\r\n";

r3 = r1 * r2;
buffer << r1 << " * " << r2 << " = " << r3 << "\r\n";

r3 = r1 / r2;
buffer << r1 << " / " << r2 << " = " << r3 << "\r\n";
buffer << "\r\n";

r1(-11,21);
r2(21,31);

r3 = r1 + r2;
buffer << r1 << " + " << r2 << " = " << r3 << "\r\n";

r3 = r1 - r2;
buffer << r1 << " - " << r2 << " = " << r3 << "\r\n";

r3 = r1 * r2;
buffer << r1 << " * " << r2 << " = " << r3 << "\r\n";

r3 = r1 / r2;
buffer << r1 << " / " << r2 << " = " << r3 << "\r\n";
buffer << "\r\n";

r1(-11,21);
r2(21,-31);

r3 = r1 + r2;
buffer << r1 << " + " << r2 << " = " << r3 << "\r\n";

r3 = r1 - r2;
buffer << r1 << " - " << r2 << " = " << r3 << "\r\n";

r3 = r1 * r2;
buffer << r1 << " * " << r2 << " = " << r3 << "\r\n";

r3 = r1 / r2;
```

```
    buffer << r1 << " / " << r2 << " = " << r3 << "\r\n";
    buffer << "\r\n";

    r1(-11,21);
    r2(21,31);

    buffer << r1 << " = " << float(r1) << "\r\n";
    buffer << r1 << " = " << double(r1) << "\r\n";
    buffer << r2 << " = " << float(r2) << "\r\n";
    buffer << r2 << " = " << double(r2) << "\r\n";
    buffer << "\r\n";

    r1 = -r1;
    r2 = -r2;

    buffer << r1 << "\r\n";
    buffer << r2 << "\r\n";
    }
```

The program will output the following:

```
1/2 + 2/3 = 7/6
1/2 - 2/3 = -1/6
1/2 * 2/3 = 1/3
1/2 / 2/3 = 3/4


-1/2 + 2/3 = 1/6
-1/2 - 2/3 = -7/6
-1/2 * 2/3 = -1/3
-1/2 / 2/3 = -3/4


-1/2 + -2/3 = -7/6
-1/2 - -2/3 = 1/6
-1/2 * -2/3 = 1/3
-1/2 / -2/3 = 3/4


-1/2 = -0.5
-1/2 = -0.5
2/3 = 0.666667
2/3 = 0.666667


1/2
-2/3
```

ONWARD

From here, I move on to a more complicated class with broader applicability: a dynamically allocated `String` type that supports sophisticated searching and editing facilities.

CHAPTER 5

RANDOM NUMBER GENERATORS

A random number is a number whose value cannot be predicted in advance of its existence. Although the human mind has been known to be unpredictable, it isn't very good at generating a completely unrelated ating a list of 20 random integers selected from the range one through 100, inclusive. Are those numbers really random? And wouldn't it be tedious if you had to generate a thousand, or a million, random numbers?

Computers are supposed to be good at reducing tedious numeric operations. Unfortunately, computers perform calculations by means of algorithms, and truly random numbers cannot be generated by an algorithm. By definition, an algorithm is a specific sequence of operations that produces a predictable output for a given set of parameters. In the case of random numbers, the last thing we want is something predictable!

The best we can do with a computer is to create an algorithm that *appears* to generate a random sequence of numbers. The numbers aren't really random; a human with a sharp mind or a calculator could predict the numbers in the sequence by following the algorithm. But the sequence of numbers is difficult to follow, and a human looking at the values will not be able to see any algorithmic pattern to them. For practical applications, pseudo-random numbers suffice.

ALGORITHMS

In general, a pseudo-random number generator is initialized with a *seed* value that begins a sequence of apparently unpredictable values. A set of mathematical operations is performed on the seed, generating a number that is reported as a pseudo-random number. That return value is also used as the next seed value.

Researchers have devoted copious time to inventing and analyzing pseudo-random number generators. The goal of this research has been to produce the most unpredictable sequence of values. Designing a good random number generator involves solving two problems:

- Increasing the size of the repetition cycle. As the algorithm is applied, the seed will eventually return to its starting value, and the values will start repeating themselves. An algorithm that repeats after generating a million numbers is more useful than a generator that repeats itself every 100 numbers.

- Avoiding predictability. A random number generator that always returns values with the same last digit is worthless. An algorithm that generates only odd numbers is equally useless.

Although there are many fancy and complicated algorithms that generate pseudo-random numbers, one of the most commonly used algorithms is also one of the simplest. First introduced by D. Lehmer in 1951, the *linear congruential* method involves only two mathematical operations. Standard C, as defined by ANSI, uses the following linear congruential generator in implementing the rand and srand functions:

```
static unsigned long next = 1;

int rand(void)
    {
    next = next * 1103515245 + 12345;
    return ((unsigned int) (next / 65536UL) % 0x32767UL);
    }
```

```
void srand(unsigned int seed)
    {
    next = seed;
    }
```

Why not use the rand function defined by ANSI? Because the ANSI C algorithm is inadequate for many applications. And what's wrong with a simple random number generator? Nothing, as long as your random numbers don't need to be very unpredictable and the repetition of those values is not a problem in your work.

The first problem with rand is that its output is limited to int values lying between 0 and 32,767, inclusive. That range isn't great enough for many applications—and many algorithms work best with floating-point numbers. You could get around this limitation by using division to obtain numbers between 0 and 1:

```
float f = rand() / (RAND_MAX + 1.0);
```

Now we can get floating-point values, but only 32,767 different ones. Such a limited range can be disastrous for some applications, such as genetic algorithms, in which a program may generate millions, or even billions, of random values as it examines a large search space. An even more serious problem lies with the "randomness" of a simple algorithm; if it is implemented poorly, rand produces sequences that repeat every few thousand values. I once wrote a program that plotted dots at random positions within a window, only to have the dots appear in ragged diagonal lines because of imperfections in the compiler's rand function. Even worse, some mathematically inept compiler vendors try to improve on rand by using cute little byte-swapping tricks that only shorten the period of repetition!

In 1988, S.K. Park and L.W. Miller studied a variety of random number generators before suggesting what they called the *minimum standard.* I've seen several implementations of this function, but here's the one I've used in many C programs:

```
static long rseed = 1;

void setseed(long s)
    {
    rseed = s;
    }

float random()
    {
    static const long  A =       16807L;
    static const long  M = 2147483647L;
    static const long  Q =      127773L;
    static const long  R =        2836L;
    static const long  X =   123459876L;
    static const float F =    1.0F / K2;

    long k;
    float res;

    rseed ^= X;

    k = rseed / Q;

    rseed = A * (rseed - k * Q) - R * k;

    if (rseed < 0)
        rseed += M;

    res = F * rseed;

    rseed ^= X;

    return res;
    }
```

Note that the random assumes a 32-bit long type. The exclusive ORs prevent the seed from containing simple values that would produce poor sequences of values. random will produce more than two billion pseudo-random values before repeating itself, and the values will be spread evenly throughout the positive range of 0 to LONG_MAX - 2. However, random does have its limitations; successive values of the seed will differ only by a multiple of 16,807, allowing sequences of small values to emerge.

I used `random` for many years, until I read about better generators in *Mathematical Recipes in C,* by William H. Press and others.

UNIFORM RANDOM DEVIATES

As I mentioned, no algorithm can produce a truly random value. Number theorists prefer the term *uniform deviate* for the kind of number we're trying to get from a computer's `rand` function. For the purposes of this book, uniform deviates are floating-point numbers that fall within a given range, usually 0 and 1. All numbers within the range have a statistically equal probability of being generated upon a call to the deviate generator. The best deviate generators have been thoroughly studied in the computer science literature, and a basic model known as the Minimal Standard has passed numerous theoretical tests of its efficacy. Yet even the Minimal Standard can show weaknesses when generating millions of values.

In a 1988 issue of *Communications of the ACM,* Paul L'Ecuyer suggests a variety of algorithms for the production of reliable, long-period random deviates. By combining two generators based on the Minimal Standard, L'Ecuyer creates a routine that avoids the pitfalls of simpler algorithms. The generator, which I've used in the `RandDev` class discussed in the next section, produces uniform random deviates between 0.0 and 1.0. In a nutshell, L'Ecuyer's algorithm uses an approximate factorization, shuffling the result to remove correlation in low-order bits. A single generator of that type will have a repetition period of about 10^8, a period that believe it or not, may not be adequate for some complex stochastic algorithms. But combining two such generators with a judicious selection of factors produces a generator with a period of approximately 2.3×10^{18}, which should be more than effective in algorithms of any practical scope.

RANDDEV CLASS

I implemented a uniform deviate generator via a C++ class. C++ classes can often provide a better way of accomplishing a task normally performed using stand-alone functions. Aside from their numerical limitations, rand and srand have several faults from a software engineering standpoint:

- A program must explicitly call srand to initialize the seed. If srand isn't called, the default value of seed will be used, and every execution of the program will generate the same sequence of pseudo-random numbers.

- Because srand and rand are two separate functions, seed is defined as a global variable. Good programmers avoid global variables, even those that can be hidden using the static keyword.

- Because there is only one seed value, only one sequence of pseudo-random numbers is generated in a program. Often, I like to have separate random number generators for different parts of a program.

- The ANSI rand function returns values between 0 and UINT_MAX. In most cases, I want to retrieve random values that are within a specific range, say from 1 to 100.

With all this discussion in mind, I defined my RandDev class as follows:

```
class RandDev
    {
    protected:
        // sets default seed argument from system time
        static long TimeSeed()
            {
            return (long)time(NULL);
            }

    public:
        // constructor
        RandDev
            (
            long initSeed = TimeSeed()
            );

        // set seed value
```

```
void SetSeed
    (
    long newSeed = TimeSeed()
    );

// get a uniform deviate between 0.0 and 1.0
float operator () ();

// get a uniform deviate between 0 and max
size_t operator ()
    (
    size_t max
    );

int operator ()
    (
    int max
    );

private:
    long Seed;
};
```

I defined the `TimeSeed` function to automatically initialize the constructor's `seed` parameter with the current system time. You can supply a specific seed, ensuring the creation of identical sequences of values.

```
inline RandDev::RandDev
    (
    long initSeed
    )
    {
    if (initSeed < 0)
        Seed = initSeed;
    else
        Seed = -initSeed;
    }
```

`SetSeed` resets the generator using a new seed.

```
inline void RandDev::SetSeed
    (
```

```
long initSeed
)
{
if (initSeed < 0)
    Seed = initSeed;
else
    Seed = -initSeed;
}
```

The operator () function returns the next deviate in the sequence.

```
static const long    IM1 = 2147483563L;
static const long    IM2 = 2147483399L;
static const long   IMM1 = IM1 - 1L;
static const long    IA1 = 40014L;
static const long    IA2 = 40692L;
static const long    IQ1 = 53668L;
static const long    IQ2 = 52774L;
static const long    IR1 = 12211L;
static const long    IR2 =  3791L;
static const long   NTAB =    32L;
static const long   NDIV = 1L + IMM1 / long(NTAB);
static const float  RNMX = 1.0F - FLT_EPSILON;
static const float    AM = 1.0F / 2147483563.0F;

float RandDev::operator () ()
    {
    long j, k;
    static long idum2 = 123456789L;
    static long iy    = 0L;
    static long iv[NTAB];
    float temp;

    if (Seed <= 0L)
        {
        if (-Seed < 1L)
            Seed = 1L;
        else
            Seed = -Seed;

        idum2 = Seed;

        for (j = NTAB + 7; j >= 0; —j)
            {
```

```
          k = Seed / IQ1;
          Seed = IA1 * (Seed - k * IQ1) - k * IR1;

          if (Seed < 0L)
              Seed += IM1;

          if (j < NTAB)
              iv[size_t(j)] = Seed;
          }

      iy = iv[0];
      }

k = Seed / IQ1;

Seed = IA1 * (Seed - k * IQ1) - k * IR1;

if (Seed < 0L)
    Seed += IM1;

k = idum2 / IQ2;

idum2 = IA2 * (idum2 - k * IQ2) - k * IR2;

if (idum2 < 0L)
    idum2 += IM2;

j  = iy / NDIV;
iy = iv[size_t(j)] - idum2;
iv[size_t(j)] = Seed;

if (iy < 1L)
    iy += IMM1;

temp = AM * float(iy);

if (temp > RNMX)
    return RNMX;
else
    return temp;
}
```

I also created two convenience functions to obtain `int` and `size_t` values from a `RandDev` object:

```
inline size_t RandDev::operator ()
    (
    size_t max
    )
    {
    return size_t(float(max) * (*this)());
    }

inline int RandDev::operator ()
    (
    int max
    )
    {
    return int(float(max) * (*this)());
    }
```

With an ANSI-compliant C++ compiler, I could define the following template function to get values of specific types from a `RandDev`:

```
template <class T>
    T GetRand ()
        (
        T max,
        RandDev & r
        )
        {
        return T(float(max) * r());
        }
```

I'd call the `GetRand` function using explicit template arguments:

```
RandDev rdev;
long x = GetRand<long>(100L,rdev);
```

The primary calculations in `RandDev` rely on integer math to avoid the performance costs of floating-point arithmetic. If you want an in-depth theoretical explanation of this code, the classic text *Numerical Recipes in C* provides an excellent discussion of random number generators, and I highly recommend that you read it for detailed analysis of this topic.

RANDOM NUMBER TABLES

Generating random numbers one by one is fine for some applications; for other problems, however, it can be advantageous to have a set of pre-generated random values. In the days before computers, math books often contained tables of random numbers; you simply started at the beginning of the list and moved sequentially through it as you needed numbers.

Some algorithms work well with tables of random numbers. If, for example, an inner loop constantly requests random values, calling RandGen's () function will slow processing with constant multiplications and divisions. By pregenerating a table, the inner loop can quickly read an extant value.

Many algorithms use a series of random values, and it's often necessary to use the same set of random values in more than one place. That need led me to create RandTable, a class that uses RandGen to build random number tables.

```
template
    <
    size_t Size
    >
    class RandTable : private RandDev
        {
        public:
            // constructors
            RandTable
                (
                unsigned long seed = TimeSeed()
                );

            RandTable
                (
                const RandTable<Size> & table
                );

            // assignment
            void operator =
                (
```

```
                const RandTable<Size> & table
                );

            // get next value
            float operator () ();

    private:
            size_t Index;
            float   Values[Size];

            // initialize an array
            void Initialize();
        };
```

RandTable is a template derived from RandDev; it has a template argument that specifies the number of values in the table. The table is an array named Values; the Index data member points to the element of Values that will be returned by the next call to the operator() function.

Upon construction, a RandTable fills the Value array with random numbers by calling Initialize:

```
template
    <
    size_t Size
    >
    inline RandTable<Size>::RandTable
        (
        unsigned long seed
        )
        : RandDev(seed)
        {
        Initialize();
        }


template
    <
    size_t Size
    >
    void RandTable<Size>::Initialize()
        {
        for (size_t n = 0; n < Size; ++n)
            Values[n] = RandDev::operator ()();
```

```
Index = 0;
}
```

Index begins at zero; when the operator() routine returns a value from the table, it also increments Index. When Index reaches the end of the table, operator() calls Initialize to reload Values with a new set of random numbers.

```
template
    <
    size_t Size
    >
    float RandTable<Size>::operator () ()
        {
        float result = Values[Index];

        ++Index;

        if (Index == Size)
            Initialize();

        return result;
        }
```

Just for the record, the copy constructor and assignment operator look like this:

```
template
    <
    size_t Size
    >
    inline RandTable<Size>::RandTable
        (
        const RandTable<Size> & table
        )
        : RandDev(table)
        {
        Index = table.Index;
        memcpy(Values,table.Values,sizeof(float) * Size);
        }

template
    <
```

```
size_t Size
>
inline void RandTable<Size>::operator =
    (
    const RandTable<Size> & table
    )
    {
    Index = table.Index;
    memcpy(Values,table.Values,sizeof(float) * Size);
    }
```

RandTable demonstrates that templates have application far beyond the creation of container classes. By including the size of the table in the template argument, I can create a static Values array without having to allocate dynamic memory. This is a technique you'll see me use in other classes throughout this book.

The complete source code for RandDev can be found in **RandDev.h** and **RandDev.cpp**, both of which are found on the accompanying source diskette. The RandTable class is completely implemented in the file **RandTable.h**.

ONWARD

In Chapter 3, I introduced a simple String class as an example in my discussion of error handling. Over the years, I've developed a String class that is now an integral part of my C++ library. Originally, C++ didn't come with a string type, although some vendors implemented a string class based on an AT&T design. The ANSI C++ committee has defined a standard basic_string class, but it has yet to be implemented by any compilers I've used—so I continue to use my home-grown String class.

And so, in the next chapter, I present String, along with an additional class that supports a sophisticated searching algorithm.

CHAPTER 6

STRINGS

Developing a string class was one of my first C++ projects, and over the years the class has undergone substantial changes. As my understanding of C++ has grown, so has my ability to build a better class; for example, the `String` class has undergone five major revisions. I'm quite happy with the incarnation presented here, which works well in applications ranging from databases to text editors.

My goal was to create a dynamically allocated string class that provides all the functionality of standard, NULL-terminated C character arrays (which I call *C-strings*). However, I wanted to avoid the pitfalls of C-strings. For instance, errors often occur when you're working with C-strings because the string library functions fail to do any sort of range or validity checking. In addition, the library functions defined in **string.h** are missing important features. For strings to be useful in a wide variety of applications, they need manipulation routines, such as those for inserting and deleting data, that are normally not found in C function libraries.

ENUMERATED TYPES

The `String` class uses three enumerated types: `StrCompVal`, `StrCompMode`, and `StrError`.

139

```
enum StrCompVal
    {
    SC_LESS,
    SC_EQUAL,
    SC_GREATER,
    SC_ERROR
    };

enum StrCompMode
    {
    SM_SENSITIVE,
    SM_IGNORE
    };

enum StrError
    {
    SE_OKAY,
    SE_ALLOC,
    SE_TOO_LONG,
    SE_INVALID
    };
```

StrCompVal is the return value of the Compare member function.
StrCompMode is used to indicate whether String comparisons are case-sensitive. StrError is used by the error-processing function.

I use enumerations for these types to control the validity of values passed to and returned from member functions. Because some C++ compilers still don't correctly support nested type definitions, I defined these types outside the String class definition.

DATA MEMBERS

A String is defined as having three private instance variables: Siz, Len, and Txt.

```
class String
    {
    .
    .
    .
```

```
private:
    size_t Siz;
    size_t Len;
    char * Txt;

    static size_t AllocIncr;
    .
    .
    .
};
```

Txt is a pointer to a buffer allocated in dynamic memory; in it are stored the characters that constitute the String, as a NULL-terminated array of characters. Siz contains the currently allocated length of the buffer pointed to by the Txt pointer. Len holds the actual number of characters stored in the String.

AllocIncr is a private static class member. It defines the "chunk" size used in allocating memory for the Txt members of String objects. The Siz of a String will always be the smallest multiple of AllocIncr that can hold Len characters. By default, AllocIncr is assigned the value 8 in the implementation file **str.cxx**.

```
size_ t String::AllocIncr = 8;
```

ERROR HANDLING

Any class that allocates memory should implement an error-reporting mechanism. For this edition of *C++ Components and Algorithms*, I employed exceptions in the String class. To do so, I created two exception classes, StringEx and DebugString. I won't go into great detail explaining their design, because they're based on the classes and ideas I presented in the previous chapter.

StringEx is an incredibly simple type:

```
class StringEx
    : public ExceptionBase
    {
```

```
    public:
        StringEx(StrError err);

        StrError WhatsWrong();

         void Explain(DiagOutput & out);
    protected:
        StrError Error;
    };

StringEx::StringEx(StrError err)
    {
    Error = err;
    }


void StringEx::Explain(DiagOutput & out)
    {
    switch (Error)
        {
        case SE_OKAY :
            out.DisplayMsg("String test object");
            break;

        case SE_ALLOC :
            out.DisplayMsg("String allocation failure",
                        DIAG_FATAL);
            break;

        case SE_TOO_LONG :
            out.DisplayMsg("String is too long",
                        DIAG_ERROR);
            break;

        case SE_INVALID :
            out.DisplayMsg("String invalid parameters",
                        DIAG_WARNING);
        }
    }
```

A StringEx object contains an error code that determines the message to be handled by a DiagOutput object. For errors in which I want to examine the internal data of the erroneous String object, I derived DebugString from StringEx and DiagnosticBase. Its implementation looks like this:

```
class DebugString
    : public StringEx,
      public DiagnosticBase
    {
    public:
        DebugString(const String & str, StrError err);
        DebugString(const DebugString & dstr);
        void operator = (const DebugString & dstr);

        void Dump(DiagOutput & out);
        void ShowInternals(DiagOutput & out);
        Boolean CheckIntegrity();
    private:
      size_t   Siz;   // allocated size
      size_t   Len;   // current length
      char *   Txt;   // pointer to text
    };


DebugString::DebugString(const String & str, StrError err)
    : StringEx(err)
    {
    Len = str.Len;
    Siz = str.Siz;
    Txt = str.Txt;
    }


DebugString::DebugString(const DebugString & dstr)
    : StringEx(dstr.Error)
    {
    Len = dstr.Len;
    Siz = dstr.Siz;
    Txt = dstr.Txt;
    }


void DebugString::operator = (const DebugString & dstr)
    {
    Len = dstr.Len;
    Siz = dstr.Siz;
    Txt = dstr.Txt;
    Error = dstr.Error;
    }


void DebugString::Dump(DiagOutput & out)
    {
    strstream strm;
```

```
    strm << "len: " << Len
         << " size: " << Siz
         << " text pointer: " << (void *)Txt << endl
         << " text: " << Txt << ends;

    out.DisplayMsg(strm.str());
    }

void DebugString::ShowInternals(DiagOutput & out)
    {
    Dump(out);
    }


Boolean DebugString::CheckIntegrity()
    {
    if (Len > Siz)
        return BOOL_FALSE;

    if (Txt != NULL)
        {
        if (strlen(Txt) != Len)
            return BOOL_FALSE;
        }

    return BOOL_TRUE;
    }
```

In looking over the code for String, you'll see where I've thrown StringEx and DebugString exceptions. The class throws StringEx objects for exceptions, because they don't require complicated processing. I use DebugString objects in testing the String class.

In general, it's best to keep your exception objects as simple as possible to avoid having them become entangled in the problem that caused their creation. For example, if a memory allocation failed for an object, it's unlikely that it can generate an exception object that must allocate memory.

UTILITY FUNCTIONS

In general, I make class member functions public to facilitate their use by user-defined objects. In the case of the String class, however, some utilitarian functions are used only internally by the class, and I defined them as private members.

```
class String
    {
    .
    .
    .
    public:
        static int Version();

        size_t Length() const;
        size_t Size() const;

    private:
        static size_t CalcSiz(size_t needed);
    .
    .
    .
    };
```

CalcSiz computes the smallest allocated buffer size for a given String length. CalcSize is not meant to be called from outside the class scope, so it is declared in the private section of the String class definition. Its implementation is inline in the class implementation file (**str.cxx**) to improve efficiency.

```
inline size_t String::CalcSiz(size_t needed)
    {
    size_t x = ((needed + AllocIncr) / AllocIncr) * AllocIncr;
    return x;
    }
```

The Length and Size member functions simply return, respectively, the current length and allocation size of a string. Length corresponds to the ANSI function strlen, but Length is considerably faster by virtue of its simply returning an already calculated value.

```
inline size_t String::Length() const
    {
    return Len;
    }
```

Size was originally created to help test the class. Because it is so simple, I just left it in for future use. As with Length, I defined Size as an inline function.

```
inline size_t String::Size() const
    {
    return Siz;
    }
```

CONSTRUCTORS AND THE DESTRUCTOR

I defined several constructors for the String class.

```
class String
    {
    .
    .
    .
    public:
        // constructors

        // default constructor to create empty string
        String();

        // copy constructor
        String(const String & str);

        // create string from char array
        String(const char * cstr);

        // create string containing count fillCh
        String(size_t count,   char fillCh = ' ');
        // create string containing formatted output
        String(size_t maxSize, const char * format, ...);

        // destructor
        ~String();
    .
    .
    .
    };
```

The default constructor creates an empty, uninitialized string.

```
String::String()
    {
    Len = 0;
    Siz = 0;
    Txt = NULL;
    }
```

The class also defines a copy constructor to create a new `String` from an existing one:

```
String::String(const String & str)
    {
    Len = str.Len;
    Siz = str.Siz;

    // if source string is empty, so is this string
    if (str.Txt == NULL)
        Txt = NULL;
    else
        {
        // allocate text buffer
        Txt = new char[Siz];

        if (Txt == NULL)
            throw StringEx(SE_ALLOC);

        // copy text from source string
        memcpy(Txt,str.Txt,Len + 1);
        }
    }
```

`String(char * Cstr)` generates a `String` from the value of a character array.

```
String::String(const char * cstr)
    {
    // if given a null char string, create an empty String
    if ((cstr == NULL) || (cstr[0] == '\x00'))
        {
        Len = 0;
        Siz = 0;
```

```
        Txt = NULL;
        }
    else
        {
        // calculate length and size
        Len = strlen(cstr);
        Siz = CalcSiz(Len);

        // allocate text buffer
        Txt = new char [Siz];

        if (Txt == NULL)
            throw StringEx(SE_ALLOC);

        // copy character array into text buffer
        memcpy(Txt,cstr,Len + 1);
        }
    }
```

The constructor String(char FillCh, unsigned int Count) creates a new String that contains Count FillCh characters:

```
String::String(char fillCh, size_t count)
    {
    // this constructor must store at least one character
    if (count == 0)
        throw StringEx(SE_INVALID);

    // calculate size and length
    Len = count + 1;
    Siz = CalcSiz(Len);

    // allocate text buffer
    Txt = new char[Siz];

    if (Txt == NULL)
        throw StringEx(SE_ALLOC);

    // fill text buffer with fillCh
    memset(Txt,fillCh,count);

    // add terminating NULL
    Txt[count] = '\x00';
    }
```

The final constructor creates a String containing formatted data. It is analogous to the sprintf function, which formats a series of data items into a character array. In the String class constructor, the first argument specifies the maximum length of the output, and the format parameter points to a character array that contains the format specifiers (as with printf, sprintf, and so on). Following format is a variable list of parameters to be formatted into the new String.

```
String::String(size_t maxsize, const char * format, ... )
    {
    // allocate temporary buffer
    char * buffer = new char[maxsize];

    if (buffer == NULL)
        throw StringEx(SE_ALLOC);

    // initialize argument list
    va_list args;

    va_start(args,format);

    // format items into buffer based on format
    Len = vsprintf(buffer,format,args);

    // end argument list processing
    va_end(args);

    // calculate required Txt length
    Siz = CalcSiz(Len);

    // allocate Txt
    Txt = new char[Siz];

    if (Txt == NULL)
        throw StringEx(SE_ALLOC);

    // duplicate data from buffer
    strcpy(Txt,buffer);

    // delete buffer
    delete buffer;
    }
```

In the constructor implementation, I allocate a temporary character array (buffer) with maxSize characters. I used ANSI-standard macros to process the variable argument list, which, along with buffer and format, is passed to the ANSI vsprintf function. Len is assigned vsprintf's return value, and I calculate Siz from Len. Finally, Txt duplicates buffer, and buffer is deleted.

Duplicating the buffer may seem like extra work. However, maxSize may be (and, in fact, should be) larger than the number of characters generated by vsprintf. By allocating new space for Txt and copying only the useful contents of buffer, I chop off any extraneous characters.

The String class requires a destructor to delete the memory allocated to the Txt instance variable when a String object is destroyed.

```
String::~String()
    {
    if (Txt != NULL)
        delete Txt;
    }
```

CONVERSION OPERATOR

A programmer will often want to use a String in place of a character array. This conversion can be accomplished with the conversion operator I defined for String.

```
class String
    {
    .
    .
    .
    public:
        operator const char * () const;
    .
    .
    .
    };
```

The conversion function allows a `String` to be cast to a `const char *`. This arrangement allows `String` objects to be used anywhere that `const char *`s are accepted, such as in ANSI library functions.

```
inline String::operator const char * () const
    {
    return (const char *)Txt;
    }
```

`Txt` points to a NULL-terminated buffer, and the conversion operator returns the value of `Txt` cast to a `const char *`. I define the conversion operator as a `const` function so that it can be used with `const String`s.

The conversion would be used like this:

```
String Str = "Hello!";
puts((const char *)Str);
```

The `const` specifier is used to prevent modification of the character array pointed to by `Txt`. In other words, the pointer conversion operator can be used to examine the value of `Str`, but it cannot change it.

ASSIGNMENT OPERATOR

Every class should define an assignment operator.

```
class String
    {
    .
    .
    .
    public:
        String operator = (const String & str);
    .
    .
    .
    };
```

The definition of the assignment operator looks like this:

```
String String::operator = (const String & str)
    {
    Len = str.Len;
    Siz = str.Siz;

    if (Txt != NULL)
        delete Txt;

    if (Siz == 0)
        Txt = NULL;
    else
        {
        Txt = new char[Siz];

        if (Txt == NULL)
            Throw StringEx(SE_ALLOC);

        memcpy(Txt,str.Txt,Len + 1);
        }

    return *this;
    }
```

CONCATENATION

I defined the + and += operators to concatenate two Strings, performing the same function as the ANSI strcat function.

```
class String
    {
    .
    .
    .
    public:
        friend String operator + (const String & str1,
                                   const String & str2);

        friend String operator + (const String & str1, char ch);
```

```
    void operator += (const String & str);
    void operator += (char ch);
    .
    .
    .
};
```

The binary + operator concatenates two strings, returning a new string object. The function begins by calculating the total length of the combined text and allocates an appropriately sized Txt buffer for temp (the return value). The Txt buffers in both source strings are then copied into **temp.Txt**, and the length of temp is calculated. The function returns temp as its result.

```
String operator + (const String & str1,
                   const String & str2)
    {
    // create an empty string
    String temp;

    // calculate length of new string
    unsigned long totalLen = str1.Len + str2.Len;

    // if both source strings are empty, so is the result
    if (totalLen == 0)
        return temp;

    // if length is greater than maximum string length
    if (totalLen > UINT_MAX)
        throw StringEx(SE_TOO_LONG);

    temp.Len = 0;
    temp.Siz = String::CalcSiz((size_t)totalLen);

    // allocate text buffer for result
    temp.Txt = new char[temp.Siz];

    if (temp.Txt == NULL)
        throw StringEx(SE_ALLOC);

    // copy str1 to result
```

```
if (str1.Txt != NULL)
    {
    memcpy(temp.Txt,str1.Txt,str1.Len);
    temp.Len = str1.Len;
    }

// copy str2 to result
if (str2.Txt != NULL)
    {
    memcpy(&temp.Txt[temp.Len],str2.Txt,str2.Len + 1);
    temp.Len += str2.Len;
    }

// return new string
return temp;
}
```

I defined the shorthand operator as a call to the binary operator.

```
inline void String::operator += (const String & str)
    {
    *this = *this + str;
    }
```

If a character array is passed to either of these member functions, the conversion constructor will convert it to a temporary String object before calling the function.

Two other member functions employ the + operator to concatenate a single character to a String.

```
inline void String::operator += (char ch)
    {
    *this = *this + ch;
    }

String operator + (const String & str, char ch)
    {
    String temp;

    if (str.Txt == NULL)
        {
        // if str is empty, the result is a string containing ch
```

```
        temp.Len = 1;
        temp.Siz = String::AllocIncr;


        // allocate text buffer
        temp.Txt = new char [temp.Siz];


        if (temp.Txt == NULL)
            throw StringEx(SE_ALLOC);


        // insert ch and terminating NULL
        temp.Txt[0] = ch;
        temp.Txt[1] = '\000';
        }
    else
        {
        // if string is max length, can't add any more characters
        if (str.Len == UINT_MAX)
            throw StringEx(SE_TOO_LONG);


        // increment string length
        temp.Len = str.Len + 1;


        // if Len is larger than Siz, increase Siz
        if (temp.Len == str.Siz)
            temp.Siz = str.Siz + String::AllocIncr;
        else
            temp.Siz = str.Siz;


        // allocate text buffer
        temp.Txt = new char[temp.Siz];


        if (temp.Txt == NULL)
            throw StringEx(SE_ALLOC);


        // copy str.Txt to text buffer
        memcpy(temp.Txt,str.Txt,str.Len);


        // append ch
        temp.Txt[str.Len]  = ch;
        temp.Txt[temp.Len] = '\000';
        }


    return temp;
    }
```

COMPARISON OPERATORS

Several comparison operators are defined for Strings.

```
class String
    {
    .
    .
    .
    public:
        int String::operator <  (const String & str) const
        int String::operator <= (const String & str) const
        int String::operator == (const String & str) const
        int String::operator != (const String & str) const
        int String::operator >= (const String & str) const
        int String::operator >  (const String & str) const
    .
    .
    .
    };
```

The symbolic comparison operators are most efficiently implemented inline, and they all call the Compare member function:

```
inline int String::operator <  (const String & str) const
    {
    return (Compare(str) == SC_LESS);
    }


inline int String::operator >  (const String & str) const
    {
    return (Compare(str) == SC_GREATER);
    }


inline int String::operator <= (const String & str) const
    {
    return (Compare(str) != SC_GREATER);
    }


inline int String::operator >= (const String & str) const
    {
    return (Compare(str) != SC_LESS);
```

```
    }

inline int String::operator == (const String & str) const
    {
    return (Compare(str) == SC_EQUAL);
    }

inline int String::operator != (const String & str) const
    {
    return (Compare(str) != SC_EQUAL);
    }
```

These member functions use symbolic comparison operators as a shell over the Compare member function. I originally implemented individual comparison functions for each operator, only to see that all the functions were virtually identical. Compare combines all the comparisons into a single function, and the inline operator functions return appropriate results. No efficiency is lost, code size is reduced, and a program using these operators will look more natural when read.

Compare compares two Strings character for character, returning an enumeration value of type StrCompVal that indicates the relationship between the two values. This technique works much like the ANSI function strcmp, except that the caseChk parameter determines whether the comparison is case-sensitive. Here is the implementation of Compare:

```
StrCompVal String::Compare(const String & str,
                           StrCompMode caseChk) const
    {
    // handle special cases where one string is empty
    if (Txt == NULL)
        if (str.Txt == NULL)
            return SC_EQUAL;
        else
            return SC_LESS;

    if (str.Txt == NULL)
        return SC_GREATER;

    // compare the # of characters in the shorter string
    size_t count;
```

```
if (str.Len < Len)
    count = str.Len;
else
    count = Len;

// working variables
char   c1, c2;
size_t i;
if (caseChk == SM_IGNORE)
    {
    // case insensitive comparison
    for (i = 0; i < count; ++i)
        {
        // convert both characters to lowercase
        c1 = (char)tolower(Txt[i]);
        c2 = (char)tolower(str.Txt[i]);

        // if characters differ
        if (c1 != c2)
            {
            // select appropriate result
            if (c1 < c2)
                return SC_LESS;
            else
                return SC_GREATER;
            }
        }
    }
else
    {
    for (i = 0; i < count; ++i)
        {
        c1 = Txt[i];
        c2 = str.Txt[i];

        // if characters differ
        if (c1 != c2)
            {
            // select appropriate result
            if (c1 < c2)
                return SC_LESS;
            else
                return SC_GREATER;
            }
        }
    }

// at this point, no differences were found
```

```
if (Len == str.Len)
    return SC_EQUAL;
else
    {
    // if lengths differ, shorter string < longer one
    if (Len < str.Len)
        return SC_LESS;
    else
        return SC_GREATER;
    }
}
```

SUBSTRING SEARCHES

Many programs look for one string inside another. The more often programs need to perform a task, the more time is spent by computer scientists trying to find a better algorithm for accomplishing that task. Several algorithms provide techniques for searching one string for another. In this book, I'll discuss two algorithms: a brute-force algorithm for one-shot searches and a powerful, fast algorithm for performing multiple searches.

A Brute-Force Algorithm

Brute-force algorithms accomplish their task by the most direct (and usually the most inefficient) way possible. This implementation of the member function `Find` duplicates the purpose of the ANSI library function `strstr` by locating a given `String` within another `String`.

```
class String
    {
    .
    .
    .
    public:         size_t Find(const String & str,
                    size_t & pos,
                    StrCompMode caseChk = SM_IGNORE) const;
    .
    .
    .
    };
```

Find returns an index that indicates where the substring begins. As with Compare, the caseChk parameter defaults to SM_IGNORE to indicate a case-insensitive comparison. The search can be made case-sensitive by specifying the Case parameter as SM_SENSITIVE.

This is the implementation of Find:

```
Boolean String::Find(const String & str,
                      size_t & pos,
                      StrCompMode caseChk) const
    {
    // uses the brute force method
    if (Len < str.Len)
        return BOOL_FALSE;

    // duplicate buffers
    char * target = new char[Len + 1];

    if (target == NULL)
        throw StringEx(SE_ALLOC);

    strcpy(target,Txt);

    char * pattern = new char[str.Len + 1];

    if (pattern == NULL)
        throw StringEx(SE_ALLOC);

    strcpy(pattern,str.Txt);

    // create return value variable
    Boolean result;

    // convert to all lowercase if case-insensitive search
    if (caseChk == SM_IGNORE)
        {
        strlwr(target);
        strlwr(pattern);
        }

    // calculate last position in *this where str could be
    size_t end = Len - str.Len;
```

```
size_t p, t;

// start at the beginning of target
pos = 0;

for (;;)
    {
    p = 0;    // beginning of pattern
    t = pos; // beginning of search position in target

    // while characters match
    // and we're not at the end of the strings

    while ((pattern[p] == target[t])
        && (pattern[p] != 0)
        && (target[t]  != 0))
        {
        // move to next character
        ++t;
        ++p;
        }

    // if we've reached the end of pattern
    //     we've found pattern in target

    if (pattern[p] == 0)
        {
        result = BOOL_TRUE;
        break;
        }

    // if we've reached the end of target
    // or we've searched far enough
    //     pattern has not been found

    if ((target[t] == 0) || (pos >= end))
        {
        result = BOOL_FALSE;
        break;
        }

    // keep looking, starting at the mismatch

    ++pos;
```

```
        }

    // delete temporary buffers
    delete target;
    delete pattern;

    // outta here
    return result;
    }
```

Brute-force algorithms, such as the one used in Find, work in a direct and simplistic manner. The brute-force string-searching algorithm examines every possible position in the target string for the pattern string.

For example, let's assume that I've written an application that searches an electronic copy of Dante's *The Divine Comedy*. When the brute-force algorithm is asked to find the pattern string "unto" in the target string "Pure and disposed to mount unto the stars" (from canto XXXIII, line 145), the search begins like this:

```
target:    Pure, disposed to mount unto the stars
pattern:   unto
```

The algorithm can best be understood by placing the pattern parallel to the target. The algorithm compares the characters in the pattern to those directly above it in the target. For example, the *u* in "unto" does not match the corresponding *p* in the target. This is not a match, and the algorithm moves the pattern right one character.

```
target:    Pure, disposed to mount unto the stars
pattern:    unto
```

The *u*'s in both strings match, but the second character of the pattern, *n*, does not match the corresponding character in the target, *r*. So it moves the pattern right one more character.

```
target:    Pure, disposed to mount unto the stars
pattern:     unto
```

The brute-force algorithm keeps looking for the pattern string by sliding it to the right one character every time the pattern is not found. After several more comparisons, the pattern is situated below the *u* in "mount":

```
target:     Pure, disposed to mount unto the stars
pattern:                      unto
```

Four comparisons (one for each character in the pattern) are made before the algorithm realizes it doesn't have a match. The pattern is moved right four more times before it finally lands under the matching word.

```
target:     Pure, disposed to mount unto the stars
pattern:                           unto
```

In the example, the brute-force algorithm performs 32 comparisons to find the pattern string. In a worst case situation, where the pattern isn't found in the target, the brute-force algorithm will need to perform `strlen(target) - strlen(pattern)` comparisons—and more comparisons if there are any partial matches. When performing a search many times or when the target string is very large, the brute-force algorithm is brutally slow.

Boyer-Moore String Searching

One goal of computer science is to develop algorithms that operate using rudimentary intelligence. Robert S. Boyer and J. Strother Moore developed a very intelligent (and efficient) string-searching algorithm in 1977. The basic implementation of the Boyer-Moore algorithm builds a table that is used to make decisions while searching for a substring.

The table contains a number of values equal to the size of the character set being used. In most environments, characters are represented by eight-bit values; this arrangement requires a table of 256 entries to hold values for all possible characters. In an ASCII environment, the value associated with *A* would be in entry 65; the value for a black space would be located in entry 32.

Initially, the array should contain zeros in all entries. Then a "delta" value is computed for each character in the pattern, as shown by this pseudo-code:

```
for index = 1 to (pattern_length)
    delta [pattern [ index - 1 ] ] = pattern_length - index
```

The delta value for a character is the position of the leftmost occurrence of that character relative to the end of the pattern. For the word *unto*, *u* would be assigned three, *n* would be assigned two, *t* would be assigned one, and *o* would be assigned zero.

In the brute-force algorithm, comparisons are performed from left to right; the first character of the pattern is compared against the first search position in the target; then the second character in the pattern is compared against the second target character, and so on. The Boyer-Moore algorithm is a right-to-left algorithm; it begins by comparing the *last* character in the pattern to the corresponding character in the target.

```
target:    Pure, disposed to mount unto the stars
pattern:   unto
```

The character *o* is not equal to *e*; the pattern must be moved to the right. The pattern is moved to the right the number of characters from the entry in the delta table that corresponds to the target character from the mismatch. Because *e* does not appear in the pattern string, its delta value is four (the length of the pattern), and the pattern is moved four characters to the left relative to the target string.

```
target:    Pure, disposed to mount unto the stars
pattern:       unto
```

Again, the *o* in the pattern fails to match the corresponding character in the target. Because *i* is not in the pattern, the pattern is again moved four positions to the right.

```
target:    Pure, disposed to mount unto the stars
pattern:           unto
```

Another mismatch. Again, the pattern is shifted to the right by its length, where it reaches this position:

```
target:    Pure, disposed to mount unto the stars
pattern:              unto
```

Although the pattern's *o* does not match the corresponding *u* in the target string, the *t* does match a character in the pattern. Again, the pattern is shifted to the right by the delta value for *t*, which is one.

```
target:    Pure, disposed to mount unto the stars
pattern:               unto
```

The last two characters of the pattern match the target, but *n* does not match a space. The pattern is once again shifted by its length.

```
target:    Pure, disposed to mount unto the stars
pattern:                unto
```

The *o* does not match the *u* in the target. *u* is a member of the string "unto," and its table entry has a delta value of three. So the pattern is shifted right by three characters, placing together the *u*'s in the target and pattern strings.

```
target:    Pure, disposed to mount unto the stars
pattern:                   unto
```

The *o* in "unto" does not match the corresponding space in the target. Again, the pattern is shifted right by its length.

```
target:    Pure, disposed to mount unto the stars
pattern:                   unto
```

And the pattern is found! Whereas the brute-force algorithm requires more than 30 comparisons to find the pattern, the Boyer-Moore algorithm needs only 13.

The Boyer-Moore algorithm is faster because it has information about the pattern string stored in the delta table. The character that caused the mismatch in the target string tells Boyer-Moore how to move the pattern in relation to the target. If the mismatching character in the target does not exist in the pattern, Boyer-Moore can safely move the pattern its length to the right, because it is a waste of time to compare the pattern against a character it doesn't contain. When the mismatched character in the target is also resident in the pattern, the delta value for that character aligns the rightmost occurrence of that character in the pattern with the character in the target.

The Boyer-Moore Class

Once the delta table has been created, it can be used to search for the pattern string in any target string. The overhead of creating the table is sufficient that I wanted to create the table once and use it again and again. When searches are being performed for several patterns, I wanted to be able to define unique delta tables for each pattern.

A class that defines a Boyer-Moore delta table is exactly what I needed. The BoyerMoore class is defined like this:

```
class BoyerMoore
    {
    public:
        // constructors
        BoyerMoore(const String & pattern);
        BoyerMoore(const BoyerMoore & bm);

        // destructor
        ~BoyerMoore();

        // assignment operator
        void operator = (const BoyerMoore & bm);

        // get character from pattern string
        char operator [] (size_t index) const;
```

```
        // get delta value from table
        size_t GetDelta(char ch) const;

        // get length of pattern used to create table
        size_t GetPatternLen() const;

        // Assign an exception handler
        static void SetErrOut(const ErrReporter & er);

    private:

        // error display object
        static ErrReporter * ErrOut;

        // pointer to error handler
        static void ReportError();

        // size of delta table
        static const size_t DeltaSize;

        // pointer to delta table
        size_t * Delta;
        String Pattern;
    };
```

Inside a BoyerMoore object is a pointer, Delta, that references a dynamically allocated table of delta values. A BoyerMoore object also includes a duplicate of the pattern String; the duplicate is named Pattern. The static constant DeltaTableSize contains the number of characters in the character set; in this case, I assume that the characters are eight-bit values and initialize DeltaTableSize to 256.

```
const size_t BoyerMoore::DeltaSize = 256;
```

Because BoyerMoore objects allocate memory, they may need to throw an exception. The BoyerMooreEx class is even simpler than the StringEx class in that BoyerMoore objects have only one possible problem: a memory-allocation failure.

```
class BoyerMooreEx
    : public ExceptionBase
    {
    public:
        void Explain(DiagOutput & out);
    };


void BoyerMooreEx::Explain(DiagOutput & out)
    {
    out.DisplayMsg("Boyer-Moore allocation failure",
                        DIAG_FATAL);
    }
```

A BoyerMoore object can be created only from a pattern String or from another, existing BoyerMoore object. The primary constructor duplicates the pattern String and then builds a delta table from it.

```
BoyerMoore::BoyerMoore(const String & pat)
    : Pattern(pat)
    {
    // allocate delta table
    Delta = new size_t [DeltaSize];

    if (Delta == NULL)
            throw BoyerMooreEx();

    // clear table
    size_t i;

    // get length of pattern
    size_t patlen = Pattern.Length();

    for (i = 0; i < DeltaSize; ++i)
        Delta[i] = patlen;

    // set table values
    for (i = 1; i < patlen; ++i)
        Delta[(size_t)Pattern[i - 1]] = patlen - i;

    // set value for last pattern character
    Delta[(size_t)Pattern[patlen - 1]] = 1;
    }
```

The copy constructor simply duplicates the `Delta` table of the source object.

```
BoyerMoore::BoyerMoore(const BoyerMoore & bm)
    : Pattern(bm.Pattern)
    {
    // allocate delta table
    Delta = new size_t [DeltaSize];

    if (Delta == NULL)
        throw BoyerMooreEx();

    // copy contents of source
    memcpy(Delta,bm.Delta,DeltaSize);
    }
```

The destructor deletes the `Delta` table when the object is destroyed.

```
inline BoyerMoore::~BoyerMoore()
    {
    delete Delta;
    }
```

I defined an assignment operator for `BoyerMoore` objects.

```
void BoyerMoore::operator = (const BoyerMoore & bm)
    {
    Delta = bm.Delta;
    }
```

Three interrogation functions provide information about the pattern and its delta table. The [] operator is an inline function that returns a character from the `Pattern` `String`. `PatternLen` is also an inline function that returns the value from calling the `String::Length` function for `Pattern`.

```
// get length of pattern used to create table
inline size_t BoyerMoore::GetPatternLen() const
    {
    return Pattern.Length();
    }
```

```
inline char BoyerMoore::operator [] (size_t index) const
    {
    return Pattern[index];
    };
```

Why not derive BoyerMoore from String? I wanted to limit the types of operations that could be performed on the pattern String. Any modifications to the Pattern after it has been used to create the delta table will invalidate that table. The pattern String can only be examined; it cannot be changed or manipulated in any other fashion.

The remaining interrogation function returns the value from Delta for the character ch.

```
inline size_t BoyerMoore::GetDelta(char ch) const
    {
    return Delta[size_t(ch)];
    }
```

Boyer-Moore String Searching

I created a second Find function that takes a BoyerMoore object as a parameter.

```
class String
    {
    .
    .
    .
    public:
        // Boyer-Moore string search
        Boolean Find(const BoyerMoore & bm, size_t & pos);
    .
    .
    .
    };
```

The Boyer-Moore Find function is implemented like this:

```
Boolean String::Find(const BoyerMoore & bm, size_t & pos)
    {
```

```
size_t i, j, patlen;

// store pattern length locally (it gets used a lot)
patlen = bm.GetPatternLen();

// i is the index into the target
i = patlen;

while (i <= Len)
    {
    // j is an index into pattern
    j = patlen;

    // while corresponding characters match
    while (bm[j - 1] == Txt[i - 1])
        {
        if (j > 1)
            {
            // move left one character for next comparison
            --j;
            --i;
            }
        else
            {
            // we've reached the beginning of the pattern
            // pattern found!
            pos = i - 1;
            return BOOL_TRUE;
            }
        }

    // move target index by delta value of
    // mismatched character
    i += bm.GetDelta(Txt[i - 1]);
    }

return BOOL_FALSE;
}
```

The delta table in the BoyerMoore object is used to change the position in the target string where the pattern is being compared. The function returns BOOL_FALSE if the pattern was not found. If the pattern was found, BOOL_TRUE is returned and the variable parameter pos is set to hold the index within the target at which the first occurrence of the pattern was found.

SUBSTRING DELETION

The Delete member function removes a specified number of characters from a string.

```
class String
    {
    .
    .
    .
    public:
        void String::Delete(size_t pos, size_t count = 1);
    .
    .
    .
    };
```

The parameter pos provides the index of the first character to be deleted, and the count parameter indicates how many characters should be deleted. If count isn't specified, it defaults to one, so the Delete removes a single character from the string. Here is the implementation of Delete:

```
void String::Delete(size_t pos, size_t count)
    {
    if (Txt == NULL)
        return;

    size_t newLen, i;

    // error if deleting outside of string
    if ((pos + count - 1) > Len)
        throw StringEx(SE_INVALID);

    // length of new string
    newLen = Len - count;

    if ((Siz - newLen) > AllocIncr)
        {
```

```
    // allocation size has changed
    // calculate new size

    Siz = CalcSiz(newLen);

    // create new buffer

    char * temp = new char[Siz];

    if (temp == NULL)
        throw StringEx(SE_ALLOC);

    // copy characters into new buffer
    char * tptr = temp;

    for (i = 0; i <= Len; ++i)
        {
        // when count is reached, skip deleted characters
        if (i == pos)
            i += count;

        *tptr = Txt[i];
        ++tptr;
        }

    // delete old buffer
    delete Txt;

    // assign new buffer
    Txt = temp;
    }
else
    {
    // just "slide" characters down
    for (i = pos + count; i <= Len; ++i)
        Txt[i] = Txt[i + count];
    }

Len = newLen;
}
```

STRING INSERTION

Characters and strings can be inserted into a String at any position using the Insert member functions.

```
class String
    {
    .
    .
    .
    public:
        void Insert(size_t pos, char ch);
        void Insert(size_t pos, const String & str);
    .
    .
    .
    };
```

The first Insert member function listed inserts a single character:

```
void String::Insert(size_t pos, char ch)
    {
    if (pos > Len)
        throw StringEx(SE_INVALID);

    if (Txt == NULL)
        {
        // an empty string == ch
        Len = 1;
        Siz = AllocIncr;

        Txt = new char [Siz];

        if (Txt == NULL)
            throw StringEx(SE_ALLOC);

        Txt[0] = ch;
        Txt[1] = '\000';
        }
    else
        {
        size_t newLen = Len + 1;
```

```
    size_t i;

if (newLen == Siz)
    {
    // need a larger buffer
    Siz += AllocIncr;

    // create temporary buffer
    char * temp = new char[Siz];
    char * tptr = temp;

    if (temp == NULL)
        throw StringEx(SE_ALLOC);

    // copy in old buffer, inserting ch when needed
    for (i = 0; i <= Len; ++i)
        {
        if (i == pos)
            {
            *tptr = ch;
            ++tptr;
            }

        *tptr = Txt[i];
        ++tptr;
        }

    // delete old buffer
    delete Txt;

    // assign new buffer and length
    Txt = temp;
    Len = newLen;
    }
else
    {
    // slide characters right
    for (i = newLen; i > pos; --i)
        Txt[i] = Txt[i-1];

    // insert character
    Txt[pos] = ch;

    // adjust length
```

```
            Len = newLen;
            }
        }
    }
```

The second `Insert` member function inserts an entire `String`:

```
void String::Insert(size_t pos, const String & str)
    {
    if (str.Txt == NULL)
        return;

    if (pos > Len)
        throw StringEx(SE_INVALID);

    if (Txt == NULL)
        {
        // empty string = str
        *this = str;
        }
    else
        {
        // calculate new length
        unsigned long totalLen = str.Len + Len;

        if (totalLen > UINT_MAX)
            throw StringEx(SE_TOO_LONG);

        size_t i, j;

        // if new  length > current size
        if (totalLen > Siz)
            {
            // allocate new buffer
            Siz = CalcSiz((size_t)totalLen);

            char * temp = new char [Siz];
            char * tptr = temp;

            // copy buffers from source strings
            for (i = 0; i <= Len; ++i)
                {
                if (i == pos)
                    {
```

```
                    for (j = 0; j < str.Len; ++j)
                        {
                        *tptr = str.Txt[j];
                        ++tptr;
                        }
                    }

                *tptr = Txt[i];
                ++tptr;
                }

            // delete old buffer
            delete Txt;

            // assign new buffer
            Txt = temp;
            }
        else
            {
            // slide section old buffer to right
            for (i = Len + str.Len; i > pos + str.Len; —i)
                Txt[i] = Txt[i - str.Len];

            // insert new string
            for (i = 0; i < str.Len; ++i)
                Txt[pos + i] = str.Txt[i];
            }

        Len = (size_t)totalLen;
        }
    }
```

Once again, the conversion constructor permits the use of a character array in place of the String parameter in both Insert member functions.

SUBSTRING EXTRACTION

The various "cut" member functions extract portions of a string.

```
class String
    {
```

```
        .
        .
        .
    public:
        String Cut(size_t start, size_t count);
        String CutHead(size_t count);
        String CutTail(size_t count);
        .
        .
        .
    };
```

The Cut function extracts count characters beginning at start.

```
String String::Cut(size_t start, size_t count)
    {
    if ((start + count) > Len)
        throw StringEx(SE_INVALID);

    String temp;

    if ((start < Len) && (count > 0))
        {
        temp.Len = count;
        temp.Siz = CalcSiz(count);
        temp.Txt = new char[temp.Siz];

        if (temp.Txt == NULL)
            Throw StringEx(SE_ALLOC);

        memcpy(temp.Txt,&Txt[start],count);

        temp.Txt[count] = '\000';
        }

    return temp;
    }
```

CutHead cuts count characters from the front of the String, and CutTail extracts count characters from the end of a String.

```
String String::CutHead(size_t count)
```

```
    {
    if (count > Len)
        throw StringEx(SE_INVALID);

    String temp;

    if (count > 0)
        {
        temp.Len = count;
        temp.Siz = CalcSiz(count);
        temp.Txt = new char[temp.Siz];

        if (temp.Txt == NULL)
            throw StringEx(SE_ALLOC);

        memcpy(temp.Txt,Txt,count);

        temp.Txt[count] = '\000';
        }

    return temp;
    }

String String::CutTail(size_t count)
    {
    if (count > Len)
        throw StringEx(SE_INVALID);

    String temp;

    if (count > 0)
        {
        temp.Len = count;
        temp.Siz = CalcSiz(count);
        temp.Txt = new char[temp.Siz];

        if (temp.Txt == NULL)
            throw StringEx(SE_ALLOC);

        memcpy(temp.Txt,&Txt[Len - count - 1],count);

        temp.Txt[count] = '\000';
        }
```

```
    return temp;
    }
```

All these member functions create a new string that contains the characters extracted from the implicit object.

INDEXING

Single characters at indexed positions within a String can be examined by using the operator [] function.

```
class String
    {
    .
    .
    .
    public:
        char operator [] (size_t pos) const;
    .
    .
    .
    .
    };
```

The String operator function [] is used exactly like the [] operators are used on a C-like array of characters. However, although you can index outside a C-like string, the [] operator implementation prevents indexing into areas outside a String's boundaries. If the position given is beyond the last character of the String, a NULL character is returned. I implement the [] operator inline.

```
inline char String::operator [] (size_t pos) const
    {
    if (pos >= Len)
        return '\x00';
    else
        return Txt[pos];
    }
```

CASE CONVERSION

The last four member functions for `String` are `ToUpper`, `ToLower`, `AsUpper`, and `AsLower`.

```
class String
    {
    .
    .
    .
    public:
        void ToUpper();
        void ToLower();

        String AsUpper();
        String AsLower();
    .
    .
    .
    };
```

These member functions convert all the characters in a `String` to uppercase or lowercase. The `To...` functions change the `String` object directly.

```
void ToUpper()
    {
    if (Txt != NULL)
        strupr(Txt);
    }

void ToLower()
    {
    if (Txt != NULL)
        strlwr(Txt);
    }
```

The `As...` functions return a new `String` with the same text as the original but with the case changed.

```
String String::AsUpper()
    {
```

```
    String temp = *this;

    if (temp.Txt != NULL)
        strupr(temp.Txt);

    return temp;
    }

String String::AsLower()
    {
    String temp = *this;

    if (temp.Txt != NULL)
        strlwr(temp.Txt);

    return temp;
    }
```

STREAM I/O

C++ allows the creation of operators that read and write objects to I/O streams. For the String class, I defined input and output operator functions.

```
class String
    {
    .
    .
    .

    public:
        friend ostream & operator << (ostream & strm,
                                        const String & str);

        friend istream & operator >> (istream & strm,
                                        String & str);
    .
    .
    .

    };
```

The output function is simple; it simply uses the character array insertion function to write str.Txt to strm.

```
inline ostream & operator << (ostream & strm, const String & str)
    {
    strm << str.Txt;

    return strm;
    }
```

The input function was more difficult to implement. I wanted to avoid overflowing str.Txt, but I also wanted to allow for the creation of a string of any length that was input. I reached a compromise in my implementation of the stream extraction operator.

```
istream & operator >> (istream & strm, String & str)
    {
    static char buf[128];

    if ((str.Txt == NULL) || (str.Len == 0))
        {
        strm >> setw(128) >> buf;

        #ifdef __ZTC__
            str = (const char *)buf;
        #else
            str = buf;
        #endif
        }
    else
        strm >> setw(str.Siz) >> str.Txt;

    return strm;
    }
```

If str is empty, I create a temporary buffer 128 characters in length, insert characters into that buffer from strm, and then duplicate the contents of buffer in Txt and assign values to Len and Siz based on the input data. If str has already allocated Txt, I use the Siz of that buffer as the maximum length of the input. In both cases, I use the setw manipulator to prevent overflowing of the input array.

I'm certain this isn't a perfect solution, but it has worked well enough for me to live with it.

MOVING ON

The String has been immensely useful to me. I now use Strings everywhere I can to replace C's NULL-terminated character arrays. In particular, the searching, substring, insertion, and deletion features of String objects make them useful for interactive programs such as word processors and data entry programs. Strings are also more reliable than character arrays; program bugs common to char arrays include a failure to allocate enough space, forgetting to add the terminating NULL, or simply writing into an area of a char array that is outside the array bounds. The String class shows how a C++ class can improve programs by providing reliable and powerful new data types.

I implemented the String classes in the files **Str.h** and **Str.cpp**, which I've included on this book's diskette.

ONWARD

Almost every program contains at least one array of values; most of my programs seem filled with arrays. And so it is that I developed an entire set of array types, with supporting classes for sorting and statistical calculations. The next chapter begins looking at my array library.

CHAPTER 7

ARRAY FUNDAMENTALS

When I first began working with C++, I built an application for manipulating large arrays of numbers. The result was a set of type-specific classes, one for each of the numeric data types manipulated in the program. By providing strong type checking and bounds checking, my classes were an improvement on C's simple pointers and arrays. But they were clumsy and bloated by virtue of having to explicitly define a class for every array type.

As C++ has matured, my array classes have benefited from new language features. Templates allowed me to create generic array types and from them create type-specific arrays as needed. Exception handlers allowed me to centralize and standardize my error handling. For the next four chapters, I'll present my array classes and also explain applications such as sorting and statistical calculations. I'll begin by showing you some of the classes that support my arrays.

BOUNDARIES

In some cases, it's valuable to have an integral numeric data type that is bounded by a high and a low value. Pascal and Modula-2 support sub-range data types that allow programmers to define the specific range for an integral value. In the case of C++, classes can provide the ability to create a subrange feature.

I created a Bounds data type that simply defines the upper and lower bounds of a template-defined type. In the previous edition of this book, the Bounds class was named Range and was limited to working with int values. Each Bounds object knows its high and low values; a Bounds also keeps track of the magnitude of its range. For the purposes of my arrays (and to maintain compatibility with the previous editions of this book), I defined the type Range as a Bounds<int> object.

BOUNDS CLASS

Why use Bounds? Wouldn't it be simpler to define the high and low values for an array in its constructor rather than use another object?

I created Range from Bounds to define a specific set of integer values. In most of my applications, I'm working with several arrays at once; each array has the same range of values. It seems logical to create a type that defines, controls, and manipulates a range of values and to use objects of that data type in defining the range of indexes in an array. If nothing else, it promotes consistency; a single Range object can define the bounds of several arrays, thus ensuring that the arrays are compatible.

Exceptions

The Bounds class throws exceptions of the BoundsEx type:

```
class BoundsEx : public ExceptionBase
    {
    private:
        BoundsError Error;

    public:
        BoundsEx(BoundsError err)    { Error = err; }
```

```
    void Explain(DiagOutput & out);
};
```

The enumerated type BoundsError defines values representing the variety of problems that can occur in a Bounds object:

```
enum BoundsError
    {
    BEX_INVALID,
    BEX_ADDOUT,
    BEX_BOUNDS,
    BEX_UNDER,
    BEX_OVER
    };
```

Note that the BEX_UNDER and BEX_OVER errors apply only to Index objects, which I'll introduce shortly.

Bounds::WhatsWrong is a helpful function when you're trapping a specific Bounds problem. For example, in this block of code, I'm processing BEX_BOUNDS:

```
try { /* do something */ }

catch (BoundsEx & bex)
    {
    if (bex.WhatsWrong() == BEX_BOUNDS)
        HandleBoundsProblem();
    else
        throw; // send exception up handler chain
    }
```

I implemented the Bounds::Explain function using a switch statement:

```
void Bounds::Explain(DiagOutput & out)
    {
    switch (Error)
        {
        case BEX_INVALID:
            out.DisplayMsg("Range created with max > min"
```

```
                         ,DIAG_ERROR);
        break;
    case BEX_ADDOUT:
        out.DisplayMsg("Range addition out of range"
                         ,DIAG_ERROR);
        break;
    case BEX_BOUNDS:
        out.DisplayMsg("Range value out of bounds"
                         ,DIAG_ERROR);
        break;
    case BEX_UNDER:
        out.DisplayMsg("Index underflow"
                         ,DIAG_ERROR);
        break;
    case BEX_OVER:
        out.DisplayMsg("Index overflow"
                         ,DIAG_ERROR);
    }
  }
```

Class Definition

The template class definition of Bounds looks like this:

```
template <class T>
    class Bounds
        {
        public:
            // constructors
            Bounds
                (
                T rmin,
                T rmax
                );

            Bounds
                (
                T rmax
                );

            Bounds
                (
                const Bounds<T> & r
                );
```

```
    // assignment operator
    Bounds<T> & operator =
        (
        const Bounds<T> & r
        );

    // add ranges
    friend Bounds<T> operator +
        (
        const Bounds<T> & r1,
        const Bounds<T> & r2
        );

    // comparison operator
    bool operator ==
        (
        const Bounds<T> & r
        ) const;

    bool operator !=
        (
        const Bounds<T> & r
        ) const;

    // information retrieval functions
    T GetMin() const;
    T GetMax() const;
    T GetMagnitude() const;

    // report error if 'n' is invalid
    bool Check(T n) const;

    // check for 'n' or range within bounds
    bool Includes(T n) const;
    bool Includes(const Bounds<T> & r) const;
    bool Excludes(T n) const;
    bool Excludes(const Bounds<T> & r) const;

    // range-checking functions
    static void CheckOn();
    static void CheckOff();
    static bool GetCheck();

protected:
    // minimum and maximum values
```

```
        T Minimum;
        T Maximum;
        T Magnitude;

        // range-checking switch
        static bool BoundsCheck;
    };
```

The `Minimum` and `Maximum` data members of `Range` define its lower and upper bounds. `Magnitude` is the number of values between `Minimum` and `Maximum`, or, in other words, the size of the `Range`.

The static `Switch` `BoundsCheck` turns on and off exception generation by `Bounds` objects. `BoundsCheck` is on by default, and you can use the `CheckOn` and `CheckOff` functions to change its setting. The `GetCheck` function returns the current value of `BoundsCheck`:

```
template <class T>
    inline void Bounds<T>::CheckOn()
        {
        BoundsCheck = true;
        }


template <class T>
    inline void Bounds<T>::CheckOff()
        {
        BoundsCheck = false;
        }


template <class T>
    inline bool Bounds<T>::GetCheck()
        {
        return BoundsCheck;
        }
```

Constructors

I provided `Bounds` with four constructors. I didn't define a default (no argument) constructor, because I saw no way of determining a "default" range of values.

The first constructor creates a Bounds with specified minimum and maximum values. An exception is raised if rmax is less than rmin; otherwise, Minimum is assigned rmin, Maximum is assigned rmax, and Magnitude is calculated:

```
template <class T>
    Bounds<T>::Bounds
        (
        int rmin,
        int rmax
        )
        {
        if (BoundsCheck && (rmax < rmin))
            throw BoundsEx(BEX_INVALID);

        Minimum = rmin;
        Maximum = rmax;

        if (Minimum < 0)
            {
            if (Maximum < 0)
                Magnitude = (unsigned int)(Minimum - Maximum);
            else
                Magnitude = (unsigned int)(-Minimum)
                                    + (unsigned int)Maximum;
            }
        else
            Magnitude = Maximum - Minimum;

        ++Magnitude;
        }
```

The second constructor assumes that the Minimum value is 1. The rmax value defines the upper bound of the Range:

```
template <class T>
    Bounds<T>::Bounds
        (
        int rmax
        )
        {
        if (BoundsCheck && (rmax <= 1))
            throw BoundsEx(BEX_INVALID);
```

```
Minimum   = 1;
Maximum   = rmax;
Magnitude = rmax + 1;
}
```

The last constructor is the obligatory copy constructor. I almost always define a copy constructor, even though the compiler can generate one for me. In this case, the copy constructor simply copies the instance variables of the source object. Simple constructors like this can be implemented inline.

```
template <class T>
    inline Bounds<T>::Bounds
        (
        const Bounds<T> & r
        )
        {
        Minimum   = r.Minimum;
        Maximum   = r.Maximum;
        Magnitude = r.Magnitude;
        }
```

Operators

I defined four basic operator functions for Bounds. The assignment operator looks similar to the copy constructor. It returns a pointer to this so that assignments can be chained (For example, a = b = c).

```
template <class T>
    inline Bounds<T> & Bounds<T>::operator =
        (
        const Bounds<T> & r
        )
        {
        Minimum   = r.Minimum;
        Maximum   = r.Maximum;
        Magnitude = r.Magnitude;

        return *this;
        }
```

You can combine, or concatenate, two Bounds objects using the + operator. The lower bound of r1 is used as the Minimum value for the new Bounds; the Magnitude of r2 is added to the Maximum value of r1 to obtain the new Maximum of the Bounds .

```
template <class T>
    Bounds<T> operator +
        (
        const Bounds<T> & r1,
        const Bounds<T> & r2
        )
        {
        if (Bounds<T>::BoundsCheck
        && ((INT_MAX - r1.Maximum) < r2.Magnitude))
                throw BoundsEx(BEX_ADDOUT);

        return Bounds<T>(r1.Minimum,r1.Maximum + r2.Magnitude);
        }
```

To compare Bounds objects, use the == and != operators. Two Bounds objects are defined as equal if they have the same Minimum and Maximum. I declared the comparison functions as const to allow their use in comparing constant Bounds objects, and I implemented them inline.

```
template <class T>
    inline bool Bounds<T>::operator ==
        (
        const Bounds<T> & r
        ) const
        {
        return ((Minimum == r.Minimum)
                    && (r.Maximum == r.Maximum));
        }

template <class T>
    inline bool Bounds<T>::operator !=
        (
        const Bounds<T> & r
        ) const
        {
        return ((Minimum != r.Minimum)
                    || (r.Maximum != r.Maximum));
        }
```

Interrogation Functions

It's bad C++ programming practice to make the data members of a class public. Although a public data member can be easily read when needed, it can also be directly modified from outside the class scope. The use of interrogation functions allows data members to be examined without leaving them open to modification.

The GetMin, GetMax, and Magnitude functions return respectively, the Minimum, Maximum, and Magnitude members of a Bounds. Implementing these functions inline actually produces smaller (and vastly faster) code than the use of callable functions would .

```
template <class T>
    inline T Bounds<T>::GetMin() const
        {
        return Minimum;
        }

template <class T>
    inline T Bounds<T>::GetMax() const
        {
        return Maximum;
        }

template <class T>
    inline T Bounds<T>::GetMagnitude() const
        {
        return Magnitude;
        }
```

Checking Values

Five functions can compare a T value against a Bounds. If the given T is out of range, the Check function raises an exception. I did not implement this function inline because it contains a throw statement. In general, compilers will not inline functions that can generate exceptions.

```
template <class T>
    inline bool Bounds<T>::Check(T n) const
        {
        return ((n < Minimum) || (n > Maximum));
        }
```

The `Includes` functions return a nonzero value if the given `int` or `Bounds` is within bounds; otherwise, they return 0. The `Excludes` functions return 0 if the parameter is in bounds; otherwise, they return 1. For simplicity's sake, I implemented these functions inline.

```
template <class T>
    inline bool Bounds<T>::Includes(T n) const
        {
        return ((n >= Minimum) && (n <= Maximum));
        }

template <class T>
    inline bool Bounds<T>::Includes
        (
        const Bounds<T> & r
        ) const
        {
        return ((Minimum <= r.Minimum)
                && (Maximum >= r.Maximum));
        }

template <class T>
    inline bool Bounds<T>::Excludes(T n) const
        {
        return ((n < Minimum) || (n > Maximum));
        }

template <class T>
    inline bool Bounds<T>::Excludes
        (
        const Bounds<T> & r
        ) const
        {
        return ((Minimum > r.Minimum)
                || (Maximum < r.Maximum));
        }
```

The class definitions and functions for Bounds are in the files **Bounds.h** and **Bounds.cxx**, which can be found on the accompanying source diskette.

INDEXES

Arrays have a lower and an upper bound; the index used to reference array elements should be within these bounds. Keeping a value within bounds is the job of a Bounds object; therefore, an Index is simply a Bounds<int> to which you can assign a value. To make the syntax simpler, I defined the following Range type:

```
typedef Bounds<int> Range;
```

For exceptions, Index uses the BoundsEx type defined earlier.

Class Definition

When I derived the Index class from Range, I added a new data member named Value. I then implemented complementary constructors and member functions and added a few new features related to Value.

```
class Index : public Range
    {
    public:
        // constructors
        Index(int imin, int imax);
        Index(const Range & r);
        Index(const Range & r, int i);
        Index(const Index & i);

        // conversions
        operator int() const;     // returns exact value
        operator size_t() const; // returns zero-based value

        // value checks
        bool IsMin() const;
```

```
    bool IsMax() const;

    // explicit assignments
    void SetMin();
    void SetMax();

    // assignment operators
    Index & operator = (int n);
    Index & operator = (const Index & i);

    // math operators
    Index operator + (const Index & i);
    Index operator - (const Index & i);
    Index operator + (int i);
    Index operator - (int i);

    // shorthand operators
    Index & operator += (const Index & i);
    Index & operator -= (const Index & i);
    Index & operator += (int n);
    Index & operator -= (int n);

    // increment and decrement
    Index & operator ++ ();
    Index & operator - ();

    // comparison operators
    bool operator >  (const Index & i) const;
    bool operator >= (const Index & i) const;
    bool operator == (const Index & i) const;
    bool operator != (const Index & i) const;
    bool operator <= (const Index & i) const;
    bool operator <  (const Index & i) const;
    bool operator >  (int i) const;
    bool operator >= (int i) const;
    bool operator == (int i) const;
    bool operator != (int i) const;
    bool operator <= (int i) const;
    bool operator <  (int i) const;

protected:
    // current index value
    int Value;
};
```

Constructors

Four constructors build `Index` objects. The first constructor calls the `Range` constructor with `rmin == imin` and `rmax == imax`. It then sets `Value` equal to `imin`.

```
inline Index::Index(int imin, int imax)
    : Range(imin,imax)
    {
    Value = Minimum;
    }
```

The second constructor creates an `Index` from a `Range`. As you'll see in subsequent chapters, a constant `Range` can be used to define consistent bounds for `Arrays` and their related `Indexes`. The initial `Value` will be `Minimum`.

```
inline Index::Index(const Range & r)
    : Range(r)
    {
    Value = Minimum;
    }
```

A variation on the second constructor allows an `Index` to be created from a `Range` with a `Value` other than `Minimum`.

```
Index::Index(const Range & r, int i)
    : Range(r)
    {
    if ((RangeCheck == ON) && ((i < Minimum) || (i > Maximum)))
        throw RangeEx(RE_BOUNDS);

    Value = i;
    }
```

The last constructor is the copy constructor. Note that the simplest constructors have been implemented inline; in essence, they are extensions of the `Range` constructors, with additional code for handling `Value`.

```
inline Index::Index(const Index & i)
    : Range(i)
    {
    Value = i.Value;
    }
```

Conversions

The `Index` class defines two conversion operators. The `int()` operator returns `Value`, and it is an inline function.

```
inline Index::operator int () const
    {
    return Value;
    }
```

The `size_t()` operator returns the value of the `Index` relative to zero. As you'll see in the next chapter, the `size_t()` conversion is very useful when you're indexing from a pointer, such as the pointer to data inside an array object.

```
Index::operator size_t () const
    {
    unsigned long result;

    if (Minimum < 0)
        {
        result = (size_t)(-Minimum);

        if (Value < 0)
            result -= (size_t)(-Value);
        else
            result += (size_t)Value;
        }
    else
        result = (size_t)(Value - Minimum);

    return result;
    }
```

Setting and Checking Values

I use four functions to handle special Values of an Index. Two bool interrogation functions check to see whether Value is equal to Minimum or Maximum.

```
inline int Index::IsMin() const
    {
    return (Value == Minimum);
    }

inline int Index::IsMax() const
    {
    return (Value == Maximum);
    }
```

The last two functions set Value to Minimum or Maximum. This method makes it easier to handle "unknown" Index objects that are passed as parameters to functions.

```
inline void Index::SetMin()
    {
    Value = Minimum;
    }
```

Operators

These operator functions define assignment, addition, and subtraction operations. When an int is assigned to an Index, the class reports an error if it is not within bounds.

```
Index & Index::operator = (int i)
    {
    if ((RangeCheck == ON) && ((i < Minimum) || (i > Maximum)))
        throw RangeEx(RE_BOUNDS);

    Value = i;
```

```
    return *this;
    }
```

The assignment of one Index to another may not act exactly as you would expect. Only the Value of the source Index is copied; the destination retains its Minimum, Maximum, and Magnitude. This arrangement allows Indexes with overlapping ranges to be mutually assignable. An error will be reported if the source Value is out of range.

```
Index & Index::operator = (const Index & i)
    {
    this->Range::operator = (i);
    Value = i.Value;
    return *this;
    }
```

Index defines both the binary and the shorthand forms of addition and subtraction; ints and Indexes can be used as operands.

```
Index Index::operator + (int i)
    {
    if (BoundsCheck == ON)
        {
        if (i < 0)
            {
            if ((Value - Minimum) < -i)
                throw RangeEx(BEX_UNDER);
            }
        else
            {
            if ((Maximum - Value) < i)
                throw RangeEx(BEX_OVER);
            }
        }

    Index result(*this);
    result.Value += i;
    return result;
    }

Index Index::operator - (int i)
    {
```

```
    if (BoundsCheck == ON)
        {
        if (i > 0)
            {
            if ((Value - Minimum) < i)
                throw BoundsEx(BEX_UNDER);
            }
        else
            {
            if ((Maximum - Value) < -i)
                throw BoundsEx(BEX_OVER);
            }
        }


    Index result(*this);
    result.Value -= i;
    return result;
    }
```

I built all the other mathematical operators on the functions shown in the preceding code. This technique centralizes basic operations and allows me to extend the available nomenclature by simply defining inline "shell" functions for variant operators.

```
inline Index Index::operator + (const Index & i)
    {
    return *this + i.Value;
    }


inline Index Index::operator - (const Index & i)
    {
    return *this - i.Value;
    }


inline Index & Index::operator += (const Index & i)
    {
    return *this += i.Value;
    }


inline Index & Index::operator -= (const Index & i)
    {
    return *this -= i.Value;
    }
```

```
inline Index & Index::operator += (int i)
    {
    return *this = *this + i;
    }

inline Index & Index::operator -= (int i)
    {
    return *this = *this - i;
    }
```

More often than not, the operation performed on an Index is an increment or decrement. Like the addition and subtraction operators, increment and decrement will report an error if the calculation results in an out-of-range Value.

```
Index & Index::operator ++ ()
    {
    if ((BoundsCheck == ON) && (Value == Maximum))
        throw BoundsEx(BEX_OVER);

    ++Value;
    return *this;
    }

Index & Index::operator — ()
    {
    if ((BoundsCheck == ON) && (Value == Minimum))
        throw BoundsEx(BEX_UNDER);

    —Value;
    return *this;
    }
```

Comparisons

Using the following operator functions, you can compare Indexes against other Indexes and ints. All these operator functions are simple enough to be implemented inline.

```
inline int Index::operator > (const Index & i) const
    {
    return (Value > i.Value);
    }


inline int Index::operator >= (const Index & i) const
    {
    return (Value >= i.Value);
    }


inline int Index::operator == (const Index & i) const
    {
    return (Value == i.Value);
    }


inline int Index::operator != (const Index & i) const
    {
    return (Value != i.Value);
    }


inline int Index::operator <= (const Index & i) const
    {
    return (Value <= i.Value);
    }


inline int Index::operator < (const Index & i) const
    {
    return (Value < i.Value);
    }


inline int Index::operator > (int i) const
    {
    return (Value > i);
    }


inline int Index::operator >= (int i) const
    {
    return (Value >= i);
    }


inline int Index::operator == (int i) const
    {
    return (Value == i);
    }


inline int Index::operator != (int i) const
```

```
    {
    return (Value != i);
    }

inline int Index::operator <= (int i) const
    {
    return (Value <= i);
    }

inline int Index::operator < (int i) const
    {
    return (Value < i);
    }
```

The class definition and member functions for `Index` are in the files **Index.h** and **Index.cpp**, which you will find on the accompanying source diskette.

BASIC ARRAYS

The goal in creating a C++ class is to build on other classes and on the data types intrinsic to the language. In other words, either we want to add a new data type (such as complex) or we want to make a "better" version of an existing data type. In the first case, we are expanding our tools; in the second case, we are enhancing them. In some situations, a new class enhances an existing part of the language while adding new features.

A review of C-style arrays will help us in seeing how a C++ array class should be designed and where C++ can improve on C. If you're an experienced C programmer with a solid understanding of the intricacies of arrays, feel free to skip this section and turn to the discussion about implementing an `Array` class in C++.

Programs often need to work with homogeneous sets of data. In a financial application, you may need to keep track of the profits for each month in a year. This type of data is often represented in a program by an array. In C++, arrays are the same as C arrays; as such, C++ arrays inherit the limitations and problems of C arrays. Fortunately, a C++ class can be used to improve on the traditional C-style array.

Let's work with my example of a financial application that stores a monthly numeric value. In C, we could declare an array of 12 `doubles`:

```
double profit[12];
```

The variable `profit` designates an area of memory in which 12 `doubles` are stored. Each `double` is an element of the array, and an integer value can be used as an `Index` to specify an array element. The elements of an array are numbered from 0; thus, the elements of the `profit` array have integer `Indexes` ranging from 0 to 11. For example:

```
profit[1]  = 1200.00; // the second element (February)
profit[11] = 1750.00; // the last    element (December)
profit[4]  = 2398.00; // the fifth   element (May)
profit[0]  =  900.00; // the first   element (January)
```

An array does not include any information on its size; the programmer is responsible for knowing the size of the array. Usually, a constant is used to define the number of elements in an array, as in this example:

```
const int MON_PER_YR = 12;

double Profit[MON_PER_YR];

// fill Profit with zeros
for (int i = 0; i < MON_PER_YR; ++i)
    Profit[i] = 0.0;
```

When you're passing an array as a function argument, things get a bit stickier. You can't specify the exact size of an array in the function declaration. Instead, you must specify a blank set of brackets, as in this function:

```
void ClearProfits(double prof[])
    {
```

```
    for (int i = 0; i < MON_PER_YR; ++i)
        prof[i] = 0.0;
}
```

Or, because array arguments are passed as pointers, this declaration could be used:

```
void ClearProfits(double * prof)
    {
    for (int i = 0; i < MON_PER_YR; ++i)
        prof[i] = 0.0;
    }
```

This function definition is illegal:

```
void ClearProfits(double prof[MON_PER_YR])
    {
    // does something
    }
```

A C-style array does not keep track of the number of elements it contains. Unlike Pascal and Modula-2, a C++ compiler does not perform a check to see whether the number of elements specified for the parameter matches the number of elements in the argument. So a function that handles a fixed-size array would have to assume that the array argument has the expected number of elements:

```
void ShowMonthlies(double prof[])
    {
    for (int i = 0; i < MON_PER_YR; ++i)
        prof[i] = 0.0;
    }
```

If you want a function that can work with any size array, the number of elements in the array will have to be passed as an addition argument. For example, a function that prints an array of doubles might look like this:

```
void PrintDoubleArray(double darray[], int size)
    {
```

```
for (int i = 0; i < size; ++i)
    cout << "element " << i << " = " << darray[i];
}
```

Arrays of Objects

An array of objects is created just as an array of an intrinsic type is:

```
class Integer
    {
    private:
        int Value;
    public:
        // constructor
        Integer(int i = 0) { Value = i; };

        // other function members
    };

Integer IntArray[10];
```

In this case, the compiler generates calls to the default constructor (`Integer(int i)` with `i` equal to the default value of `0`) for each element of `IntArray`. If you want to assign specific values to each member of `IntArray`, you could provide explicit constructor values:

```
Integer IntArray[10] = {Integer(1),  Integer(2),
                        Integer(3),  Integer(4),
                        Integer(5),  Integer(6),
                        Integer(7),  Integer(8),
                        Integer(9),  Integer(10));
```

If a class does not have a default constructor, an array of that class's objects must be created using explicit constructor values.

Pros and Cons of Arrays

C-style arrays are efficient, because your program works directly with the underlying memory map of the data. Unfortunately, this efficiency comes with a cost: Arrays are error-prone.

If you try to index outside the bounds of an array, C++ will not complain. This statement will compile without so much as a peep from your C++ compiler:

```
Profit[20] = 0.0; // set value of 21st element
```

If you run a program containing the preceding statement, what will happen is anybody's guess. `Profit` has only 12 elements; the memory in the "21st element" may be a piece of executable code, or it might be a part of another data item. When a function such as `PrintDoubleArray` is passed an array address and size, problems are likely. If the size is too small, some array elements will be ignored. If the size is too large, memory outside the array will be manipulated. And manipulating pointers has always involved a certain risk of wandering outside the memory owned by an array.

Whenever a program mysteriously dies or your data is corrupted, you can bet that an out-of-bounds array reference or pointer is to blame.

Arrays are not only dangerous but also inconvenient. You can't simply assign one array to another, as in these statements:

```
double Profit1[MON_PER_YR];
double Profit2[MON_PER_YR];

// assign values to Profit1
for (int i = 0; i < MON_PER_YR; ++i
    Profit1 = 0.0;

// copy Profit1 into Profit2
Profit2 = Profit1; // ERROR!
```

Instead, you must copy one array to another, element by element:

```
for (int i = 0; i < MON_PER_YR; ++i)
    Profit2[i] = Profit1[i];
```

Or you can use a library function such as memcpy:

```
memcpy(Profit2,Profit1,MON_PER_YR * sizeof(double));
```

In either case, it is the programmer's responsibility to ensure that the correct number of elements is copied and that the two arrays are compatible.

One reason to use an array is so that several data items of the same type can be handled as a group. When you're collecting data into an array, it's often necessary to apply the same operation or function to each element. Using C-type arrays, a loop must be used:

```
// function prototype
double Adjust(double n);

for (int i = 0; i < MON_PER_YR; ++i)
    Profit[i] = Adjusted(Profit[i]);
```

Again, it's necessary to know the number of array elements. And you need to put a loop in the program every time you want to perform the same operation on all an array's elements.

The index of an array's first element is always zero. This arrangement is inconvenient, to say the least, when you're working with values that are not normally numbered from zero. The months of the year would better be indexed from 1 through 12 rather than from 0 to 11 as is required by a C-style array. And, in some cases, you may want to number the elements of an array from a different base, say from 1981 through 2001. Unfortunately, the only base value allowed for arrays is zero.

You can't compare two arrays with a simple statement:

```
if (Profit2 == Profit1) // won't work!
    // do something
```

In some cases, we want to know whether all the elements in one array equal those in another array of the same size and type. Also, it can be useful to know how the corresponding elements of two arrays compare. Again, the comparison of two C-type arrays requires the use of loops and knowledge of an array's size.

Can you use a C++ class to create a better array type? Of course you can! Otherwise, I wouldn't be writing this book...

Class Requirements

Before building the Array class, I developed a list of goals that I wanted to accomplish:

- I need to create type-specific Arrays.

- An Array will be similar in use to C-type arrays. It will be possible to convert a C-type array to an Array and vice versa.

- An Array knows its upper and lower bounds and prevents access to "elements" outside those bounds.

- When an Array is created, it will be possible to assign values to its elements, similar to the way in which constructors are used to assign initial values to the elements of a C-type object array.

- The Indexes used to reference an Array will have a programmer-defined base value instead of always being based from zero.

- It will be possible to compare Arrays as a whole and on an element-by-element basis.

- Arithmetic operators will be defined to apply the same operation to all Array elements.

A base template class named Array, provides a common foundation. To keep things simple, I decided to define an Array as a C-type array with enhancements. An Array object contains a member that is a pointer to a traditional array; another data member stores the size of the C-style array, which is dynamically allocated. I added a Range member to specify the upper and lower bounds of the array. To keep the base class generic, an

`Array` also needs a member that stores the size of an element. And I'll use exceptions for reporting errors in `Array` objects.

A single `Array` class should be capable of handling any type of data, and I'll be using templates. The `Array` class defines member functions that create, destroy, index, copy, compare, and otherwise manipulate `Array`s. Future chapters will build on this foundation to create numeric and sortable array classes.

Exceptions

Following the pattern I set with `Range` and `Index`, I use a simple class to define exceptions raised by `Array`. The `ArrayError` enumeration defines the various exception types:

```
enum ArrayError
    {
    AEX_TOOBIG,
    AEX_ALLOC,
    AEX_INVALID,
    AEX_SORTOVER,
    AEX_INCOMPAT,
    AEX_NULLBUFF,
    AEX_LOCKED,
    AEX_LOCKERR
    };
```

When a problem arises, the `Array` class throws an `ArrayEx` object constructed from an `ArrayError` value:

```
class ArrayEx : public ExceptionBase
    {
    private:
        ArrayError Error;

    public:
        ArrayEx(ArrayError err) { Error = err; }

        void Explain(DiagOutput & out);
    };
```

You can use the WhatsWrong function to selectively process specific ArrayEx exceptions, as in the RangeEx class. The virtual Explain function, inherited from the ExceptionBase class, is implemented like this:

```
void ArrayEx::Explain(DiagOutput & out)
    {
    switch (Error)
        {
        case AEX_TOOBIG:
            out.DisplayMsg("Combined arrays exceed memory ",
                           DIAG_ERROR);
            break;
        case AEX_ALLOC:
            out.DisplayMsg("Array memory allocation failed",
                           DIAG_FATAL);
            break;
        case AEX_INVALID:
            out.DisplayMsg("Array parameters invalid",
                           DIAG_ERROR);
            break;
        case AEX_SORTOVER:
            out.DisplayMsg("Sort stack overflow",
                           DIAG_ERROR);
            break;
        case AEX_INCOMPAT:
            out.DisplayMsg("Incompatible arrays in math",
                           DIAG_ERROR);
            break;
        case AEX_NULLBUFF:
            out.DisplayMsg("Destructor found NULL array buffer",
                           DIAG_ERROR);
            break;
        case AEX_LOCKED:
            out.DisplayMsg("Can't destroy locked array",
                           DIAG_ERROR);
            break;
        case AEX_LOCKERR:
            out.DisplayMsg("Too many array locks deleted",
                           DIAG_ERROR);
            break;
        default:
            out.DisplayMsg("Unknown array error",
                           DIAG_ERROR);
        }
    }
```

Class Definition

Following is the Array class template. For now, ignore the declarations of
the friend templates ArrayPtr and ArrayManipulator. The ArrayPtr will be
discussed in the next chapter, and ArrayManipulator is the subject of
Chapter 9.

```
template <class T> class ArrayPtr;
template <class T> class ArrayManipulator;

template <class T>
    class Array
        {
        friend class ArrayPtr<T>;
        friend class ArrayManipulator<T>;

        public:
            // constructors
            Array
                (
                const Range & r
                );

            Array
                (
                const Array<T> & a
                );

            Array
                (
                const T * a,
                size_t n
                );

                // concatenate constructor
            Array
                (
                const Array<T> & a1,
                const Array<T> & a2
                );

                // subrange
```

```
Array
    (
    const Array<T> & a,
    const Index & first,
    const Index & last
    );

Array
    (
    const Array<T> & a,
    int first,
    int last);

// destructor
~Array();

// assignment operator
Array<T> & operator =
    (
    const Array<T> & a
    );

// conversion operator
operator const T * () const;

// create an appropriate index
 Index MakeIndex() const;

// get the range
 Range GetRange() const;

// get number of elements
 size_t GetCount() const;

// index operators
T & operator []
    (
    const Index & i
    );

T & operator []
    (
    int i
    );
```

```
const T Read
    (
    const Index & i
    ) const;

const T Read
    (
    int i
    ) const;

// comparison operators
bool Equals
    (
    const Array<T> & ia
    ) const;

friend Array<bool> operator <
    (
    const Array<T> & ia1,
    const Array<T> & ia2
    );

friend Array<bool> operator <=
    (
    const Array<T> &ia1,
    const Array<T> &ia2
    );

friend Array<bool> operator ==
    (
    const Array<T> &ia1,
      const Array<T> &ia2
    );

friend Array<bool> operator !=
    (
    const Array<T> &ia1,
    const Array<T> &ia2
    );

friend Array<bool> operator >=
    (
    const Array<T> &ia1,
    const Array<T> &ia2
    );
```

```
friend Array<bool> operator >
    (
    const Array<T> &ia1,
    const Array<T> &ia2
    );


// apply function to elements
Array & Apply
    (
    T (* func)(T)
    );


friend Array<T> Apply
    (
    const Array<T> & ia,
    T (* func)(T)
    );


// fill functions
void Fill(T i);

protected:
    Range   IndexRange;
    T *     Buffer;
    size_t Count;
    size_t LockCount;
};
```

The class defines only three data members. IndexRange defines the upper and lower bounds of the Array. Buffer is a pointer to the dynamically allocated memory that holds the Array elements. Count holds the number of elements in the Array.

In this edition of the book, I've added a new member, LockCount, to Array. This value is incremented every time an associated object—an ArrayPtr or Manipulator—is created for an Array. Those objects are created to directly reference or alter the values stored in an Array, and it would be dangerous to delete an Array object if it is attached to any ArrayPtrs or ArrayManipulators. The section in Chapter 8 about ArrayPtr demonstrates this concept.

Constructors and the Destructor

Array defines six constructors and a destructor. The primary constructor creates a new Array based on a Range:

```
template <class T>
    Array<T>::Array
        (
        const Range & r
        )
        : IndexRange(r)
        {
        // make sure this array will fit in memory
        if (r.GetMagnitude() > UINT_MAX / sizeof(T))
            throw ArrayEx(AEX_TOOBIG);

        Count   = IndexRange.GetMagnitude();

        // allocate new buffer
        Buffer = new T [Count];

        if (Buffer == NULL)
            throw ArrayEx(AEX_ALLOC);

        // set iterator count to zero
        LockCount = 0;
        }
```

The constructor begins by making sure that the size of the Array does not exceed the maximum amount of memory that can be allocated. The constructor then allocates Buffer, throwing an exception if the allocation fails. Note that the elements of Buffer will automatically be constructed when new allocates Buffer.

The copy constructor duplicates an existing Array object. To ensure that elements are identical between the two arrays, the copy constructor uses a loop to assign elements from the source Array to the new one. Duplication of the contents of Buffer via a call to memcpy would not invoke constructors that might be required if the Array is holding objects.

```
template <class T>
    Array<T>::Array
        (
        const Array<T> & a
        )
        : IndexRange(a.IndexRange)
        {
        IndexRange = a.IndexRange;
        Count      = a.Count;

        Buffer = new T [Count];

        if (Buffer == NULL)
            throw ArrayEx(AEX_ALLOC);

        // I don't use memcpy because these might be
        // object-array needing constructor calls

        T * dest = Buffer;
        T * src  = a.Buffer;

        for (size_t i = 0; i < Count; ++i)
            {
            *dest = *src;
            ++dest;
            ++src;
            }

        // set iterator count to zero
        LockCount = 0;
        }
```

To create an `Array` object from a C-style array, use the following constructor, which specifies the address of the source data and the number of elements to be read:

```
template <class T>
    Array<T>::Array
        (
        const T * a,
        size_t n
        )
```

```
        : IndexRange(n)
        {
        // verify size
        if (n > UINT_MAX / sizeof(T))
            throw ArrayEx(AEX_TOOBIG);


        Count   = n;
        Buffer = new T [Count];


        if (Buffer == NULL)
            throw ArrayEx(AEX_ALLOC);


        // copy data
        T * dest = Buffer;
        const T * src  = a;


        for (size_t i = 0; i < Count; ++i)
            {
            *dest = *src;
            ++dest;
            ++src;
            }


        // set iterator count to zero
        LockCount = 0;
        }
```

This constructor concatenates two Arrays. The elements of the second array follow those of the first; the two Ranges combine via the Bounds<int> operator + function. The IndexRange of the new Array will extend from the minimum IndexRange value for a1 to the maximum of a1's IndexRange plus the number of elements in a2.

```
template <class T>
    Array<T>::Array
        (
        const Array<T> & a1,
        const Array<T> & a2
        )
        : IndexRange(a1.IndexRange + a2.IndexRange)
        {
        Count = IndexRange.GetMagnitude();
        Buffer = new T [Count];
```

```
if (Buffer == NULL)
    throw ArrayEx(AEX_ALLOC);

T * dest = Buffer;
T * src  = a1.Buffer;
size_t i;

for (i = 0; i < a1.Count; ++i)
    {
    *dest = *src;
    ++dest;
    ++src;
    }

src = a2.Buffer;

for (i = 0; i < a2.Count; ++i)
    {
    *dest = *src;
    ++dest;
    ++src;
    }

// set iterator count to zero
LockCount = 0;
}
```

It's often handy to extract a segment of an array for individual process-ing. I created a constructor that copies a range of Array values into a new Array object of the same type. The parameters first and last create the IndexRange for the new Array. A loop then copies the elements of the two source Arrays into the newly created Array.

```
template <class T>
    Array<T>::Array
        (
        const Array<T> & a,
        const Index & first,
        const Index & last
        )
        : IndexRange((int)first,(int)last)
        {
        if (IndexRange.Includes(first)
```

```
      &&  IndexRange.Includes(last))
          {
          Count  = IndexRange.GetMagnitude();
          Buffer = new T [Count];

          if (Buffer == NULL)
              throw ArrayEx(AEX_ALLOC);

          T * dest = Buffer;
          T * src  = a.Buffer + (size_t)first;

          for (size_t i = 0; i < Count; ++i)
              {
              *dest = *src;
              ++dest;
              ++src;
              }
          }
      else
          throw ArrayEx(AEX_INVALID);

      // set iterator count to zero
      LockCount = 0;
      }

template <class T>
    Array<T>::Array
        (
        const Array<T> & a,
        int first,
        int last
        )
        : IndexRange(first,last)
        {
        if (IndexRange.Includes(first)
        &&  IndexRange.Includes(last))
            {
            Count  = IndexRange.GetMagnitude();
            Buffer = new T [Count];

            if (Buffer == NULL)
                throw ArrayEx(AEX_ALLOC);

            T * dest = Buffer;
            T * src  = a.Buffer
```

```
                + (size_t)Index(a.IndexRange,first);

        for (size_t i = 0; i < Count; ++i)
            {
            *dest = *src;
            ++dest;
            ++src;
            }
        }
    else
        throw ArrayEx(AEX_INVALID);

    // set iterator count to zero
    LockCount = 0;
    }
```

The `Array` destructor is implemented simply to delete the dynamic `Buffer`. The destructor throws exceptions if it attempts to destroy a locked `Array` or if `Buffer` has somehow been set to NULL. In theory, exceptions thrown in the constructors should prevent `Buffer` from ever being NULL in the destructor; however, checking `Buffer` before deleting it is a good programming practice:

```
template <class T>
    Array<T>::~Array()
        {
        if (LockCount > 0)
            throw ArrayEx(AEX_LOCKED);

        if (Buffer == NULL)
            throw ArrayEx(AEX_NULLBUFF);

        delete [] Buffer;
        }
```

Interrogation Functions

Several functions provide information about an `Array`. `MakeIndex` is a convenience function; it returns an `Index` built from the `IndexRange` of the `Array`. `Indexes` can thus be created without the need to know anything about the `Array`.

```
template <class T>
    inline Index Array<T>::MakeIndex() const
        {
        return Index(IndexRange);
        }
```

GetRange and GetCount return the values of the data members IndexRange and Count, and I've implemented them inline:

```
template <class T>
    inline Range Array<T>::GetRange() const
        {
        return IndexRange;
        }
```

```
template <class T>
    inline size_t Array<T>::GetCount() const
        {
        return Count;
        }
```

Assignment Operator

The assignment operator allows one Array to be assigned to another:

```
template <class T>
    Array<T> & Array<T>::operator =
        (
        const Array<T> & a
        )
        {
        if (IndexRange != a.IndexRange)
            {
            // create a new array since sizes differ
            delete [] Buffer;

            IndexRange = a.IndexRange;
            Count = a.Count;
            Buffer = new T [Count];
```

```
        if (Buffer == NULL)
            throw ArrayEx(AEX_ALLOC);
        }

    T * dest = Buffer;
    T * src  = a.Buffer;

    for (size_t i = 0; i < Count; ++i)
        {
        *dest = *src;
        ++dest;
        ++src;
        }

    return *this;
    }
```

Element Functions

Four functions provide access to the members of an Array. The Read functions return an element from a const Array, as specified by either an Index or an int.

```
template <class T>
    inline const T Array<T>::Read(const Index & i) const
        {
        return Buffer[(size_t)i];
        }

template <class T>
    inline const T Array<T>::Read(int i) const
        {
        return Buffer[(size_t)Index(IndexRange,i)];
        }
```

For a non-const Array, the [] operator works perfectly for accessing an Array's elements. Unlike Read, which returns an element directly, the [] operator returns a reference to an element, thus allowing it to be changed.

```
template <class T>
    inline T & Array<T>::operator [] (const Index & i)
        {
        return Buffer[(size_t)i];
        }


template <class T>
    inline T & Array<T>::operator [] (int i)
        {
        return Buffer[(size_t)Index(IndexRange,i)];
        }
```

Comparisons

Equals produces a bool answer: true when all elements of the two arrays are equal, and false when the arrays have any elements that differ.

```
template <class T>
    bool Array<T>::Equals
        (
        const Array<T> & ia
        ) const
        {
        bool result = true;

        if (IndexRange == ia.IndexRange)
            {
            T *  left = Buffer;
            T * right = ia.Buffer;

            for (size_t i = 0; i < Count; ++i)
                {
                if (*left != *right)
                    {
                    result = false;
                    break;
                    }

                ++left;
                ++right;
```

```
        }
     }
else
    result = false;

return result;
}
```

The comparison operators compare corresponding elements of two Array<T> functions, creating a new Array<bool> in which the elements are true or false based on the "truth" of the comparison. For brevity, I'll show only the operator < function here:

```
template <class T>
    Array<bool> operator <
        (
        const Array<T> & ia1,
        const Array<T> & ia2
        )
        {
        if (ia1.IndexRange != ia2.IndexRange)
            throw ArrayEx(AEX_INCOMPAT);

        Array<bool> result(ia1.IndexRange);

        ArrayPtr<bool> dest(result);
        T * left  = ia1.Buffer;
        T * right = ia2.Buffer;

            for (size_t i = 0; i < ia1.Count; ++i)
             {
             *dest = (*left < *right);

             ++dest;
             ++left;
             ++right;
             }

        return result;
        }
```

Miscellaneous Functions

It's often useful to apply a function to every element of an `Array`. I created two versions of the `Apply` function, the first of which modifies the target array, and the second to create a new `Array` that is the result of calling the function for each element of the original array.

```
template <class T>
    Array<T> & Array<T>::Apply
        (
        T (* func)(T)
        )
        {
        T * ptr = Buffer;

        for (size_t i = 0; i < Count; ++i)
            {
            *ptr = func(*ptr);
            ++ptr;
            }

        return *this;
        }


template <class T>
    Array<T> Apply
        (
        const Array<T> & ia,
        T (* func)(T)
        )
        {
        NumericArray<T> result(ia);

        T * ptr = result.Buffer;

        for (size_t i = 0; i < result.Count; ++i)
            {
            *ptr = func(*ptr);
            ++ptr;
            }

        return result;
        }
```

I also created a `Fill` function to assign a constant value to all elements of an `Array`. Note that the creation constructors do not initialize the data contained in the new `Array`, unless type `T` is an object class for which a default constructor is defined.

```
template <class T>
    void Array<T>::Fill(T n)
        {
        T * ptr = Buffer;

            for (size_t i = 0; i < Count; ++i)
                {
                *ptr = n;
                ++ptr;
                }
        }
```

Conversions

Defining conversion between various `Array` types is, at first, problematic. Things would be so much easier if I could simply define a template function such as this one:

```
template
    <
    class T1,
    class T2
    >
    Array<T2> Convert
        (
        const Array<T1> & a
        )
        {
        Range r(a.GetRange());
        Array<T2> result(r);

        for (Index i = r.GetMin(); i <= r.GetMax(); ++i)
            result[i] = T2(a.Read(i));

        return result;
        }
```

An `Array` conversion could be carried out as follows:

```
Array<int> ia(1,10);
Array<float> fa(1,10) = Convert<int,float>(ia);
```

Unfortunately, the explicit use of template arguments in a function call is a new ANSI C++ feature that's not yet implemented by any compilers.

I defined an operator `const T *` function to allow an `Array` to be treated just like a C-style array by many existing, C-like functions:

```
template <class T>
    inline Array<T>::operator const T * () const
        {
        return Buffer;
        }
```

Because the `Array` class is a template, its class definition and function's are contained in the file **Array.h**; only the `ArrayEx::Explain` function is a precompiled function, and it is defined in **Array.cpp**.

ONWARD

Now that we have a core `Array` class in hand, it is a simple matter to add new capabilities through derived classes. The next chapter begins by looking at the `ArrayPtr` template class, which provides an iterator for `Array`s. Then I'll continue by implementing arrays specifically for working with numbers.

CHAPTER 8

ARRAY POINTERS AND NUMERIC ARRAYS

One difference between my `Array` type and standard C-type arrays comes when you're using pointers. As mentioned in the previous chapter, the relationship between arrays and pointers is intimate; they are, essentially, different techniques for addressing a block of memory. Often, pointers to array elements can be more efficient than direct indexing—and many C programmers feel more comfortable with pointers.

With that in mind, I created a pointer type that works with `Array`s. The template class is an example of an *iterator*: an object that references elements of another object. And whereas standard pointers know nothing about the bounds (or continued existence) of their associated array, an `ArrayPtr` object is intimately connected to the `Array` it references.

ARRAYPTR CLASS

This is the definition of the `ArrayPtr` template class:

```
template
    <
    class T
    >
    class ArrayPtr
        {
        public:
            // constructors
            ArrayPtr
                (
                Array<T> & a
                );

            ArrayPtr
                (
                const ArrayPtr<T> & aptr
                );

            // destructor
            ~ArrayPtr();

            // assignment operators
            ArrayPtr<T> & operator =
                (
                const ArrayPtr<T> & aptr
                );

            ArrayPtr<T> & operator =
                (
                const Index & i
                );

            ArrayPtr<T> & operator =
                (
                size_t i
                );

            // conversion operator
            T & operator * ();
```

```
                // increment and decrement
                ArrayPtr<T> & operator ++ ();          // prefix
                ArrayPtr<T>   operator ++ (int dummy); // postfix
                ArrayPtr<T> & operator - ();           // prefix
                ArrayPtr<T>   operator - (int dummy); // postfix

                // set to first or last element
                void SetFirst();
                void SetLast();

                // value check functions
                int IsFirst();
                int IsLast();

                // comparison operators
                int operator == (const ArrayPtr<T> & aptr);
                int operator != (const ArrayPtr<T> & aptr);

        protected:
                Array<T> & Target; // reference to target array
                T * ElemFirst;     // address of first element
                T * ElemLast;      // address of last  element
                T * ElemPtr;       // pointer to element
        };
```

The class data members include a reference Target to the <TArray> being pointed to by ElemPtr. ElemFirst marks the first element of Target's Buffer, and ElemLast marks the address of the last element in Target.

Constructor and Destructor

The creation constructor assigns the new ArrayPtr<T> to the specified Array<T>, calculating the ends of the Target Buffer and incrementing the Target's LockCount. An ArrayPtr begins with ElemPtr pointing to the first element of Target.Buffer:

```
template <class T>
    inline ArrayPtr<T>::ArrayPtr(Array<T> & a)
        : Target(a)
        {
        ElemFirst = a.Buffer;
```

```
        ElemLast   = ElemFirst
                        + Target.IndexRange.GetMagnitude()
                        - 1;


        ElemPtr    = ElemFirst;


        ++Target.LockCount;
        }
```

The copy constructor duplicates the members of an existing ArrayPtr and increments Target.LockCount:

```
template <class T>
    inline ArrayPtr<T>::ArrayPtr(const ArrayPtr<T> & aptr)
        : Target(a)
        {
        ElemFirst = aptr.ElemFirst;
        ElemLast  = aptr.ElemLast;
        ElemPtr   = aptr.ElemPtr;
        ++Target.LockCount;
        }
```

The assignment operator looks much like the copy constructor, but it also needs to decrement the LockCount of its previous Target before incrementing the LockCount of the new Array:

```
template <class T>
    inline ArrayPtr<T> & ArrayPtr<T>::operator =
        (
        const ArrayPtr<T> & aptr
        )
        {
        if (Target.LockCount == 0)
            throw ArrayEx(AEX_LOCKERR);

        —Target.LockCount;

        Target    = aptr.Target;
        ElemFirst = aptr.ElemFirst;
        ElemLast  = aptr.ElemLast;
        ElemPtr   = aptr.ElemPtr;
```

```
++Target.LockCount;

return *this;
    }
```

The destructor's only purpose is to decrement `Target.LockCount`:

```
template <class T>
    inline ArrayPtr<T>::~ArrayPtr<T>()
        {
        if (Target.LockCount == 0)
            throw ArrayEx(AEX_LOCKERR);

        —Target.LockCount;
        }
```

By incrementing the `LockCount` of its associated `Array`, the `ArrayPtr` object causes an exception to be raised by the `Array`'s destructor if an attempt is made to delete the `Array` while the `ArrayPtr` is still active.

Pointer Manipulation

Assignment operators allow you to set an `ArrayPtr` to reference a specific `Array` element by `Index`:

```
template <class T>
    ArrayPtr<T> & ArrayPtr<T>::operator = (const Index & i)
        {
        if (Target.IndexRange != Range(i))
            throw BoundsEx(BEX_BOUNDS);

        ElemPtr = ElemFirst + (size_t)i;
        return *this;
        }

template <class T>
    ArrayPtr<T> & ArrayPtr<T>::operator = (size_t i)
        {
        Target.IndexRange.Check(i);
```

```
      ElemPtr = ElemFirst + i;
      return *this;
      }
```

Like a normal pointer, an `ArrayPtr` can be "moved" through consecutive elements of the `Array` by the increment and decrement operators. I defined both prefix and postfix versions of these operators, following the appropriate language semantics regarding return values:

```
template <class T>
    inline ArrayPtr<T> & ArrayPtr<T>::operator ++ ()
        {
        // prefix
        if (ElemPtr != ElemLast)
            ++ElemPtr;

        return *this;
        }

template <class T>
    inline ArrayPtr<T> ArrayPtr<T>::operator ++ (int dummy)
        {
        // save current state
        ArrayPtr result(*this);

        // move to next element
        if (ElemPtr != ElemLast)
            ElemPtr++;

        // return previous state
        return result;
        }

template <class T>
    inline ArrayPtr<T> & ArrayPtr<T>::operator - ()
        {
        // prefix
        if (ElemPtr != ElemFirst)
            ElemPtr-;

        return *this;
        }
```

```
template <class T>
    inline ArrayPtr<T> ArrayPtr<T>::operator - (int dummy)
        {
        // save current state
        ArrayPtr result(*this);

        // move to next element
        if (ElemPtr != ElemFirst)
            ElemPtr-;

        // return previous state
        return result;
        }
```

To set an `ArrayPtr` to the beginning or end of its `Array`, use the `SetFirst` and `SetLast` functions:

```
template <class T>
    inline void ArrayPtr<T>::SetFirst()
        {
        ElemPtr = ElemFirst;
        }


template <class T>
    inline void ArrayPtr<T>::SetLast()
        {
        ElemPtr = ElemLast;
        }
```

To find out whether an `ArrayPtr` is pointing to the `Array`'s first element or to its last element, use these interrogation functions:

```
template <class T>
    inline int ArrayPtr<T>::IsFirst()
        {
        return (ElemPtr == ElemFirst);
        }


template <class T>
    inline int ArrayPtr<T>::IsLast()
        {
        return (ElemPtr == ElemLast);
        }
```

I also defined operators to compare two `ArrayPtr`s for equality:

```
template <class T>
    inline int ArrayPtr<T>::operator == (const ArrayPtr & aptr)
        {
        return (ElemPtr == aptr.ElemPtr);
        }

template <class T>
    inline int ArrayPtr<T>::operator != (const ArrayPtr & aptr)
        {
        return (ElemPtr != aptr.ElemPtr);
        }
```

The following function lets you examine the `Array` element being referenced by an `ArrayPtr`. The function works by returning a "real" pointer to that element.

```
template <class T>
    inline T & ArrayPtr<T>::operator * ()
        {
        return *ElemPtr;
        }
```

Using an ArrayPtr

An `ArrayPtr` acts very much like the standard C-type pointer it encapsulates. Here's a short piece of example code from the Testbed application (see the Appendix).

```
void ArrayTest12
    (
     strstream & buffer
    )
    {
buffer << "\r\nArrays: Iterator Tests"
            "\r\n————————\r\n";

    Range r(1,10);
    NumericArray<double> da(r);
    da.FillArithmetic(1.0,1.0);
```

```
ArrayPtr<double> dptr(da);

buffer << " forward: ";

while (1)

    {

    buffer << (*dptr) << " ";


    if (dptr.IsLast())

        break;

    ++dptr;
    }

buffer << "\r\nbackward: ";

while (1)
    {
    buffer << (*dptr) << " ";

    if (dptr.IsFirst())
        break;

    —dptr;
    }

buffer << "\r\n";
}
```

NUMERIC ARRAYS

The basic Array template works well for many data types, but for some applications, particularly those involving numbers, an extended Array implementation is useful. All numbers—integers or floating-point numbers—have

standard mathematical properties and operations that should be implemented for arrays. So I created a core template, based on `Array`, that
includes basic numeric operations:

```
template <class T>
    class NumericArray : public Array<T>
        {
        public:
            // constructors
            NumericArray
                (
                const Range & r
                );

            NumericArray
                (
                const Array<T> & a
                );

            NumericArray
                (
                const NumericArray<T> & n
                );

            NumericArray
                (
                const T * a, size_t n
                );

            NumericArray
                (
                const NumericArray<T> & a1,
                const NumericArray<T> & a2
                );

            NumericArray
                (
                const NumericArray & a,
                const Index & first,
                const Index & last
                );

            NumericArray
                (
```

```
      const NumericArray & a,
      int first,
      int last
      );

// assignment operator
NumericArray & operator =
      (
      const NumericArray & a
      );

// unary operators
NumericArray operator + ();
NumericArray operator - ();

// basic math operators
NumericArray operator + (const NumericArray & ia);
NumericArray operator + (T n);
NumericArray operator - (const NumericArray & ia);
NumericArray operator - (T n);
NumericArray operator * (const NumericArray & ia);
NumericArray operator * (T n);
NumericArray operator / (const NumericArray & ia);
NumericArray operator / (T n);

// shorthand operators
NumericArray & operator += (const NumericArray & ia);
NumericArray & operator += (T n);
NumericArray & operator -= (const NumericArray & ia);
NumericArray & operator -= (T n);
NumericArray & operator *= (const NumericArray & ia);
NumericArray & operator *= (T n);
NumericArray & operator /= (const NumericArray & ia);
NumericArray & operator /= (T n);

// fill functions
void FillArithmetic
      (
      T first,
      T incr
      );

void FillGeometric
      (
      T first,
```

```
                    T mult
                    );


            // absolute value function
            NumericArray & Abs();

            friend NumericArray<T> Abs
                (
                const NumericArray<T> & ia
                );
    };
```

Constructors and Assignment

The NumericArray constructors and assignment operator simply make inline calls to the constructors inherited through Array.

```
template <class T>
    inline NumericArray<T>::NumericArray
        (
        const Range & r
        )
        : Array<T>(r)
        {
        // simple inline call to base class constructor
        }


template <class T>
    inline NumericArray<T>::NumericArray
        (
        const NumericArray<T> & a
        )
        : Array<T>(a)
        {
        // simple inline call to base class constructor
        }


template <class T>
    inline NumericArray<T>::NumericArray
        (
        const Array<T> & a
        )
```

```
    : Array<T>(a)
    {
    // simple inline call to base class constructor
    }


template <class T>
    inline NumericArray<T>::NumericArray
        (
        const T * a, size_t n
        )
        : Array<T>(a,n)
        {
        // simple inline call to base class constructor
        }


template <class T>
    inline NumericArray<T>::NumericArray
        (
        const NumericArray<T> & a1,
        const NumericArray<T> & a2
        )
        : Array<T>(a1,a2)
        {
        // simple inline call to base class constructor
        }


template <class T>
    inline NumericArray<T>::NumericArray
        (
        const NumericArray<T> & a,
        const Index & first,
        const Index & last
        )
        : Array<T>(a,first,last)
        {
        // simple inline call to base class constructor
        }


template <class T>
    inline NumericArray<T>::NumericArray
        (
        const NumericArray<T> & a,
        int first,
        int last
        )
        : Array<T>(a,first,last)
```

```
            {
            // simple inline call to base class constructor
            }

template <class T>
    inline NumericArray<T> & NumericArray<T>::operator =
            (
            const NumericArray<T> & a
            )
            {
            this->Array<T>::operator = (a);
            return *this;
            }
```

Operators

I defined the unary operators + and −, of which the former is a do-nothing function included for cosmetic purposes. The operator - function applies the unary - operation to each array element:

```
template <class T>
    inline NumericArray<T> NumericArray<T>::operator + ()
            {
            return *this;
            }

template <class T>
    NumericArray<T> NumericArray<T>::operator - ()
            {
            NumericArray<T> result (*this);

            T * res  = result.Buffer;
            T * orig = Buffer;

            for (size_t i = 0; i < Count; ++i)
                {
                *res = -(*orig);
                ++res;
                ++orig;
                }

            return result;
            }
```

Each binary math operator has two forms. When the parameter is an array, the functions check to see whether the two arrays have equivalent Ranges before performing operations on corresponding elements. Because these functions are repetitive, I'll just show the implementation of the + operators here. Full implementations of the other operators can be found in the **NumArray.h** file located on the accompanying source disk.

```
template <class T>
    NumericArray<T> NumericArray<T>::operator +
        (
        const NumericArray<T> & ia
        )
        {
        if (IndexRange != ia.IndexRange)
            throw ArrayEx(AEX_INCOMPAT);

        NumericArray<T> result(*this);

        T * ptr1 = result.Buffer;
        T * ptr2 = ia.Buffer;

        for (size_t i = 0; i < Count; ++i)
            {
            *ptr1 += *ptr2;
            ++ptr1;
            ++ptr2;
            }

        return result;
        }
```

When the parameter is a single T value, it is applied by the appropriate operation to each element:

```
template <class T>
    NumericArray<T> NumericArray<T>::operator + (T n)
        {
        NumericArray<T> result(*this);

        T * ptr = result.Buffer;

        for (size_t i = 0; i < Count; ++i)
```

```
        {
        *ptr += n;
        ++ptr;
        }

    return result;
    }
```

The unary operators follow a scheme similar to the one I employed for the binary operators. The difference is that the binary operators produce a new NumericArray<T>, whereas the unary operators change an existing object. Again, in the interest of brevity, I show only two of several nearly identical functions here, leaving the others to be implemented in **NumArray.h**.

```
template <class T>
    NumericArray<T> & NumericArray<T>::operator +=
        (
        const NumericArray<T> & ia
        )
        {
        if (IndexRange != ia.IndexRange)
            throw ArrayEx(AEX_INCOMPAT);

        T * ptr1 = Buffer;
        T * ptr2 = ia.Buffer;

        for (size_t i = 0; i < Count; ++i)
            {
            *ptr1 += *ptr2;
            ++ptr1;
            ++ptr2;
            }

        return *this;
        }

template <class T>
    NumericArray<T> & NumericArray<T>::operator += (T n)
        {
        T * ptr = Buffer;

        for (size_t i = 0; i < Count; ++i)
            {
```

```
    *ptr += n;
    ++ptr;
    }

return *this;
}
```

Numerical Functions

The `Relation` function returns a `NumericArray<int>` in which each element is based on the relationship between the corresponding elements of two arrays. The resulting element contains a −1 if the target array's element is less than the parameter array; zero indicates equality, and 1 results when the target array's element is greater than the parameter array element.

```
template <class T>
    NumericArray<int> NumericArray<T>::Relation
        (
        const NumericArray & ia
        ) const
        {
        if (IndexRange != ia.IndexRange)
            throw ArrayEx(AEX_INCOMPAT);

        NumericArray<int> result(IndexRange);

        int * dest  = &result[0];
        T   * left  = Buffer;
        T   * right = ia.Buffer;

        for (int i = 0; i < Count; ++i)
            {
            if (*left == *right)
                *dest = 0;
            else
                {
                if (*left < *right)
                    *dest = -1;
                else
                    *dest = 1;
                }

            ++dest;
```

```
        ++left;
        ++right;
        }


    return result;
    }
```

All numbers have an absolute value, which in essence makes a negative value into a positive one. For arrays, I implemented two versions of the Abs function: One version creates a new array that contains the absolute values from a target, and the other version changes the values in an Array.

```
template <class T>
    NumericArray<T> & NumericArray<T>::Abs()
        {
        T * ptr = Buffer;

        for (size_t i = 0; i < Count; ++i)
            {
            *ptr = ((*ptr < 0) ? -(*ptr) : (*ptr));
            ++ptr;
            }

        return *this;
        }


template <class T>
    NumericArray<T> Abs
        (
        const NumericArray<T> & ia
        )
        {
        NumericArray<T> result(ia);

        T * ptr = result.Buffer;

        for (size_t i = 0; i < result.Count; ++i)
            {
            *ptr = ((*ptr < 0) ? -(*ptr) : (*ptr));
            ++ptr;
            }

        return result;
        }
```

The Array base class provides functions to iterate a function through each element of an Array, and it also allows all the elements of an array to be set to a specific value. Sometimes, we want to fill an array with a series of values based on a mathematical progression. FillArithmetic fills an array using an arithmetic progression:

```
template <class T>
    void NumericArray<T>::FillArithmetic
        (
        T first,
        T incr
        )
        {
        T value = first;
        T * ptr = Buffer;

        for (size_t i = 0; i < Count; ++i)
            {
            *ptr = value;
            value += incr;
            ++ptr;
            }
        }
```

FillGeometric fills an array with a geometric progression:

```
template <class T>
    void NumericArray<T>::FillGeometric
        (
        T first,
        T mult
        )
        {
        T value = first;
        T * ptr = Buffer;

        for (size_t i = 0; i < Count; ++i)
            {
            *ptr = value;
            value *= mult;
            ++ptr;
            }
        }
```

INTEGER ARRAYS

Integer values can be manipulated using a set of bit-oriented operators. Because these operators have no application for floating-point values, I created a special template just for integer data types. Called IntegerArray, it implements bitwise and logical operators:

```
template <class T>
    class IntegerArray : public NumericArray<T>
        {
        public:
            // constructors
            IntegerArray
                (
                const Range & r
                );

            IntegerArray
                (
                const IntegerArray<T> & n
                );

            IntegerArray
                (
                const Array<T> & n
                );

            IntegerArray
                (
                const T * a, size_t n
                );

            IntegerArray
                (
                const IntegerArray<T> & a1,
                const IntegerArray<T> & a2
                );

            IntegerArray
                (
                const IntegerArray<T> & a,
                const Index & first,
```

```
        const Index & last
        );

    IntegerArray
        (
        const IntegerArray<T> & a,
        int first,
        int last
        );

    // assignment operator
    IntegerArray<T> & operator =
        (
        const IntegerArray<T> & a
        );

    // unary operators
    IntegerArray<T> operator ~ ();
    IntegerArray<T> operator ! ();

// modulus, shift, and bitwise operators
IntegerArray<T> operator %  (const IntegerArray<T> & ia);
IntegerArray<T> operator %  (T n);
IntegerArray<T> operator << (const IntegerArray<T> & ia);
IntegerArray<T> operator << (T n);
IntegerArray<T> operator >> (const IntegerArray<T> & ia);
IntegerArray<T> operator >> (T n);
IntegerArray<T> operator &  (const IntegerArray<T> & ia);
IntegerArray<T> operator &  (T n);
IntegerArray<T> operator |  (const IntegerArray<T> & ia);
IntegerArray<T> operator |  (T n);
IntegerArray<T> operator ^  (const IntegerArray<T> & ia);
IntegerArray<T> operator ^  (T n);

    // shorthand operators
    IntegerArray<T> & operator %=
                (const IntegerArray<T> & ia);
    IntegerArray<T> & operator %=  (T n);
    IntegerArray<T> & operator <<=
                (const IntegerArray<T> & ia);
    IntegerArray<T> & operator <<= (T n);
    IntegerArray<T> & operator >>=
                (const IntegerArray<T> & ia);
    IntegerArray<T> & operator >>= (T n);
    IntegerArray<T> & operator &=
```

```
                                (const IntegerArray<T> & ia);
              IntegerArray<T> & operator &=  (T n);
              IntegerArray<T> & operator |=
                                (const IntegerArray<T> & ia);
              IntegerArray<T> & operator |=  (T n);
              IntegerArray<T> & operator ^=
                                (const IntegerArray<T> & ia);
              IntegerArray<T> & operator ^=  (T n);
              };
```

The constructors and assignment operator make inline calls to base class
constructors. The only new functions added by IntegerArray are the operators, which follow the same implementation pattern as do the operators
defined by NumericArray. Here are some sample functions from the
implementation:

```
template <class T>
    IntegerArray<T> IntegerArray<T>::operator ~ ()
        {
        IntegerArray<T> result(*this);

        T * res  = result.Buffer;
        T * orig = Buffer;

        for (size_t i = 0; i < Count; ++i)
            {
            *res = ~(*orig);
            ++res;
            ++orig;
            }

        return result;
        }

template <class T>
    IntegerArray<T> IntegerArray<T>::operator %
        (
        const IntegerArray<T> & ia
        )
        {
        if (IndexRange != ia.IndexRange)
            throw ArrayEx(AEX_INCOMPAT);

        IntegerArray<T> result(*this);
```

```
        T * ptr1 = result.Buffer;
        T * ptr2 = ia.Buffer;

        for (size_t i = 0; i < Count; ++i)
            {
            *ptr1 %= *ptr2;
            ++ptr1;
            ++ptr2;
            }

        return result;
        }

template <class T>
    IntegerArray<T> & IntegerArray<T>::operator <<=
        (
        const IntegerArray<T> & ia
        )
        {
        if (IndexRange != ia.IndexRange)
            throw ArrayEx(AEX_INCOMPAT);

        T * ptr1 = Buffer;
        T * ptr2 = ia.Buffer;

        for (size_t i = 0; i < Count; ++i)
            {
            *ptr1 <<= *ptr2;
            ++ptr1;
            ++ptr2;
            }

        return *this;
        }
```

The complete implementation of `IntegerArray` is in the file **IntArray.h**, which you'll find on the accompanying source disk.

ONWARD

Now it's time to look at sorting, one of the more interesting and most discussed areas of programming. In the next chapter, I introduce the concept of manipulators: objects that alter other objects. I'll describe (in detail) and implement both the ShellSort and the QuickSort algorithms through `Array` manipulator objects.

CHAPTER 9

SORTING TECHNIQUES

Classes tend to evolve with time, and it's wise to build in capabilities for expansion. In older editions of this book, the ability to sort an array was defined by deriving a `SortableArray` from the basic `Array` type, providing a basis for "sortable" classes. That approach worked, but it was inflexible; not every `NumericArray` needed sorting capability, and the `SortableArray` class added only one function—`Sort`—to those inherited from `Array`.

When I had the time to redesign my class libraries, I began with a philosophy that sorting was something applied to an `Array` instead of being an attribute of the `Array` itself. That line of thinking led me to develop a generalized mechanism for creating tools to manipulate `Array`s effectively.

ARRAY MANIPULATORS

An `ArrayManipulator` is an object attached to an `Array`; an `ArrayManipulator` has special access to the `Array`'s internal structure to allow for efficient manipulation of data. `ArrayManipulator` is a simple template class that defines basic `Array`-handling tools:

```
template <class T>
    class ArrayManipulator
        {
        public:
            // constructor
            ArrayManipulator
                (
                Array<T> & a
                );

            // destructor
            ~ArrayManipulator();

        protected:
            Array<T> & Target;
            T * BufBase;
        };
```

`Target` references the `Array` being manipulated, and `BufBase` is a pointer to the first element of `Target`'s `Buffer`. The constructor sets the values of `Target` and `BufBase` and increments `Target.LockCount`. The destructor decrements the `LockCount`:

```
template <class T>
    ArrayManipulator<T>::ArrayManipulator
        (
        Array<T> & a
        )
        : Target(a)
        {
        ++Target.LockCount;
        BufBase = Target.Buffer;
        }

// destructor
template <class T>
    ArrayManipulator<T>::~ArrayManipulator()
        {
        if (Target.LockCount == 0)
            throw ArrayEx(AEX_LOCKERR);

        -Target.LockCount;
        }
```

Because ArrayManipulator<T> is a friend of Array<T>, a manipulator has complete access to Target. Although some object-oriented programming purists will complain that such access violates an Array's integrity, I found that unrestricted access allowed me to implement some very efficient manipulators.

I derived a sort-specific, polymorphic template class from ArrayManipulator to provide a foundation for algorithm-specific sorting manipulators:

```
template <class T>
    class ArraySorter : public ArrayManipulator<T>
        {
        public:
            // constructor
            ArraySorter
                (
                Array<T> & a
                );

            // pure virtual sorting function
            virtual void Sort
                (
                bool reverse = false
                ) = 0;
        };

// constructor
template <class T>
    inline ArraySorter<T>::ArraySorter
        (
        Array<T> & a
        )
        : ArrayManipulator<T>(a)
        {
        }
```

The Sort function is a pure virtual function, thus allowing ArraySorter to act as a polymorphic base class for any child class. The reverse parameter indicates the direction of the sort; the default value of false produces an ascending sort, whereas setting reverse to true will sort an Array in descending order.

SORTING

Sorting a few items isn't difficult—in fact, it can be trivial. For example, a function that sorts two ints can be written like this:

```
void sort2(int & a, int & b)
    {
    int temp;

    if (a > b)
        {
        temp = a;
        a = b;
        b = temp;
        }
    }
```

A similar technique sorts three items:

```
void sort3(int & a, int & b, int & c)
    {
    int temp;
    if (a > b)
        {
        temp = a;
        a = b;
        b = temp;
        }

    if (a > c)
        {
        temp = a;
        a = c;
        c = temp;
        }

    if (b > c)
        {
        temp = b;
        b = c;
        c = temp;
        }
    }
```

ShellSort Algorithm

Once we get beyond three items, sorting gets complicated. The books on my shelves describe insertion sorts, selection sorts, heap sorts, and all sorts of sorts. Although bubble and insertion sorts may have their places, they tend to be limited and slow routines that can easily be replaced by a simple and effective routine known as ShellSort.

ShellSort organizes an array by stepping through every n elements, sorting those elements into relative order, and then successively reducing n and repeating the process until the entire array is in order. For example, in an array with 15 elements, ShellSort might begin with an "increment" of 13, which would allow it to sort the element pairs {0, 13} and {1, 14}. That finished, ShellSort would reduce the increment to four, sorting element sets {0, 4, 8, 12}, {1, 5, 9, 13}, and {2, 6, 10, 14}. The next increment is one, leaving the ShellSort to perform a quick insertion sort on the nearly ordered array.

How are the increments chosen? Experimentation and numerical analysis show that the following formula generates an excellent set of increment values: $inc_{n+1} = inc_n * 3 + 1$. That formula generates the series of values 1, 4, 13, 40, 121, 364, 1093, 3280…. Pick the starting increment that is less than the number of elements in the array, and then work your way down to one. Implementing this algorithm is remarkably simple, as you can see in this function template for ShellSort:

```
template
    <
    class  T
    >
    void ShellSort
        (
        T * a,
        size_t n
        )
        {
        size_t inc, i, j;
        T t;

        // algorithm relies on one-based arrays
```

```
    —a;

    for (inc = 1; inc <= n / 9; inc = 3 * inc + 1) ;

    for ( ; inc > 0; inc /= 3)
        {
        for (i = inc + 1; i <= n; i += inc)
            {
            t = a[i];
            j = i;

            while ((j > inc) && (a[j - inc] > t))
                {
                a[j] = a[j - inc];
                j -= inc;
                }

            a[j] = t;
            }
        }
    }
```

ShellSort Manipulator

To implement ShellSort as an `Array` manipulator, I derived an
`ArrayShellSort` template class from `ArraySorter`:

```
template <class T>
    class ArrayShellSort : public ArraySorter<T>
        {
        public:
            // constructor
            ArrayShellSort
                (
                Array<T> & a
                );

            // sorting function
            void Sort
                (
                bool reverse = false
                );
        };
```

```
// constructor
template <class T>
    inline ArrayShellSort<T>::ArrayShellSort
        (
        Array<T> & a
        )
        : ArraySorter<T>(a)
        {
        // empty
        }
```

The sorting function uses the information inherited from ArrayManipulator to access the elements of an Array:

```
template <class T>
    void ArrayShellSort<T>::Sort
        (
        bool reverse
        )
        {
        T v;
        size_t i, j, inc;
        T * ptr    = BufBase - 1;
        size_t len = Target.GetCount();

        for (inc = 1; inc <= len / 9; inc = 3 * inc + 1) ;

        if (reverse)
            {
            for ( ; inc > 0; inc /= 3)
                {
                for (i = inc + 1; i <= len; i += inc)
                    {
                    v = ptr[i];
                    j = i;

                    while ((j > inc) && (ptr[j - inc] < v))
                        {
                        ptr[j] = ptr[j - inc];
                        j -= inc;
                        }

                    ptr[j] = v;
                    }
```

```
              }
          }
      else
          {
          for ( ; inc > 0; inc /= 3)
              {
              for (i = inc + 1; i <= len; i += inc)
                  {
                  v = ptr[i];
                  j = i;

                  while ((j > inc) && (ptr[j - inc] > v))
                      {
                      ptr[j] = ptr[j - inc];
                      j -= inc;
                      }

                  ptr[j] = v;
                  }
              }
          }
      }
```

ShellSort, like many common algorithms, is most easily written to work
with an array whose first element is indexed as 1. C-style arrays, of course,
begin with index zero; however, a sneaky kludge can get around this
apparent conflict. In the previous routine, `ptr` references the element
preceding the actual array data. This arrangement allows access to the
array's first element with an index of 1. This technique should be used
with caution—but it should be used, as it is in this example, to efficiently
implement algorithms that work best when indexes begin at 1.

QuickSort Algorithm

Sorting involves two actions: comparing values and exchanging values.
An efficient sorting routine minimizes the number of comparisons and
exchanges. QuickSort, invented by C.A.R. Hoare in 1960, is just such an
algorithm. Although several minor improvements have been made to
QuickSort, no one has developed a sorting algorithm that is faster or
more elegant.

The basic QuickSort algorithm can be stated simply, even if its implementation is complex. Let's assume that we have an array. An array element is selected as the *pivot value*. All elements less than the pivot value are moved to its left; all the elements that come after the pivot value are placed on the right. The pivot value is then placed in the appropriate position within the array. Then the elements to the left of the pivot are processed using the same technique, as are the elements to the right of the pivot. This process goes on, with smaller and smaller sections being processed, until the entire array is sorted.

Let's see how this technique works, using a simple 11-element array of characters.

index:	0	1	2	3	4	5	6	7	8	9	10
value:	S	T	A	N	J	F	U	B	X	R	G

Any element can be chosen for the pivot value; in this case, I'll use G, the rightmost element in the array. Two indexes will scan the array; one will begin with the leftmost element, and the other will start with the element just to the left of the pivot value. So the left index begins at 0, and the right index begins at 9.

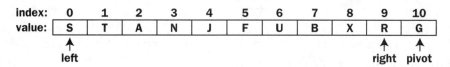

The left index is incremented while the element it references is less than the pivot value. In other words, all the elements that are already less than the pivot value are ignored; what we're interested in is an element that is out of place by virtue of being greater than the pivot value G. In the example above, the very first element is S, so the left index simply stays at 0. The right index is decremented until it references an element that is less than the pivot value; in this case, it stops on B with a value of 7.

index:	0	1	2	3	4	5	6	7	8	9	10
value:	S	T	A	N	J	F	U	B	X	R	G

B and S are out of order; therefore, they need to be swapped. Then the left and right indexes are moved to start scanning anew. The array now looks like this:

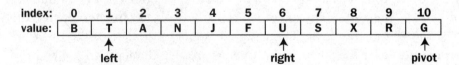

The left and right indexes begin scanning again from their new positions. The left index stays on element 1 (T), the right index moves to element 5 (F).

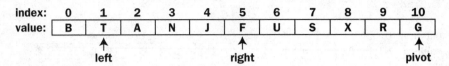

Again, the elements are swapped, and the indexes are moved to continue the scanning.

The scan continues. The left index will stop at element 3 (N), and the right index will stop at 2 (A).

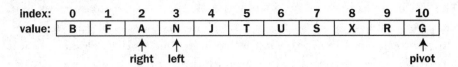

At this point, the indexes have passed each other, and the scanning is complete. All that remains is to swap the pivot element with the element in the position where the left index stopped.

All the elements to the left of G are smaller than G; all the elements larger than G are now on its right. What we have just done is known as *partitioning* the array.

The partially sorted array can now be viewed as two pieces that need to be sorted further by partitioning: the elements to the right of G and the elements to its left. It doesn't matter which section is partitioned first; for example's sake, I use the right partition. When partitioning begins, the section looks like this:

This section doesn't take much time to partition! The right index stays just where it is, pointing to B (which is larger than the pivot value, A). The left index moves to point to B also, ending the partitioning process.

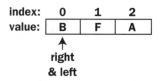

A is then swapped with B as the final act of the partitioning process.

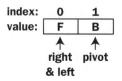

This leaves two sections: A by itself, and B with F. A single-element section can be ignored, because it can't be sorted. So, the two-element section needs to be partitioned, beginning like this:

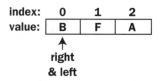

The right and left indexes have nowhere to go; all that needs to be done is to swap the pivot value (B) with the value pointed to by the left index (F). This action ends the processing of everything to the left of G, and the array now looks like this:

index:	0	1	2	3	4	5	6	7	8	9	10
value:	A	B	F	G	J	T	U	S	X	R	N

Now the elements to the left of G need to be processed by the partition-ing routine. Here's how the pivot and indexes start out:

index:	4	5	6	7	8	9	10
value:	J	T	U	S	X	R	N

↑ left   ↑ right   ↑ pivot

The left index will scan to element 5 (T), and the right index will scan to element 4 (J), ending the scanning process. The only thing that will happen is that the pivot element (N) is exchanged with T.

index:	4	5	6	7	8	9	10
value:	J	N	U	S	X	R	T

↑ right   ↑ left

Because J is in a section by itself, it doesn't need any further processing. Partitioning the section containing elements 6 through 10 begins like this:

index:	6	7	8	9	10
value:	U	S	X	R	T

↑ left   ↑ right   ↑ pivot

The indexes start out referencing elements that need to be exchanged. After the exchange, the next scan begins like this:

index:	6	7	8	9	10
value:	R	S	X	U	T

↑ left   ↑ right   ↑ pivot

After scanning, the indexes will be positioned like this:

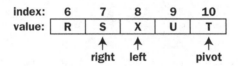

The left and right indexes have crossed, and the scanning ends. To complete the partitioning, element 8 (X) will be exchanged with the pivot value T.

index:	6	7	8	9	10
value:	R	S	T	U	X

Although the entire array is sorted, the two-element sections will still be partitioned, because the program doesn't know that they are already in order. The result of all this processing is that the array now looks like this:

index:	0	1	2	3	4	5	6	7	8	9	10
value:	A	B	F	G	J	N	R	S	T	U	X

It may not be obvious that QuickSort is efficient. Sections that have already been sorted are sometimes partitioned, a useless process. Indexes scan back and forth through the data, often scanning over the same item several times.

But QuickSort is fast, because it performs very few comparisons and exchanges. Incrementing and decrementing indexes do not use CPU time; comparing values and moving data do use CPU time. In the example, only seven swaps were required to sort 11 elements. Overall, empirical testing has shown that QuickSort is by far the fastest sorting routine so far invented—unless the wrong circumstances get it into trouble. QuickSort has an Achilles heel that turns it into SlowSort.

Sorted arrays and QuickSort do not get along. For example, let's say that we tried to QuickSort this array:

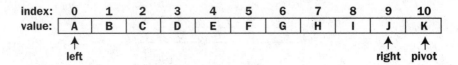

Although it may seem silly to sort sorted data, it often happens that incoming data is either sorted or nearly sorted.

QuickSort will begin as it did before: by picking a pivot value and the starting points for right- and left-scanning indexes.

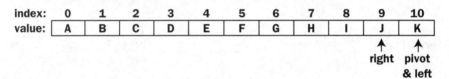

The left index will scan forward until it reaches the first element that is greater than or equal to the pivot element (K); the right index will stay where it is, because J is less than K.

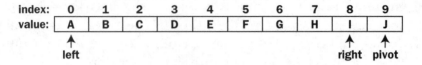

The left and right indexes have passed each other, ending the partitioning process. Because the left index now points to the pivot element, no exchanges have taken place.

Since there are no elements to the right of the pivot element, QuickSort will proceed to partition the elements on the left, 0 through 9.

index: 0   1   2   3   4   5   6   7   8   9

value: A   B   C   D   E   F   G   H   I   J

      left   right   pivot

Again, the left index will slide all the way over to the left, and the right index will remain stationary. No exchanges will take place.

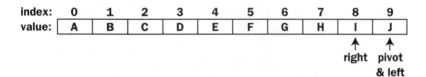

If you see a pattern developing, you're right! QuickSort will continue to partition sections of the array that are one element smaller than the last section. Many comparisons will be performed, but no exchanges will take place. The result? QuickSort takes a very long time to sort sorted information. It doesn't matter which element is selected as the pivot value; changing the pivot selection changes the order of partitioning, but it doesn't reduce the amount of work that is done.

All is not lost, however. A simple improvement to QuickSort can make it perform quickly on sorted arrays. That, however, is a subject for later in this chapter. For now, let's get the basic QuickSort algorithm implemented before we proceed to improve on it.

QuickSort: The Basics

To simplify the exploration of QuickSort, I'll demonstrate how it can be implemented for sorting a C-type array of ints. This technique eliminates some additional complexities introduced when you incorporate a QuickSort into the Array class.

The basic algorithm can be expressed like this:

```
void quicksort1(int array[], int l, int r)
    {
    int temp, pivot, scanl, scanr;

    if (r > l)
        {
        // select pivot element
        pivot = array[r];
```

```
    // set scanning indexes
    scanl = 1;
    scanr = r - 1;

    for (;;)
        {
        // scan from left
        while (array[scanl] < pivot)
            ++scanl;

        // scan from right
        while (array[scanr] > pivot)
            —scanr;

        // if scans have met, exit inner loop
        if (scanl >= scanr)
            break;

        // exchange elements
        temp        = array[scanl];
        array[scanl] = array[scanr];
        array[scanr] = temp;

        // move scans to next elements
        ++scanl;
        —scanr;
        }

    if (scanl != r)
        {
        // exchange final element
        temp        = array[r];
        array[r]     = array[scanl];
        array[scanl] = temp;
        }

    // process the sections
    quicksort1(array,1,scanl - 1);
    quicksort1(array,scanl + 1,r);
    }
}
```

The pivot value is selected as the rightmost element in the section. The for loop partitions the segment. scanl begins pointing to the first element in the section, and it scans to the right, looking for elements that are greater than pivot. scanr beings with the element just to the right of the pivot element; it scans to the left looking for elements that are less than the pivot element. If scanl and scanr cross each other, the partitioning process ends. Otherwise, two out-of-order elements have been found, and they are swapped.

Once the partitioning process is complete, quicksort1 calls itself to partition the sections l through scanl - 1 and scanl + 1 through r. This makes the quicksort1 function recursive. The statement if (r > l) ends the recursive cycle; once quicksort1 is called with a section containing less than two elements, it returns without calling itself.

QuickSort: Removing Recursion

Recursion is expensive. Every time quicksort1 is called, a pointer and two integers must be pushed onto the stack, and a function call is executed. When each call to quicksort1 ends, it must remove arguments from the stack and return to the function call that invoked it. In any environment, this process is expensive in terms of time and resources. Pushing, calling, popping, and returning take time. Arguments on the stack use what may be limited stack space.

Removing recursion isn't difficult. Analysis by computer scientists has shown that any algorithm that can be expressed recursively can also be expressed iteratively. We need to replace the recursion in quicksort1 with a loop that tracks the sizes of partitions.

Most recursive routines call themselves only once, making it easier to remove recursion. Let's look at a simple example before removing recursion from QuickSort.

A factorial is the value obtained when a whole number is multiplied by all the whole numbers that precede it in sequence. For example, the factorial of 4 (4! in mathematical notation) is 4 * 3 * 2 * 1, or 26. And 5! is 5 * 4 * 3 * 2 * 1, or 120. An observant person will notice a pattern here:

```
for x > 1, x! = x * (x - 1)!
for x = 1, x! = 1;
```

The last statement declares that the factorial of 1 is defined explicitly as 1. All other factorials can be defined in terms of other factorials, leading to this recursive implementation of a factorial function:

```
int factorial(int n)
    {
    if (n == 1)
        return 1;
    else
        return n * factorial(n - 1);
    }
```

The function calls itself with successively smaller values of n, until n equals 1. When n == 1, the recursion "unfolds," providing the correct answer.

Although the recursive implementation is simple, it isn't fast. Assuming a large range for an int, it's possible that the factorial of a very large number could cause a stack overflow. And, as I mentioned before, function calls are not generally efficient.

The solution is to remove the recursion by implementing factorial as an iterative function:

```
int factorial(int n)
    {
    int result = 1;

    while (n > 1)
        {
        result *= n;
        —n;
        }

    return result;
    }
```

The iterative version of factorial is longer, and it looks more complex than does its recursive cousin. However, we have removed the need for function calls and stack overhead.

Note that the factorial function could be implemented as a table lookup, removing the need for repeated multiplications at the expense of allocating static memory for the table. But that's a story for another book.

The same principles can be applied to create an iterative version of quicksort1. The task is complicated by the fact that quicksort1 calls itself twice rather than just once as in factorial. What we need is a mechanism that will allow us to store information about sections that have not yet been partitioned. Information about one section can be imparted through variables; information about the other section will need to be stored so that it can be retrieved.

The solution is to use a simple internal stack. Create two arrays of ints that represent the left and right bounds of sections that need to be processed. An index can be used as a stack pointer to indicate how many sections are stored in the arrays. Then, once partitioning is done, the bounds of one partition can be stored in the internal stack, and the other bounds can be used to reset the parameters of the loop that replaces recursion.

This is how the QuickSort function looks after I removed the recursion by adding a loop and a stack:

```
// set the size of the stack based on the size of an int
const int STKSZ = sizeof(int) * CHAR_BIT;

void quicksort2(int array[], int l, int r)
    {
    int temp, pivot, scanl, scanr;

    // stack data
    int stackl[STKSZ], stackr[STKSZ], sptr = 0;

    for (;;)
        {
        while (r > l)
            {
            // select pivot element
            pivot = array[r];
```

```
// set scanning indexes
scanl = l;
scanr = r - 1;

for (;;)
    {
    // scan from left
    while (array[scanl] < pivot)
        ++scanl;

    // scan from right
    while (array[scanr] > pivot)
        --scanr;

    // if scans have met, exit inner loop
    if (scanl >= scanr)
        break;

    // exchange elements
    temp         = array[scanl];
    array[scanl] = array[scanr];
    array[scanr] = temp;

    // move scans to next elements
    ++scanl;
    --scanr;
    }

if (scanl != r)
    {
    // exchange final element
    temp         = array[r];
    array[r]     = array[scanl];
    array[scanl] = temp;
    }

// place left-side section on stack
++sptr;

if (sptr == STKSZ)
    {
    cerr << "\aError: stack overflow";
    exit(EXIT_FAILURE);
    }
```

```
        stackl[sptr] = l;
        stackr[sptr] = scanl - 1;

        l = scanl + 1;
        }

    // iterate with values from the stack (if any)
    if (sptr)
        {
        l = stackl[sptr];
        r = stackr[sptr];

        —sptr;
        }
    else
        break;
    }
}
```

The core of quicksort2 is the same as the core of quicksort1: A for loop performs partitioning on a section of the array. When the loop is done, the left and right bounds of the section to the left of the pivot are stored in the arrays stackl and stackr. The stack pointer, sptr, keeps track of the number of sections stored in the stack arrays. The right-side section has bounds of scanl + 1 and r; to iterate, I simply assigned scanl + 1 to l, and looped back. The looping will continue, storing data on the left-side section in the stack and iterating with the bounds of the right-side section, until the right-side section contains fewer than two elements. At that point, the values stored in stackl and stackr are retrieved to start the loop process for the unpartitioned sections. When the stack arrays are empty, the iteration ends and the array is sorted.

The number of bits in the index data type determines the maximum size of the array and thus the size of the stack; in this case, for a C-type array, ints are used as indexes. The size of an int in bytes is multiplied by the number of bits per byte to obtain the size of the stack. Because QuickSort is essentially a binary algorithm—dividing sections into two smaller sections—the average number of sections stored in the stack arrays should be no larger than log2(sizeof(int)), or the number of bits in an int.

Note that CHAR_BIT was created by the ANSI standard as a constant representing the number of bits in a char. It is defined in the header file **limits.h**.

When you're sorting an already sorted array, the number of sections to be stored will equal the number of elements in the array. Clearly, we don't want create an internal stack large enough to handle the largest possible sorted array. In 16-bit MS-DOS programs, an array of ints may have as many as 30,000+ elements, requiring two stack arrays of 30,000+ elements. Fortunately, we can make a simple modification to QuickSort that eliminates the need to store all that section information.

QuickSort: Improvements

In my tests, quicksort2 performs slightly faster than quicksort1. However, quicksort2 has a hard-coded limitation: Its internal stack may not be adequate when QuickSort degenerates into SlowSort on ordered arrays.

In every case, quicksort2 stores information on the left-side section and iterates using the right-side section. When the data in an array causes quicksort2 to generate small left-side partitions and large right-side partitions, a stack overflow is bound to occur. An ordered (or nearly ordered) array can cause just this type of behavior in quicksort2.

What needs to be done is to place the largest partition on the stack every time. Whereas quicksort2 has these statements:

```
// place left-side section on stack
++sptr;

if (sptr == STKSZ)
    {
    cerr << "\aError: stack overflow";
    exit(EXIT_FAILURE);
    }

stackl[sptr] = 1;
stackr[sptr] = scanl - 1;

l = scanl + 1;
```

quicksort3 has these statements:

```
// place largest section on stack
if ((scanl - l) > (r - scanl))
    {
    // ignore 1-element sections
    if ((scanl - l) > 1)
        {
        ++sptr;

        if (sptr == STKSZ)
            {
            cerr << "\aError: stack overflow";
            exit(EXIT_FAILURE);
            }

        stackl[sptr] = l;
        stackr[sptr] = scanl - 1;
        }

    // ignore 1-element sections
    if (rsize != 0)
        l = scanl + 1;
    else
        break;
    }
else
    {
    // ignore 1-element sections
    if ((r - scanl) > 1)
        {
        ++sptr;

        if (sptr == STKSZ)
            {
            cerr << "\aError: stack overflow";
            exit(EXIT_FAILURE);
            }

        stackl[sptr] = scanl + 1;
        stackr[sptr] = r;
        }

    // ignore 1-element sections
```

```
if (lsize != 0)
    r = scanl - 1;
else
    break;
}
```

The sizes of the left and right sections are compared, and the larger of the two sections is placed on the stack. The smaller section is then used to iterate the partitioning loop. This technique guarantees that no more than `log2(sizeof(int))` elements will be needed in the stack arrays. As an additional benefit, the program now avoids iterating or storing partitions that have fewer than two elements. The overall gain in speed is about 5%.

With a sorted array, `quicksort3` places the largest section on the stack; the smallest section, consisting of a single element, ends the loop. `quicksort3` then retrieves the largest section from the stack and processes it. In other words, for a sorted array, `quicksort3` uses only one element of stack space for iteration. It isn't very efficient, but it avoids the problem of overrunning the stack.

QuickSort: Median-of-Three Partitioning

Now it's time to solve QuickSort's problem with ordered arrays. The solution involves finding a better way of selecting the pivot element. Two techniques have been presented in various texts:

- Use a random number generator to pick an element for the pivot value. Picking a random element avoids the possibility that a consistent selection (such as always using the rightmost element in a section) will generate many partitions.
- Pick three elements, sort them, and pick the middlemost element for the pivot value. This is known as median-of-three partitioning.

Good random number functions use multiplication or division to generate values. Multiplication and division are the most costly operations that can be performed on two numbers, and I like to avoid slow math whenever possible. Also, I don't like hit-and-miss techniques for solving problems; I prefer to use an empirical method that leaves as little as possible to chance.

For these reasons, I decided to implement median-of-three partitioning. For a theoretical section, let L represent the index of the leftmost element, R represent the index of the rightmost element, and M represent the index of the middle element.

index:	0	1	2	3	4	5	6	7	8	9	10
value:	S	T	A	N	J	F	U	B	X	R	G

L at 0, M at 5, R at 10

I begin by sorting L, M, and R into order relative to each other.

index:	0	1	2	3	4	5	6	7	8	9	10
value:	F	T	A	N	J	G	U	B	X	R	S

L at 0, M at 5, R at 10

Then the middlemost element is exchanged with the element just to the left of the rightmost element.

index:	0	1	2	3	4	5	6	7	8	9	10
value:	F	T	A	N	J	R	U	B	X	G	S

L at 0, M at 5, R at 10

Partitioning now proceeds, with the left scan starting at L + 1 and the right scan at R–2.

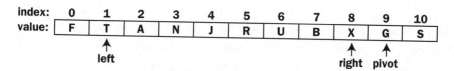

index:	0	1	2	3	4	5	6	7	8	9	10
value:	F	T	A	N	J	R	U	B	X	G	S

left at 1, right at 8, pivot at 9

It may not seem obvious, at first, how median-of-three partitioning could improve QuickSort's performance. Why does shuffling a few elements make QuickSort run faster?

QuickSort performs best when the pivot value is the median of the values in a section. The original QuickSort algorithm always picked the rightmost element in a section as the pivot element. For an unordered section, any element has an equal chance of being close to the median value; thus, always picking the rightmost element (or any other element, for that matter) works well. When a section is sorted or almost sorted, the rightmost element will be the largest value, causing a SlowSort to occur.

Median-of-three partitioning selects the median of three values in a section, increasing the chance of picking a good pivot value. To see how this method helps, let's look at how median-of-three partitioning affects a sorted array such as this one:

index:	0	1	2	3	4	5	6	7	8	9	10
value:	A	B	C	D	E	F	G	H	I	J	K

After performing the median-of-three operation, the array and its scanning indexes look like this before partitioning begins:

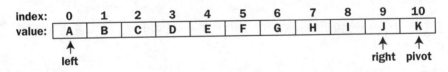

Without a median-of-three setup, partitioning would begin like this:

index:	0	1	2	3	4	5	6	7	8	9	10
value:	A	B	C	D	E	F	G	H	I	J	K

left   right   pivot

The median-of-three approach selects a pivot value of F, which is closer to being a median value than is the element K selected without median-of-three. Strange as it may seem, median-of-three partitioning improves sorting performance by "unsorting" sorted data!

For small sections, the added overhead of median-of-three partitioning overshadows the benefits. In testing, I found that I saw the best performance when I used median-of-three partitioning for sections of eight

or more elements. I defined a variable named Threshold that defines the
size of the largest section that will not be partitioned with median-of-
three. Threshold should not be set to a value less than 3, because you
need at least three elements (right, left, and middle) for median-of-three
partitioning.

In the earlier QuickSort functions, the following three lines were
used to set the pivot and index values for partitioning:

```
pvidx = r;
scanl = l;
scanr = r - 1;
```

To implement median-of-three partitioning, quicksort4 replaces the previous lines with these lines:

```
if ((r - l) > Threshold)
    {
    // "median-of-three" partitioning
    mid = (l + r) / 2;

    // three-sort left, middle, and right elements
    if (array[l] > array[mid])
        {
        temp      = array[l];
        array[l]   = array[mid];
        array[mid] = temp;
        }

    if (array[l] > array[r])
        {
        temp      = array[l];
        array[l] = array[r];
        array[r] = temp;
        }

    if (array[mid] > array[r])
        {
        temp       = array[mid];
        array[mid] = array[r];
        array[r]   = temp;
        }
```

```
    // select pivot element index
    pvidx = r - 1;

    // exchange pivot with the middle element
    temp        = array[mid];
    array[mid]  = array[pvidx];
    array[pvidx] = temp;

    // setup for partitioning
    scanl = l + 1;
    scanr = r - 2;
    }
else
    {
    // select pivot element index
    pvidx = r;

    // set scanning indexes
    scanl = l;
    scanr = r - 1;
    }
```

The if statement selects between median-of-three partitioning and normal partitioning by comparing the difference in r and l to Threshold.

When writing quicksort4, I realized that the sizes of the left and right
sections could be precalculated. In the earlier QuickSort functions, three
subtractions are performed when a section is stored in the internal stack.
Precalculating the sizes of the sections eliminates duplicate subtractions.
The speed gain is minimal, but every little bit helps.

The complete quicksort4 function looks like this:

```
// set the size of the stack based on the size of an int
const int STKSZ = sizeof(int) * CHAR_BIT;

// minimum size of a section for median-of-3 processing
const int Threshold = 7;

void quicksort4(int array[], int l, int r)
    {
    int temp, pivot, scanl, scanr, mid, pvidx, lsize, rsize;
```

```
// stack data
int stackl[STKSZ], stackr[STKSZ], sptr = 0;

for (;;)
    {
    while (r > l)
        {
        if ((r - l) > Threshold)
            {
            // "median-of-three" partitioning
            mid = (l + r) / 2;

            // three-sort left, middle, and right elements
            if (array[l] > array[mid])
                {
                temp       = array[l];
                array[l]   = array[mid];
                array[mid] = temp;
                }

            if (array[l] > array[r])
                {
                temp     = array[l];
                array[l] = array[r];
                array[r] = temp;
                }

            if (array[mid] > array[r])
                {
                temp       = array[mid];
                array[mid] = array[r];
                array[r]   = temp;
                }

            // select pivot element index
            pvidx = r - 1;

            // exchange pivot with the middle element
            temp        = array[mid];
            array[mid]  = array[pvidx];
            array[pvidx] = temp;

            // setup for partitioning
            scanl = l + 1;
```

```
            scanr = r - 2;
            }
    else
        {
        // select pivot element index
        pvidx = r;

        // set scanning indexes
        scanl = 1;
        scanr = r - 1;
        }

    // select pivot element
    pivot = array[pvidx];

    for (;;)
        {
        // scan from left
        while (array[scanl] < pivot)
            ++scanl;

        // scan from right
        while (array[scanr] > pivot)
            --scanr;

        // if scans have met, exit inner loop
        if (scanl >= scanr)
            break;

        // exchange elements
        temp        = array[scanr];
        array[scanr] = array[scanl];
        array[scanl] = temp;

        // move scans to next elements
        ++scanl;
        --scanr;
        }

    if (scanl != pvidx)
        {
        // exchange final element
        temp        = array[pvidx];
        array[pvidx] = array[scanl];
        array[scanl] = temp;
```

```
        }

    // calculate section sizes
    lsize = scanl - l;
    rsize = r - scanl;

    // place largest section on stack
    if (lsize > rsize)
        {
        // ignore 1-element sections
        if (lsize > 1)
            {
            ++sptr;

            if (sptr == STKSZ)
                {
                cerr << "\aError: stack overflow";
                exit(EXIT_FAILURE);
                }

            stackl[sptr] = l;
            stackr[sptr] = scanl - 1;
            }

        // ignore 1-element sections
        if (rsize != 0)
            l = scanl + 1;
        else
            break;
        }
    else
        {
        // ignore 1-element sections
        if (rsize > 1)
            {
            ++sptr;

            if (sptr == STKSZ)
                {
                cerr << "\aError: stack overflow";
                exit(EXIT_FAILURE);
                }

            stackl[sptr] = scanl + 1;
            stackr[sptr] = r;
```

```
            }

        // ignore 1-element sections
        if (lsize != 0)
            r = scan1 - 1;
        else
            break;
        }
    }

// iterate with values from the stack (if any)
if (sptr)
    {
    l = stackl[sptr];
    r = stackr[sptr];

    —sptr;
    }
else
    break;
    }
}
```

A template-based version of `quicksort4` could effectively sort arrays holding any type of data. The accompanying source code disk contains just such a routine, along with other sorting utilities, in the header file **SortTools.h**.

QuickSort Thoughts

Some texts talk about using alternative sorting routines for small partitions. It makes sense to handle small sections using simpler sorts. For example, a two-element section can be sorted using a simple `if` statement; three-element partitions can be sorted using the three-sort method I showed at the beginning of the chapter. Some texts suggest that for partitions of fewer than 20 elements, a simple insertion or selection sort is faster than the partitioning process.

I wrote versions of QuickSort that used alternative sorts for array elements ranging from two to 10 elements. In every case, the alternative sorts produced a slower QuickSort. Profiling the results, I found that the overhead of additional conditional statements was sufficient to cancel out the advantage of having little sorts for small sections.

Speaking of assumptions, my design for a simple QuickSort function quickly caused me problems when I implemented it for Arrays. While I was developing the sorting routines for C-type arrays, I assumed that it would be easy to modify the best routine for use with an Array. How wrong I was! Decisions that I made about the workings of an Array did not mesh with the way quicksort4 goes about its task.

For example, it is possible that the scanl and scanr indexes will be incremented or decremented outside the bounds of the array during the partitioning process. This doesn't cause a problem when you're working with C-type arrays, because they don't perform bounds checking. An Index object, however, knows what its bounds are and will report an error when those bounds are crossed. I had to add several checks to be sure that increments and decrements did not exceed the ranges of Indexes for a given Array.

QuickSort: An Array Manipulator

QuickSort is, quite obviously, more involved than ShellSort. That's why ShellSort is often the routine of choice when you're sorting arrays with fewer than 1000 elements. Although QuickSort performs fewer exchanges and comparisons than does ShellSort, QuickSort requires considerable overhead and bookkeeping not needed by ShellSort. QuickSort can be nearly twice as fast as ShellSort, but the smaller routine uses fewer resources.

I derived an ArrayQuickSort manipulator from ArraySorter:

```
template <class T>
    class ArrayQuickSort : public ArraySorter<T>
        {
        public:
            // constructor
            ArrayQuickSort
                (
                Array<T> & a
                );
```

```
        // sorting function
        void Sort
            (
            bool reverse = false
            );

    protected:
        // pointer to selected function
        bool (ArrayQuickSort<T>::*IsBefore)
            (
            const Index & i1,
            const Index & i2
            );

        // sorting in ascending order
        bool Ascending
            (
            const Index & i1,
            const Index & i2
            );

        // sorting in descending order
        bool Descending
            (
            const Index & i1,
            const Index & i2
            );

        // exchange two elements
        void Exchange
            (
            const Index & i1,
            const Index & i2
            );

        // struct for sorting stack
        struct stackItem
            {
            int left;
            int right;
            };
    };
```

The private Exchange function is an inline swap of two values from the array, based on Index values:

```
template <class T>
    inline void ArrayQuickSort<T>::Exchange
        (
        const Index & i1,
        const Index & i2
        )
        {
        static T tmp;

        tmp        = Target[i1];
        Target[i1] = Target[i2];
        Target[i2] = tmp;
        }
```

To control the direction of the Sort, I included a function pointer and two comparison functions. The ArrayQuickSort<T>::Sort function assigns IsBefore the address of either Ascending or Descending depending on the setting of reverse.

```
template <class T>
    bool ArrayQuickSort<T>::Ascending
        (
        const Index & i1,
        const Index & i2
        )
        {
        return (Target[i1] < Target[i2]);
        }

template <class T>
    bool ArrayQuickSort<T>::Descending
        (
        const Index & i1,
        const Index & i2
        )
        {
        return (Target[i1] > Target[i2]);
        }
```

The meat of the SortableArray class is the Sort function, which implements the QuickSort algorithm using IsBefore, Exchange, and the stackItem struct.

```
template <class T>
    void ArrayQuickSort<T>::Sort
        (
        bool reverse
        )
        {
        // determine direction of sort
        if (reverse)
            IsBefore = Descending;
        else
            IsBefore = Ascending;

        // create stack
        const size_t stackSize = CHAR_BIT * sizeof(int);
        stackItem * stack = new stackItem [stackSize];

        if (stack == NULL)
            throw ArrayEx(AEX_ALLOC);

        size_t stackPtr = 0;

        // size of minimum partition to median-of-three
        const int Threshold = 7;

        // sizes of left and right partitions
        int lsize, rsize;

        // create working indexes
        Index l(Target.GetRange()),      // left    partition index
              r(Target.GetRange()),      // right   partition index
              mid(Target.GetRange()),    // middle partition index
              scanl(Target.GetRange()),  // index scanning from left
              scanr(Target.GetRange()),  // index scanning from right
              pivot(Target.GetRange());  // pivot element index

        // set initial values
        l.SetMin();
        r.SetMax();

        // main loop
        for (;;)
            {
            while (r > l)
                {
```

```
if (((int)r - (int)l) > Threshold)
    {
    // "median-of-three" partitioning
    mid = ((int)l + (int)r) / 2;

    // three-sort left, middle, and right elements
    if ((this->*IsBefore)(mid,l))
        Exchange(mid,l);

    if ((this->*IsBefore)(r,l))
        Exchange(r,l);

    if ((this->*IsBefore)(r,mid))
        Exchange(r,mid);

    // setup for partitioning
    pivot = r - 1;

    Exchange(mid,pivot);

    scanl = l + 1;
    scanr = r - 2;
    }
else
    {
    // setup for partitioning
    pivot = r;
    scanl = l;
    scanr = r - 1;
    }

for (;;)
    {
    // scan from left for element >= to pivot
    while ((this->*IsBefore)(scanl,pivot) && (scanl < r))
        ++scanl;

    // scan from right for element <= to pivot
    while ((this->*IsBefore)(pivot,scanr) && (scanr > l))
        —scanr;

    // if scans have met, exit inner loop
    if (scanl >= scanr)
        break;
```

```
            // exchange elements
            Exchange(scanl,scanr);

            if (scanl < r)
                ++scanl;

            if (scanr > l)
                --scanr;
            }

    // exchange final element
    Exchange(pivot,scanl);

    // place largest partition on stack
    lsize = (int)scanl - (int)l;
    rsize = (int)r - (int)scanl;

    if (lsize > rsize)
        {
        if (lsize != 1)
            {
            ++stackPtr;

            if (stackPtr == stackSize)
                throw ArrayEx(AEX_SORTOVER);

            stack[stackPtr].left  = int(l);
            stack[stackPtr].right = int(scanl - 1);
            }

        if (rsize != 0)
            l = scanl + 1;
        else
            break;
        }
    else
        {
        if (rsize != 1)
            {
            ++stackPtr;

            if (stackPtr == stackSize)
                throw ArrayEx(AEX_SORTOVER);

            stack[stackPtr].left  = int(scanl + 1);
```

```
                            stack[stackPtr].right = int(r);
                        }

                if (lsize != 0)
                    r = scanl - 1;
                else
                    break;
                }
            }

        // iterate with values from stack
        if (stackPtr)
            {
            l = stack[stackPtr].left;
            r = stack[stackPtr].right;

            —stackPtr;
            }
        else
            break;
        }

    delete [] stack;
    }
```

Sort begins by creating an array of stackItems that is sizeof(int) *
CHAR_BIT elements in length. Once a stack has been created and a stack
pointer has been set, Sort looks much like quicksort4. The primary differences are that the manual exchanges in quicksort4 are replaced by
calls to Exchange, and the comparisons are replaced by calls to IsBefore. I
also added checks to avoid out-of-range Indexes.

PUTTING MANIPULATORS TO WORK

Here's a function that sorts arrays using the preceding code. This code is
taken from the Testbed application (see Appendix).

```
void ArrayTest2
    (
    strstream & buffer
```

```
)
{
// banner
buffer << "\r\nArrays: Sorting"
          "\r\n----------\r\n";

// constants
int MaxVal = 1701;

// locals
int n;
Range r(1,101);
Array<int> a(r);

// fill array with random values and display it
for (n = r.GetMin(); n <= r.GetMax(); ++n)
    a[n]  = gen(MaxVal);

// duplicate array for second sort
Array<int> a2(a);

// now sort with new manipulator
buffer << "With QuickSort:\r\n";
ArrayQuickSort<int> qsorter(a);

buffer << "   Unsorted Array = " << a << "\r\n";
qsorter.Sort();
buffer << "     Sorted Array = " << a << "\r\n";
qsorter.Sort(true);
buffer << "     Reverse Sort = " << a << "\r\n";

// now sort with new manipulator
buffer << "With ShellSort:\r\n";
ArrayShellSort<int> ssorter(a2);

buffer << "   Unsorted Array = " << a2 << "\r\n";
ssorter.Sort();
buffer << "     Sorted Array = " << a2 << "\r\n";
ssorter.Sort(true);
buffer << "     Reverse Sort = " << a2 << "\r\n";
}
```

All the `ArrayManipulator` classes are implemented in the file **ArrayManip.h**, which you can find on the accompanying source diskette.

ONWARD

Data aren't worth much unless we know what they *mean,* and one way of examining data is to apply statistics. The next chapter looks at using `Array` classes for basic statistical analysis.

CHAPTER 10

STATISTICS 101

The preceding chapters introduced a set of classes for manipulating arrays of numeric values. One goal of using classes is to allow for the easy introduction of expanded capabilities. For example, I was recently required to use the `Array` class in statistical calculations. By building on my existing data types, I was able to build a complex application quickly.

The field of statistics is far too broad for me to cover in great detail; I'll admit that my own understanding is less than professorial. The copious shelving in my office contains dozens of books that discuss the ins and outs of determining exactly what a set of numbers *might* mean. That, after all, is the purpose of statistics: to find out what numbers signify and how, if at all different numbers are related.

Statistics is by far the grayest area of mathematics, in that it deals with intangibles. What a statistician tries to do is to apply certain mathematical principles to a set of data, generating a characteristic value that can be examined by a thoughtful human. Statistics in and of themselves can prove nothing; a human brain is required to determine whether the statistics mean anything.

STATISTICAL FUNCTIONS

How should a set of statistical functions be implemented? In a C program, there would be no design choices: Individual functions would be written to calculate statistical values from C-style arrays. My C++ program, however, offer two choices. I could develop a C-like library of functions to manipulate Arrays, or I could derive a new class from NumericArray to provide member functions for basic statistical calculations. The latter course simply felt the more object-oriented of the two. I derived a template class, StatArray, from NumericArray. For the most part, statistical functions require floating-point numbers, and for most mathematical work, doubles provide the best tool; therefore, you'll usually be using StatArray<float> and StatArray<double> objects.

STATARRAY CLASS

StatArray does not define any data members; it defines only new functions. Each of the following sections of code describes a set of related functions:

```
template <class T>
    class StatArray : public NumericArray<T>
        {
        public:
            // constructors
            StatArray
                (
                const Range & r
                );

StatArray

                (
                const Array<T> & a
                );

            StatArray
                (
```

```
        const StatArray<T> & a
        );

StatArray
    (
    const T * a, size_t n
    );

StatArray
    (
    const StatArray<T> & a1,
    const StatArray<T> & a2
    );

StatArray
    (
    const StatArray<T> & a,
    const Index & first,
    const Index & last
    );

StatArray
    (
    const StatArray<T> & a,
    int first,
    int last
    );

// assignment operator
StatArray & operator =
    (
    const StatArray<T> & a
    );

// minimum, maximum, and range determination
T Min() const;
T Max() const;

void MinMax
        (
    T & minimum,
    T & maximum
    ) const;

T RangeOf() const;
```

```
// series calculations
T Sum() const;
T Product() const;

// calculate moments of distribution
T Mean() const;
T Median() const;
T MedianSort();

T Variance() const;

T StdDeviation() const;
T AvgDeviation() const;

T Skew() const;
T Kurt() const;

// calculate several values at once
void Moment
    (
    T & mean,
    T & avgdev,
    T & stddev,
    T & var,
    T & skew,
    T & kurt
    ) const;

// calculate standardized scores (z-scores)
T ZScore
    (
    const Index & i
    ) const;

T ZScore
    (
    int i
    ) const;

StatArray<T> ZScore() const;

// calculate Pearson's coefficient of correlation
// for a pair of arrays
T Correlation
    (
```

```
            const StatArray<T> & dsa
            );

        void FillRandom
            (
            T low,
            T high
            );
    };
```

Constructors and Assignments

A StatArray<T> is constructed, copied, destroyed, and assigned just as a NumericArray<T> is. I implemented the constructors and the assignment operator as inline shells that call only the corresponding functions inherited from NumericArray<double>.

```
template <class T>
    inline StatArray<T>::StatArray
        (
        const Range & r
        )
        : NumericArray<T>(r)
        {
        // simple inline call to base class constructor
        }


template <class T>
    inline StatArray<T>::StatArray
        (
        const StatArray<T> & a
        )
        : NumericArray<T>(a)
        {
        // simple inline call to base class constructor
        }


template <class T>
    inline StatArray<T>::StatArray
        (
        const Array<T> & a
        )
        : NumericArray<T>(a)
```

```
        {
        // simple inline call to base class constructor
         }

template <class T>
    inline StatArray<T>::StatArray
        (
        const T * a, size_t n
        )
        : NumericArray<T>(a,n)
        {
        // simple inline call to base class constructor
        }

template <class T>
    inline StatArray<T>::StatArray
        (
        const StatArray<T> & a1,
        const StatArray<T> & a2
        )
        : NumericArray<T>(a1,a2)
        {
        // simple inline call to base class constructor
        }

template <class T>
    inline StatArray<T>::StatArray
        (
        const StatArray<T> & a,
        const Index & first,
        const Index & last
        )
        : NumericArray<T>(a,first,last)
        {
        // simple inline call to base class constructor
        }

template <class T>
    inline StatArray<T>::StatArray
        (
        const StatArray<T> & a,
         int first,
        int last
        )
        : NumericArray<T>(a,first,last)
        {
```

302

```
        // simple inline call to base class constructor
        }

template <class T>
    inline StatArray<T> & StatArray<T>::operator =
        (
        const StatArray<T> & a
        )
        {
        this->Array<T>::operator = (a);
        return *this;
        }
```

As you may have noticed, StatArray defines a conversion constructor to create a StatArray from a NumArray<double>.

Finding the Range of Values

It's often necessary to know the highest and lowest values in a data set. Min and Max return, respectively, the minimum (smallest) and maximum (largest) values in the array:

```
template <class T>
    T StatArray<T>::Min() const
        {
        const T * ptr  = Buffer;
        T result = DBL_MAX;

        for (size_t i = 0; i < Count; ++i)
            {
            if (*ptr < result)
                result = *ptr;
            ++ptr;
            }

        return result;
        }

template <class T>
    T StatArray<T>::Max() const
        {
        const T * ptr = Buffer;
```

```
T result = DBL_MIN;

for (size_t i = 0; i < Count; ++i)
    {
    if (*ptr > result)
        result = *ptr;
    ++ptr;
    }

return result;
}
```

I created `MinMax` to return both the minimum and the maximum with one function call.

```
template <class T>
    void StatArray<T>::MinMax
        (
        T & minimum,
        T & maximum
        ) const
        {
        const T * ptr = Buffer;
        minimum = DBL_MAX;
        maximum = DBL_MIN;

        for (size_t i = 0; i < Count; ++i)
            {
            if (*ptr > maximum)
                maximum = *ptr;

            if (*ptr < minimum)
                minimum = *ptr;

            ++ptr;
            }
        }
```

`RangeOf` returns the difference between the minimum and maximum values, showing how far the values range within the array. If you already have the minimum and maximum values, you can calculate this value without calling this function.

```
template <class T>
   T StatArray<T>::RangeOf() const
      {
      T minimum, maximum;

      MinMax(minimum,maximum);

      return ::fabs(maximum - minimum);
      }
```

Series Calculations

Some applications require the product or sum of an array's elements. Although these functions aren't statistical functions, they are used by other members of StatArray. The Sum function calculates the result by cycling through the array from the first element to the last element, adding each value to a result.

```
template <class T>
   T StatArray<T>::Sum() const
      {
      const T * ptr  = Buffer;
      T result = 0.0;

      for (size_t i = 0; i < Count; ++i)
         {
         result += *ptr;
         ++ptr;
         }

      return result;
      }
```

The Product is calculated by multiplying together all the elements in a StatArray. It uses the same programming techniques as Sum, using multiplication instead of addition for calculating the result.

```
template <class T>
   T StatArray<T>::Product() const
```

```
{
const T * ptr  = Buffer;
T result = 0.0;

for (size_t i = 0; i < Count; ++i)
    {
    result *= *ptr;
    ++ptr;
    }

return result;
}
```

Mean

A *moment of distribution* is a single value that describes a data set. It is a fundamental statistical value, and the StatArray class defines member functions to calculate the most commonly used moments of distribution.

The *mean* is commonly known as the average; it is merely the sum of all elements in the set, divided by the number of elements.

$$\bar{x} = \frac{1}{N} \sum_{j=1}^{N} x_j$$

The mean is a simple yardstick for determining the most common value in a data. It is calculated by dividing the result of the Sum function by the number of elements in the array.

```
template <class T>
    T StatArray<T>::Mean() const
        {
        return Sum() / (T)Count;
        }
```

Median

The *median* also tries to tell you what the most common element in the set is, in this case by returning the middlemost value. This process involves sorting the StatArray, and then returning the value of the element that falls in the middle of the values in the array. For example, consider this array of data:

```
1, 1, 2, 4, 5, 5, 6, 7, 9, 10, 10
```

The median is 5, because that value is located in the middle of the data set.

The median can be calculated easily only if the elements of the array are sorted. This requirement can be a problem when you don't want the data in your array to be rearranged by sorting. To limit the problem, I developed two implementations of the median function. The first version creates a temporary copy of a StatArray, sorts it, and returns the median. The routines uses a polymorphic ArraySorter object and a dynamically allocated sort object to choose between QuickSort and ShellSort based on the array length:

```cpp
template <class T>
    T StatArray<T>::Median() const
        {
        // create temporary for sort
        StatArray<T> temp(*this);

        // find the middle
        int middle = (IndexRange.GetMin() + IndexRange.GetMax())
                                / 2;

        // select a sort algorithm based on array size
        ArraySorter<T> * sorter;

        if (Count < 100)
            sorter = new ArrayShellSort<T> (temp);
        else
            sorter = new ArrayQuickSort<T> (temp);

        if (sorter == NULL)
            throw ArrayEx(AEX_ALLOC);

        // sort temporary
        sorter->Sort();
```

```
    // delete sorting object
    delete sorter;

    // return middle value of temporary
    return temp[middle];
    }
```

The advantage of Median is that it does not affect the ordering of elements in the StatArray it is applied to. However, creating a second duplicate array can be prohibitive, particularly when the array is very large. Also, the work that goes into sorting the array is thrown away once the median is calculated. But, because Median does not alter its object, it can be used for constant StatArrays.

The second implementation, MedianSort, directly sorts the StatArray and returns the median.

```
template <class T>
    T StatArray<T>::MedianSort()
        {
        // find middle index of array
        int middle = (IndexRange.GetMin() + IndexRange.GetMax())
                                        / 2;

        // select a sort algorithm based on array size
        ArraySorter<T> * sorter;

        if (Count < 100)
            sorter = new ArrayShellSort<T> (*this);
        else
            sorter = new ArrayQuickSort<T> (*this);

        if (sorter == NULL)
            throw ArrayEx(AEX_ALLOC);

        // sort
        sorter->Sort();

        // delete sorting object
        delete sorter;
```

```
        // return middle value
        return Read(middle);
        }
```

`MedianSort` does not create a temporary array, but it does sort the `StatArray` being examined. Choosing a median function will depend upon your requirement for maintaining the order of the elements in an array.

Variance and Standard Deviation

You'll often want to know how widely the data in a set vary from the mean. The most common characterization of differences in a data set is known as *variance*, which is calculated using the following formula.

$$Var = \frac{1}{N\text{-}1} \sum_{j=1}^{N} (xj - \bar{x})$$

The variance represents the average square of the differences between the elements of an array and its mean. I implemented it like this:

```
template <class T>
    T StatArray<T>::Variance() const
        {
        T temp, result = 0.0;
        T m = Mean();
        const T * ptr = Buffer;

        for (size_t i = 0; i < Count; ++i)
            {
            temp = *ptr - m;
            result += temp * temp;
            ++ptr;
            }

        result /= ((T)(Count - 1));
```

```
        return result;
        }
```

The square root of the variance is called the standard *deviation*; it is represented by the Greek letter σ.

$$\sigma = \sqrt{Var}$$

Standard deviation represents the range in which most data points will be found: between *mean* - σ and *mean* + σ. In other words, the standard deviation is an indicator of how far the data range from the mean. It's a useful value for seeing how close your data are to a straight, horizontal line.

I implemented the StdDeviation function as an inline function:

```
template <class T>
    inline T StatArray<T>::StdDeviation() const
        {
        return sqrt(Variance());
        }
```

Average Deviation

Another estimation of a data set's variability is the *average deviation*, which is calculated by taking the average of the difference between each data point and the mean

$$avg.\ deviation = \frac{1}{N}\sum_{j=1}^{N}\left|x_j - \bar{x}\right|$$

The AvgDeviation function implements the preceding equation in this fashion:

```
template <class T>
    T StatArray<T>::AvgDeviation() const
        {
```

```
T result = 0.0;
T m = Mean();
const T * ptr = Buffer;

for (size_t i = 0; i < Count; ++i)
    {
    result += fabs(*ptr - m);
    ++ptr;
    }

result /= (T)Count;
return result;
}
```

Skew and Kurtosis

Now, there are a couple of terms you see every day! *Skew* and kurtosis are, for the most part, variations on Variance and Standard Deviation. Here are the formulas:

$$skew = \frac{1}{N-1} \sum_{j=1}^{N} \left[\frac{x_j - \bar{x}}{\sigma} \right]^3$$

$$kurtosis = \frac{1}{N} \sum_{j=1}^{N} \left(\left[\frac{x_j - \bar{x}}{\sigma} \right]^4 \right) - 3$$

Each of these values gives a statistician an idea of how "flat" a data set is; by using higher powers in the summation, peaks and valleys in the information are more prominent than they would be with standard deviation.

Here are the function implementations:

```
template <class T>
    T StatArray<T>::Skew() const
        {
        T result = 0.0;
        T sd = StdDeviation();

        if (sd != 0.0)
            {
```

```
            T temp;
            T m  = Mean();
            const T * ptr = Buffer;

for (size_t i = 0; i < Count; ++i)
            {
            temp = (*ptr - m) / sd;
            result += (temp * temp * temp);
            ++ptr;
            }

            result /= ((T)(Count - 1));
            }

        return result;
        }

template <class T>
    T StatArray<T>::Kurt() const
        {
        T result = 0.0;
        T sd = StdDeviation();

if (sd != 0.0)
            {
            T temp;
            T m = Mean();
            const T * ptr = Buffer;

            for (size_t i = 0; i < Count; ++i)
                {
                temp = (*ptr - m) / sd;
                result += (temp * temp * temp * temp);
                ++ptr;
                }

            result /= (T)Count;
            result -= 3.0;
            }

        return result;
        }
```

Skewness is an abstract characterization of an array's asymmetry when plotted as a distribution around the mean. Data often have tails; if you graph them as a distribution, you'll see a long stretch along the x axis. A positive skewness indicates that your data have a tail of values greater than the mean, and a negative skewness tells you that the tail is less than the mean.

Kurtosis measures how flat the distribution is around the mean. A perfect bell curve has a kurtosis of zero. A positive kurtosis value indicates that your distribution has a very sharp peak in the middle, with few values near the mean; a negative kurtosis indicates that a graph of your data would show a plateau around the mean.

Moment

I developed much of the preceding code above based on an amazing text called *Numerical Recipes in C*, by Press, Flannery, Teukolsky, and Vetterling (Cambridge Press, 1988). This volume contains a treasure-trove of mathematical formulas, concepts, and tools of indescribable value to a mathematical programmer.

Press et al. suggest that a single function be used to calculate several moments of distribution simultaneously. Statisticians generally require more than one of these values, and using the individual functions can be very inefficient. For example, calculating the `Variance` and then calling `StdDeviation` will result in two calls to `Variance` and `Mean`. Generally, a statistician needs several of the values. With that in mind, I created the `Moment` function, which returns the mean, average deviation, standard deviation, and variance in one fell swoop.

```
template <class T>
    void StatArray<T>::Moment
        (
        T & mean,
        T & avgdev,
        T & stddev,
        T & var,
        T & skew,
```

```
      T & kurt
      ) const
      {
      T temp, tempsqr, cnt;
      size_t i;

      cnt    = (T)Count;
      mean   = Mean();
      var    = 0.0;
      avgdev = 0.0;

const T * ptr = Buffer;

      for (i = 0; i < Count; ++i)
          {
          temp    = *ptr - mean;
          var    += temp * temp;
          avgdev += fabs(temp);
          ++ptr;
          }

      var    /= cnt - 1.0;
      avgdev /= cnt;
      stddev  = sqrt(var);

      if (stddev == 0.0)
          {
          skew = 0.0;
          kurt = 0.0;
          }
      else
          {
          ptr  = Buffer;
          skew = 0.0;
          kurt = 0.0;

          for (i = 0; i < Count; ++i)
              {
              temp = (*ptr - mean) / stddev;
              tempsqr = temp * temp;
              kurt += (tempsqr * tempsqr);
              skew += (tempsqr * temp);
              ++ptr;
              }

          skew /= ((T)(cnt - 1));
```

```
        kurt /= cnt;
        kurt -= 3.0;
        }
    }
```

Z-Scores

In (fictitious) Hotternhell Valley, Nevada, some ecologists have been wondering if whether variations in populations of coyotes and jack rabbits are related; they also wonder whether variation in the valley's sparse rainfall has an effect on these animals. Over 20 years, the scientists collected the information shown in this table:

Year	Coyotes	Rabbits	Rainfall
1971	97	200	3
1972	86	220	11
1973	87	225	4
1974	73	233	2
1975	70	261	1
1976	81	235	4
1977	67	257	5
1978	75	250	3
1979	78	223	3
1980	93	187	4
1981	101	171	6
1982	93	167	2
1983	96	154	3
1984	82	212	2
1985	70	210	4
1986	76	219	7
1987	50	308	10
1988	69	287	1
1989	80	244	2
1990	81	218	1

Coyote and rabbit numbers represent counts of individual animals trapped and released during that year; the rainfall numbers are the inches of precipitation for the year. Looking at the data, can we tell whether the 1991 data are peculiar? Is the population of 50 coyotes in 1987 unusually low? Is there any relationship between the populations and the rainfall?

A value called a z-*score* can help answer questions such as those. A z-score is calculated for any individual member of the data set by this formula:

$$z_j = \frac{x_j - \bar{x}}{\sigma}$$

The z-score represents the number of standard deviations a given value is from the average (mean) value. A negative z-score tells us that the value is below the norm, and a positive z-score says that the value is above normal. In most cases, a "normal" value should have a z-score between −1 and +1, indicating that it is within the range of the standard deviation from the mean. A z-score with an absolute value greater than 1 will be calculated for values that fall outside the normal data distribution. The higher the absolute z-score, the more unusual the value is.

I created three functions that calculate z-scores. The first two functions calculate the z-score for any element of the array, selected either by Index or int **index**.

```
template <class T>
    T StatArray<T>::ZScore
        (
        const Index & i
        ) const
        {
        T result = 0.0;
        T sd = StdDeviation();

if (sd == 0.0)
            result = 0.0;
        else
            result = (Read(i) - Mean()) / sd;

        return result;
```

```
    }

template <class T>
    T StatArray<T>::ZScore
        (
        int i
        ) const
        {
        T result = 0.0;
        T sd = StdDeviation();

        if (sd == 0.0)
            result = 0.0;
        else
            result = (Read(i) - Mean()) / sd;

        return result;
        }
```

The result of these functions is zero when the standard deviation is zero. This technique avoids a divide overflow that would otherwise terminate the program.

The third ZScore function creates a new StatArray that contains z-scores for every element in the target array. This is a quick way of getting all the z-scores in one function call. Its implementation follows:

```
template <class T>
    StatArray<T> StatArray<T>::ZScore() const
        {
        StatArray<T> result(IndexRange);
        T sd = StdDeviation();

        if (sd == 0.0)
            result.Fill(0.0);
        else
            {
            const T * src = Buffer;
            T * dest = result.Buffer;
            T m   = Mean();

            for (size_t i = 0; i < Count; ++i)
                {
```

```
        *dest = (*src - m) / sd;
        ++src;
        ++dest;
        }
    }

    return result;
    }
```

The z-score is 2.563 for the 11 inches of rain recorded in 1972. That's considerably more than 1, telling me that 1972's rainfall was unusually high. For the 2 inches of rain recorded in 1988, however, the z-score is only -0.6859, meaning that amount is within the expected range.

Correlation

Statisticians are always trying to find out whether two sets of data are related. For example: Is there a connection between the coyote populations and rainfall in Hotternhell Valley? When two data sets follow a similar pattern of peaks and valleys in their structure, they are said to be *positively correlated*. If the high values in one data set correspond to the low values in the other data set (and vice versa), the two sets are said to be *negatively correlated*. Often, there is no correlation between the two data sets.

To correlate two data sets, we compare the z-scores of corresponding elements. Using z-scores instead of actual values eliminates scaling problems; it allows us to look at the two data sets based on how much they vary from their mean. I have implemented a function named Correlation to perform this calculation for a StatArray. A correlation value is obtained using the following formula:

$$cor = \frac{1}{N} \sum_{j=1}^{N} \frac{(x_j - \bar{x})(y_j - \bar{y})}{\sigma_x \sigma_y}$$

In other words, the correlation of two data sets can be calculated by adding the products of corresponding z-scores and dividing that sum by the number of elements in the data sets:

```
template <class T>
    T StatArray<T>::Correlation
        (
        const StatArray<T> & dsa
        )
        {
        if (IndexRange != dsa.IndexRange)
            throw ArrayEx(AEX_INCOMPAT);

        const T * ptr1 = Buffer;
        const T * ptr2 = dsa.Buffer;
        T result = 0.0;
        T  m1 = Mean();
        T  m2 = dsa.Mean();
        T sd1 = StdDeviation();
        T sd2 = dsa.StdDeviation();

        if ((sd1 == 0.0) || (sd2 == 0.0))
            {
            if (sd1 == sd2)
                result = 1.0;
            else
                result = 0.0;
            }
        else
            {
            for (size_t i = 0; i < Count; ++i)
                {
                result += ((*ptr1 - m1) / sd1)
                                * ((*ptr2 - m2) / sd2);
                ++ptr1;
                ++ptr2;
                }

            result /= Count;
            }

        return result;
        }
```

An Example

Using the data for Hotternhell Valley, I built a function to demonstrate the use of StatArrays. It displayed the following information:

Chapter 10: Statistics 101

Statistics: Coyotes, Jack Rabbits, and Temperature
—————————————————————————

coyote stats:
  mean (average) = 80.2500
  avg. deviation = 9.4500
  std. deviation = 12.3496
  variance   = 152.5132
  skewness   = -0.3356
  kurtosis   = -0.2232

jack rabbit stats:
  mean (average) = 224.0500
  avg. deviation = 28.3550
  std. deviation = 38.4454
  variance   = 1478.0500
  skewness   = 0.1911
  kurtosis   = -0.3927

rainfall stats:
  mean (average) = 3.9000
  avg. deviation = 1.9900
  std. deviation = 2.7701
  variance   = 7.6737
  skewness   = 1.2918
  kurtosis   = 0.6562

correlation of coyotes and rabbits: -0.8364
correlation of rabbits and coyotes: -0.8364
correlation of coyotes and rainfall: -0.1498
correlation of rabbits and rainfall: 0.1198

Data dump with ZScores:

Year	Coyotes		Rabbits		Rainfall	
1971:	97.0000	(1.3563)	200.0000	(-0.6256)	3.0000	(-0.3249)
1972:	86.0000	(0.4656)	220.0000	(-0.1053)	11.0000	(2.5630)
1973:	87.0000	(0.5466)	225.0000	(0.0247)	4.0000	(0.0361)
1974:	73.0000	(-0.5871)	233.0000	(0.2328)	2.0000	(-0.6859)
1975:	70.0000	(-0.8300)	261.0000	(0.9611)	1.0000	(-1.0469)
1976:	81.0000	(0.0607)	235.0000	(0.2848)	4.0000	(0.0361)
1977:	67.0000	(-1.0729)	257.0000	(0.8571)	5.0000	(0.3971)
1978:	75.0000	(-0.4251)	250.0000	(0.6750)	3.0000	(-0.3249)
1979:	78.0000	(-0.1822)	223.0000	(-0.0273)	3.0000	(-0.3249)

```
1980:    93.0000 ( 1.0324)   187.0000 (-0.9637)    4.0000 ( 0.0361)
1981:   101.0000 ( 1.6802)   171.0000 (-1.3799)    6.0000 ( 0.7581)
1982:    93.0000 ( 1.0324)   167.0000 (-1.4839)    2.0000 (-0.6859)
1983:    96.0000 ( 1.2753)   154.0000 (-1.8221)    3.0000 (-0.3249)
1984:    82.0000 ( 0.1417)   212.0000 (-0.3134)    2.0000 (-0.6859)
1985:    70.0000 (-0.8300)   210.0000 (-0.3655)    4.0000 ( 0.0361)
1986:    76.0000 (-0.3441)   219.0000 (-0.1314)    7.0000 ( 1.1191)
1987:    50.0000 (-2.4495)   308.0000 ( 2.1836)   10.0000 ( 2.2021)
1988:    69.0000 (-0.9110)   287.0000 ( 1.6374)    1.0000 (-1.0469)
1989:    80.0000 (-0.0202)   244.0000 ( 0.5189)    2.0000 (-0.6859)
```

A value of –0.8364 tells us that there is a strong *negative* correlation between coyotes amounts and jack rabbits in Hotternhell Valley. In other words, more coyotes correspond to fewer rabbits—although we can't necessarily draw the conclusion that the rabbit population drops *because* of the coyotes; some other, unknown factor might be at work. But the correlation between the two populations is strong, telling the scientists to look more closely at the relationship between the two animals. The low correlations between the animal populations and rainfall, however, indicate that rain probably has little effect on their survival. Statistics, in general, can disprove something, but it can only rarely prove anything.

The year 1981 was unusual for the large number of coyotes and the small number of rabbits; 1987 was probably the most remarkable year in that coyote numbers were abnormally small, rabbit numbers were extraordinarily high, and rainfall was remarkably abundant. Also, the high variance value for the rabbit data indicates that their population changes considerably from year to year. And the skewness value for the rainfall data shows a data tail to the positive side of the 3.9 mean annual inches.

The StatArray class implementation can be found in the files **StatArray.h** and **StatArray.cpp**, located on the accompanying source diskette.

ONWARD

Now it's time to leave numbers behind, as I begin looking at persistent objects and indexed data files.

CHAPTER 11

PERSISTENT OBJECTS

File handling is arguably the most important component of a software application. Most useful programs can store and retrieve file-based information in a speedy and reliable manner. Yet file handling is often overlooked, particularly by C++ library vendors. They give us classes for matrices, user interfaces, and containers but fail to provide for the handling of data storage. When I built my class library, one of my goals was to create a powerful set of file-handling types. I wanted a class library that was flexible, general, extensible, and understandable—so what else is new?

PERSISTENT OBJECTS

If you read the literature about object-oriented programming, you'll find discussions of persistent objects. A *persistent object* is one that can be stored outside the program, to be retrieved at a later time. They're called persistent objects because their state persists between instances of an application. In essence, persistent objects are objects that can be stored in files. However, storing objects isn't as easy as storing structures.

It's easy—and incomplete—to view objects as data structures having associated functionality. An object is a program component that has an identity and a state. The identity and state involve relationships with other objects, static class members, virtual functions, and base classes. In storing a persistent object, the identity and state of the object must be preserved.

Only an object itself can know how to preserve its state; thus, only an object can be responsible for controlling the storage of its components. When the object is retrieved, it should be able to construct itself based on the data that were stored. Consequently, objects read from files must be new objects that are constructed from the retrieved data.

Consider this: All objects, no matter how complex or "intelligent," are created from simple types. An object's constituents are nothing more than simple data items that have been assigned an extended meaning through mutual association and a functional definition. Our task, then, is to store the raw information of an object for later retrieval into a new object.

How a file goes about its business should be transparent to objects that use it. An object should not be concerned with how its data are stored or retrieved, or even where. All the object needs to know is that it formats itself and stores these data to a file from which the data can later be retrieved to reconstruct the object.

Conversely, a file should never need to know anything about the objects it stores. A file should receive a chunk of data from an object and store it without regard for what that data represent. In this fashion, files become independent of the data that are stored in them. Where and how a file is stored should never concern an object being stored, and a persistent object should be able to treat different file types as equivalent. When we make files and objects independent, file handling becomes more generalized.

To provide a bridge between objects and files, I defined an intermediate type. Persistent objects can convert themselves to and from the intermediate type; storage objects store the intermediate type directly. Persistent objects have full control over how they are represented in the intermediate type; storage objects are free to handle the intermediate type as long as they preserve its contents.

The conversion is handled by programmer-defined functions within the context of the file object; in essence, my system is similar in concept to Turbo Pascal's old FILE OF <type> system. By using a template, I tell the file object about the type of data it is storing; the file object then converts its associated data type into the storage type for writing, and back again when reading. Once you've defined conversions between a data type and the storage type, the reading and writing of objects is a transparent process.

Although it may seem a considerable amount of work to use an intermediate type, I've found that it provides sufficient flexibility and performance for my needs.

DATA BLOCKS

The DataBlock class can be thought of as a translator. Persistent objects create DataBlocks, which are collected by a storage object. Storage objects, in turn, retrieve DataBlocks, which they then use to construct objects.

Object Signatures

I needed a simple mechanism for type verification of the data in DataBlocks. Somehow, an object needed to know that it was being built from the right kind of DataBlock. Type information cannot be stored in a file; as far as a file is concerned, a block of data is a set of bytes, and it is the program's responsibility to assign meaning to those bytes.

My solution was to store a signature with each DataBlock. The signature is an unsigned long that should be unique for each persistent object class with a set of interacting applications. When a persistent object builds a DataBlock of itself, it should store the appropriate signature value. When an object is constructed from a `DataBlock`, the signature can be checked to ensure that this data block goes with this kind of object.

`Signature`s are not bulletproof. Only your diligence prevents two different object types from having the same signature. But it's a better system than no type checking at all. If a file will contain objects of several different types, it is the programmer's responsibility to guarantee that those objects have different identifiers. When we get into real programs later in the book, I'll demonstrate techniques for selecting reliable object signatures.

I define the `Signature` data type as follows:

```
typedef unsigned long Signature;
```

I also defined some constant values for `Signature`s:

```
const Signature SIG_USER_BASE = 0x00000000;
const Signature SIG_SYS_BASE  = 0xF0000000;
const Signature SIG_USER_MAX  = SYS_SIG_BASE - 1;
const Signature SIG_DELETED   = 0xFFFFFFFF;
```

User-defined `Signature`s are those that can be used by your classes; system `Signature`s are those used internally by various parts of my persistence library. In other words, objects that define persistent objects can use any value between 0 and `SIG_USER_MAX` for their signature. `SIG_DELETED` is a system signature that defines a deleted block in a storage object; it will be explained in more detail later.

Class Definition

I defined the `DataBlock` class like this:

```
class DataBlock
    {
    public:
        // constructors
        DataBlock();
```

```
DataBlock
    (
    Signature sig,
    size_t sz,
    const void * data = NULL
    );

DataBlock
    (
    const DataBlock & db
    );

// destructor
~DataBlock();

// assignment
DataBlock & operator =
    (
    const DataBlock & db
    );

// interrogation
Signature GetSig() const;
size_t GetSize() const;
operator const void * () const;
operator void * ();

// check for NULL block
bool IsNull() const;

protected:
Signature BlockSig;
size_t    BufferSize;
void *    BufferPtr;
};
```

A DataBlock consists of a Signature, a size_t value named BufferSize, and a block of data named BufferPtr. The block of data is BufferSize bytes in length.

I defined my DataBlockExceptions with the DataBlockEx class and the DataBlockError enumeration, following the same system I've used in previous chapters:

```
enum DataBlockError
    {
    DBEX_ALLOC,
    DBEX_BADSIG,
    DBEX_NULLBUF
    };


class DataBlockEx : public ExceptionBase
    {
    public:
        DataBlockEx
            (
            DataBlockError err
            )
            {
            Error = err;
            }

        DataBlockError WhatsWrong()
            {
            return Error;
            }

         void Explain
            (
            DiagOutput & out
            );

    private:
        DataBlockError Error;
    };
```

The DataBlockEx::Explain function looks like this:

```
void DataBlockEx::Explain
    (
    DiagOutput & out
    )
    {
    switch (Error)
        {
        case DBEX_ALLOC:
            out.DisplayMsg
                (
```

```
            "DataBlock memory alloc failed",
            DIAG_ERROR
            );
        break;
    case DBEX_BADSIG:
        out.DisplayMsg
            (
            "Unexpected DataBlock signature",
            DIAG_ERROR
            );
        break;
    case DBEX_NULLBUF:
        out.DisplayMsg
            (
            "Null input buffer for DataBlock",
            DIAG_ERROR
            );
        break;
    default:
        out.DisplayMsg
            (
            "Unexpected DataBlock error!",
            DIAG_ERROR
            );
    }
}
```

A new DataBlock is constructed from a Signature, a size_t value, and a
pointer to a block of memory:

```
DataBlock::DataBlock
    (
    Signature sig,
    size_t sz,
    const void * data
    )
    {
    if (sz == 0)
        {
        BufferSize = 0;
        BlockSig   = 0;
        BufferPtr  = NULL;
        }
    else
        {
```

```
        BufferSize = sz;
        BlockSig   = sig;
        BufferPtr  = (void *)new char[sz];

        if (BufferPtr == NULL)
            throw DataBlockEx(DBEX_ALLOC);

        if (data != NULL)
            memcpy(BufferPtr,data,sz);
    }
}
```

The constructor raises an exception if it cannot allocate enough memory to duplicate the data block.

The default constructor creates a DataBlock for which all values are zero. A DataBlock with no data and a zero signature is known as a *null block*.

```
inline DataBlock::DataBlock()
    {
    BufferSize = 0;
    BufferPtr  = NULL;
    BlockSig   = 0;
    }
```

You can create new DataBlocks from existing ones using the copy constructor:

```
DataBlock::DataBlock(const DataBlock & db)
    {
    BufferSize = db.BufferSize;
    BlockSig   = db.BlockSig;

    BufferPtr  = (void *)new char[BufferSize];

    if (BufferPtr == NULL)
        throw DataBlockEx(DBEX_ALLOC);

    memcpy(BufferPtr,db.BufferPtr,BufferSize);
    }
```

The destructor deletes `Buffer`:

```
inline DataBlock::~DataBlock()
    {
    if (BufferPtr != NULL)
        delete [] BufferPtr;
    }
```

`DataBlock`s can be assigned to each other:

```
DataBlock & DataBlock::operator =
    (
    const DataBlock & db
    )
    {
    BlockSig = db.BlockSig;

    if (BufferSize != db.BufferSize)
        {
        BufferSize = db.BufferSize;

        if (BufferPtr != NULL)
            delete [] BufferPtr;

        BufferPtr = (void *)new char[BufferSize];

        if (BufferPtr == NULL)
            throw DataBlockEx(DBEX_ALLOC);
        }

    memcpy(BufferPtr,db.BufferPtr,BufferSize);

    return * this;
    }
```

Several interrogation functions return the values of a `DataBlock`'s data members. The `IsNull` function returns a `Boolean` indicating that the block in question is a null block.

```
inline Signature DataBlock::GetSig() const
    {
```

```
    return BlockSig;
    }

inline size_t DataBlock::GetSize() const
    {
    return BufferSize;
    }

inline DataBlock::operator const void * () const
    {
    return BufferPtr;
    }

inline DataBlock::operator void * ()
    {
    return BufferPtr;
    }
```

Conversion

I spent a great deal of time considering how conversions should take place between objects and DataBlocks. In my original design, shown in the first edition of this book, I defined a Persistent class that defined virtual functions for conversion to and from a DataBlock. With Persistent as a base, a class would define its own versions of the conversions.

That system worked, but it had distinct disadvantages. First, it worked only with classes, but I'm often trying to store simple structures, or even simple data types such as double. I ended up creating "wrapper" classes:

```
class Pdouble : public Persistent
    {
    private:
        double Value;
    public:
        Pdouble(double d) {Value = d;}
        Pdouble(const Pdouble & pd) {Value = pd.Value;}

        operator double () {return Value;}
```

```
        Pdouble & operator = (const Pdouble & pd)
            {Value = pd.Value;}

        // functions for persistence
        Pdouble(const DataBlock & db);
        operator
    };
```

That's a great deal of superfluous effort just because I want to write dou-bles in a file! I might, of course, have used basic C-style file handling for simple types and my persistent classes for objects, but that would have led to a hodgepodge of different approaches to file handling.

Could I have defined DataBlock as a template class, thus creating a unique DataBlock type for every persistent type? I tried that approach and quickly abandoned it. Simply put, a template cannot understand the type-specific aspects of its defining data type. A template version of DataBlock would not know how to convert a given type without under-standing the type's internal structure and requirements.

My solution, albeit an imperfect one, was to define conversion func-tions with prototypes to match these templates:

```
template <class T>
    void operator <<= (T & dest, const DataBlock & src);

template <class T>
    void operator <<= (DataBlock & dest, const T & src);
```

This approach allowed me to create file objects for specific types; the template file class could assume the existence of <<= conversion func-tions, which the programmer is assumed to have created somewhere. For example, when I create an object to store ints, I created this pair of func-tions:

```
void operator <<=
    (
    int & dest,
    const DataBlock & src
```

```
    )
    {
    if (src.GetSig() != Sig_Int)
        throw DataBlockEx(DBEX_BADSIG);

    dest = *((const int *)((const void *)src));
    }

inline void operator <<=
    (
    DataBlock & dest,
    const int & src
    )
    {
    dest = DataBlock(Sig_Int,sizeof(int),&src);
    }
```

Why did I pick the <<= operator? It seemed the most "fitting" of any operators. After all, the left and right shift operators define stream insertion and deletion in C++; the <<= operator seemed to look right as a conversion operator. As in many C++ matters, the choice was a matter of taste.

My solution is not without its caveats. I assume, for example, that a data type's internal information is available through interrogation functions or direct access. A complicated class, because it is already a class, could declare the conversion operators as friends, essentially making them members of the class.

You'll find the DataBlock classes in the files **Persist.h** and **Persist.cpp** on the accompanying source file diskette.

DATA FILES

Different types of storage objects have different requirements. For example, a hash table is used differently from a binary tree, and these storage types are different from files stored on disks or in memory.

I defined a basic set of classes for disk-based data files. Basing these classes on the ANSI-standard file I/O functions provided portability. The following discussion assumes that you understand the workings of fopen, fclose, fseek, fread, and fwrite as defined by ANSI C.

The hierarchy consists of four classes: a base class that defines the characteristics of all files, a class for sequential output files, a class for sequential input files, and a powerful data file class designed for randomly accessing records.

Exception Handling

Like most of my class systems, the data file classes define an exception type and an associated enumeration.

```
enum DataFileError
    {
    FEX_EOF,
    FEX_ALLOC,
    FEX_GEN_TEMP,
    FEX_INV_MODE,
    FEX_NO_OPEN,
    FEX_NO_WRT_FHDR,
    FEX_NO_RD_FHDR,
    FEX_NO_WRT_RHDR,
    FEX_NO_RD_RHDR,
    FEX_NO_WRT_REC,
    FEX_NO_RD_REC,
    FEX_BAD_SEEK,
    FEX_NO_OPEN_TEMP,
    FEX_NO_REMOVE,
    FEX_NO_RENAME,
    FEX_NO_REWIND,
    FEX_BAD_SIG
    };

class DataFileEx : public ExceptionBase
    {
    public:
        DataFileEx(DataFileError err) { Error = err; }
        DataFileError WhatsWrong() { return Error; }
         void Explain(DiagOutput & out);
    private:
        DataFileError Error;
    };
```

```
void DataFileEx::Explain
    (
    DiagOutput & out
    )
    {
    out.DisplayMsg("File System Error: ");

    switch (Error)
        {
        case FEX_EOF:
            out.DisplayMsg("end of file reached",DIAG_WARNING);
            break;
        case FEX_ALLOC:
            out.DisplayMsg("file memory allocation failure",
                            DIAG_ERROR);
            break;
        case FEX_GEN_TEMP:
            out.DisplayMsg("can't generate temp file name",
                            DIAG_ERROR);
            break;
        case FEX_INV_MODE:
            out.DisplayMsg("invalid file mode",DIAG_ERROR);
            break;
        case FEX_NO_OPEN:
            out.DisplayMsg("can't open file",DIAG_ERROR);
            break;
        case FEX_NO_WRT_FHDR:
            out.DisplayMsg("can't write file header",DIAG_ERROR);
            break;
        case FEX_NO_RD_FHDR:
            out.DisplayMsg("can't read file header",DIAG_ERROR);
            break;
        case FEX_NO_WRT_RHDR:
            out.DisplayMsg("can't write record header",
                            DIAG_ERROR);
            break;
        case FEX_NO_RD_RHDR:
            out.DisplayMsg("can't read record header",
                            DIAG_ERROR);
            break;
        case FEX_NO_WRT_REC:
            out.DisplayMsg("can't write record",DIAG_ERROR);
            break;
        case FEX_NO_RD_REC:
            out.DisplayMsg("can't read record",DIAG_ERROR);
            break;
        case FEX_BAD_SEEK:
```

```
            out.DisplayMsg("file seek failed",DIAG_ERROR);
            break;
        case FEX_NO_OPEN_TEMP:
            out.DisplayMsg("can't open temp file",DIAG_ERROR);
            break;
        case FEX_NO_REMOVE:
            out.DisplayMsg("can't remove file",DIAG_ERROR);
            break;
        case FEX_NO_RENAME:
            out.DisplayMsg("can't rename file",DIAG_ERROR);
            break;
        case FEX_NO_REWIND:
            out.DisplayMsg("can't rewind file",DIAG_ERROR);
            break;
        case FEX_BAD_SIG:
            out.DisplayMsg("record signature mismatch",
                           DIAG_ERROR);
        }
    }
```

Data File Base Type

`DataFileBase` is the base class for the data file classes:

```
class DataFileBase
    {
    public:
        // constructor
        DataFileBase
            (
            const String & name,
            DataFileMode m = FM_TEMPORARY
            );

        // destructor
        ~DataFileBase();

        // flush buffers
        void Commit();

    protected:
        // data members
        DataFileMode Mode;
        String    FileName;
```

```
int        DOSHandle;
int        DOSMode;
int        DOSAttr;

static const int StdModeNew;
static const int StdModeExists;
static const int StdModeAppend;
static const int StdAttr;
static const int StdAttrNew;
};
```

DataFileBase defines a common data structure used by all data file classes. The FileMode enumeration defines the possible modes in which a file can be opened:

```
enum FileMode
    {
    FM_NEW,        // new file
    FM_EXISTING,   // file must already exist
    FM_TEMPORARY   // new file, deleted when closed
    };
```

The constructor begins by duplicating the file name pointed to by the parameter name. It then constructs the contents of DosMode from the FileMode value m. The fopen function uses DosMode to determine how a file is opened (new, existing, and so on). Once the file name and mode have been stored, the file is opened and its pointer is assigned to Data. If bufsize is zero, the file is unbuffered; otherwise, memory is allocated so that the Buffer points to a block of bufsize bytes, and the ANSI setvbuf function assigns that buffer to the file.

```
DataFileBase::DataFileBase
    (
    const char * name,
    DataFileMode m
    )
    {
    // store file name
    if (name == NULL)
        FileName = new char[64];
    else
```

```
    FileName = new char[strlen(name) + 1];

if (FileName == NULL)
    throw DataFileEx(FEX_ALLOC);

if (name == NULL)
    {
    if (NULL == tmpnam(FileName))
        throw DataFileEx(FEX_GEN_TEMP);
    }
else
    strcpy(FileName,name);

// generate DosMode string
Mode = m;

DOSMode = O_BINARY;
DOSAttr = 0;

switch (Mode)
    {
    case FM_NEW:
    case FM_TEMPORARY:
        DOSMode |= O_CREAT | O_TRUNC | O_RDWR;
        DOSAttr |= S_IREAD | S_IWRITE;
        break;

    case FM_EXISTING:
        DOSMode |= O_RDWR;
        break;

    case FM_APPEND:
        DOSMode |= O_APPEND | O_WRONLY;
        break;

    default:
        throw DataFileEx(FE_INV_MODE);
    }

// open file
DOSHandle = open(FileName,DOSMode,DOSAttr);

if (DOSHandle == -1)
    throw DataFileEx(FE_NO_OPEN);
}
```

The destructor closes the file, frees the memory allocated to Buffer and
FileName, and deletes the file from disk if it was temporary:

```
DataFileBase::~DataFileBase()
    {
    // close up!
    close(DOSHandle);

    // if temp file, delete it!
    if (Mode == FM_TEMPORARY)
        remove(FileName);

    // delete file name buffer (if any)
    if (FileName != NULL)
        delete FileName;
    }
```

Sequential Output Files

The DataFileOutput template class adds a single output function to the
functions it inherits from DataFileBase. The constructor simply passes its
arguments to the constructor for DataFileBase:

```
template <class D>
    class DataFileOutput : virtual public DataFileBase
        {
        public:
            DataFileOutput
                (
                const String & name,
                DataFileMode m = FM_NEW
                )
                : DataFileBase(name,m) {}

            bool Write(const D & data);
        };
```

DataFileOutput stores variable-length records. Every record has a header,
defined by the RecordHeader structure, that contains the size of the record
and a Signature value extracted from the DataBlock.

```
struct RecordHeader
    {
    size_t RecSize;
    Signature RecSig;
    };
```

The Write function stores the information in a DataBlock at the current location in a file. Write creates a record header from the DataBlock's values and stores that header. Then it writes the data portion of the DataBlock. Note that every I/O operation is followed by a check for success; Write returns false if something goes wrong.

```
template <class D>
    bool DataFileOutput<D>::Write
        (
        const D & data
        )
        {
        // create data block
        DataBlock db;
        db <<= data;

        // create record header
        RecordHeader hdr;
        hdr.RecSig  = db.GetSig();
        hdr.RecSize = db.GetSize();

        // store record header
        size_t n = write(DOSHandle,&hdr,sizeof(RecordHeader));

        if (n != sizeof(RecordHeader))
            return false;

        // store data
        n = write(DOSHandle,(void *)db,hdr.RecSize);

        if (n == hdr.RecSize)
            return true;
        else
            return false;
        }
```

Note my use of the conversion operator, which I use to copy a D object into a waiting, empty DataBlock. DataBlocks appear only inside the context of a file class. In contrast to the technique discussed in the previous edition of this book—in which the programmer worked directly with DataBlocks—my revised, template-based system requires only that conversion operators be created.

DataFileOutput sequentially writes DataBlocks into a file. There is no provision for deleting records or selecting the file position where records are written. For many applications, the simple sequential output of data will be more than adequate; however, for applications (such as database programs) that require random access to data, the DataFile class (discussed later in this chapter) provides the necessary capabilities.

Sequential Input Files

DataFileInput adds three functions to DataFileBase:

```
template <class D>
    class DataFileInput : virtual public DataFileBase
        {
        public:
            DataFileInput
                (
                const String & name
                )
                : DataFileBase(name,FM_EXISTING) {}

            D Read() const;

            bool Rewind();
            bool Skip();
        };
```

As with DataFileOutput, the constructor merely passes arguments to the base class constructor.

The Read function complements DataFileOutput's Write function. Records are read sequentially, and the Read function assumes that the file pointer is positioned at the beginning of a record. The `DataFileInput` class is designed to complement and work with the `DataFileOutput` class. Files written with the `DataOutput` class are structured so that they can be read by the `DataFileInput` class.

`Read` begins by reading a record header from the file. Then, based on `hdr.RecSize`, `Read` allocates a buffer into which data is read. The buffer and header information is used to construct a `DataBlock` that is returned as the function's value. If an error occurs, the constant value `NULL_BLOCK` (defined in the `DataBlock` class) is returned.

```
template <class D>
    D DataFileInput<D>::Read() const
        {
        RecordHeader hdr;
        size_t n;

        // read record header
        n = read(DOSHandle,&hdr,sizeof(RecordHeader));

        if (n == 0)
            throw DataFileEx(FEX_EOF);

        if (n != sizeof(RecordHeader))
            throw DataFileEx(FEX_NO_RD_RHDR);

        // allocate buffer to hold data
        DataBlock db(hdr.RecSig,hdr.RecSize);

        if (!db.IsNull())
            {
            // read data
            n = read(DOSHandle,(void *)db,hdr.RecSize);

            if (n != hdr.RecSize)
                throw DataFileEx(FEX_NO_RD_REC);
            }

        // create an D
        D result;
        result <<= db;
```

```
    // outa here
    return result;
    }
```

The `Skip` function reads a record header and then moves the file pointer past the record's data, in effect skipping a record:

```
template <class D>
    bool DataFileInput<D>::Skip()
        {
        RecordHeader hdr;
        size_t res;

        // read record header
        res = read(DOSHandle,&hdr,sizeof(RecordHeader));

        if (res != sizeof(RecordHeader))
            return false;

        // skip data
        res = (size_t)lseek(DOSHandle,hdr.RecSize,SEEK_CUR);

        if (res == 0)
            return true;
        else
            return false;
        }
```

The `Rewind` function places the file pointer at the beginning of the file:

```
template <class D>
    bool DataFileInput<D>::Rewind()
        {
        size_t res = (size_t)lseek(DOSHandle,0,SEEK_SET);

        if (res == 0)
            return true;
        else
            return false;
        }
```

You'll find the `DataFileBase`, `DataFileOutput`, and `DataFileInput` classes in the files **datafile.h** and `datafile.cpp` located on the accompanying source file disk.

An Example of Persistence

The following short program demonstrates how persistent objects and data files work together:

```
#include "persist.h"
#include "datafile.h"
#include "diagdos.h"
#include "iostream.h"
#include "str.h"
#include "string.h"
#include "stdlib.h"

void TestDataFile1();
void TestDataFile2();

DiagOutDOS dbgout(cerr);

struct Record
    {
    String Name;
    String City;

    Record(char * n = NULL, char * c = NULL)
        : Name(n == NULL ? "" : n), City(c == NULL ? "" : c)
        { /* nada */ }

    Record(const Record & obj)
        : Name(obj.Name), City(obj.City)
        { /* nada */ }

    void operator = (const Record & obj)
        {
        Name = obj.Name;
        City = obj.City;
        }
```

```
    static const Signature Sig;
    };

const Signature Record::Sig = 0x4444414C;

void operator <<= (DataBlock & dest, const Record & src)
    {
    size_t sz = src.Name.Length() + src.City.Length() + 2;

    DataBlock db(Record::Sig,sz);

    char * blk = (char *)((void *)db);

    strcpy(blk,src.Name);
    strcpy(blk + src.Name.Length() + 1,src.City);

    dest = db;
    }

void operator <<= (Record & dest, const DataBlock & src)
    {
    if (Record::Sig != src.GetSig())
        throw DataFileEx(FE_BAD_SIG);

    const char * ptr = (const char *)((const void *)src);
    dest.Name = ptr;
    ptr += dest.Name.Length() + 1;
    dest.City = ptr;
    }

const size_t ObjCount = 20;

Record TestData[ObjCount] =
    {
    Record("Larry",   "Los Angeles"),
    Record("John",    "San Mateo"),
    Record("Karyn",   "Boston"),
    Record("Fred",    "Philadelphia"),
    Record("Lucy",    "Seattle"),
    Record("Jerry",   "Newark"),
    Record("Annie",   "Houston"),
    Record("Michael", "Lincoln"),
    Record("Scott",   "Manitou Springs"),
    Record("Maria",   "Manitou Springs"),
```

```
    Record("Rebecca",  "Manitou Springs"),
    Record("Elora",    "Manitou Springs"),
    Record("Rudolph",  "North Pole"),
    Record("Robert",   "Somerset"),
    Record("Mark",     "Pheonix"),
    Record("Susan",    "Tuscon"),
    Record("Eve",      "Salt Lake City"),
    Record("Teddy",    "Boise"),
    Record("Everett",  "Portland"),
    Record("Edwin",    "Cheyenne")
    };

int main()
    {
    try
        {
        TestDataFile1();
        TestDataFile2();
        }

    catch (ExceptionBase & ex)
        {
        ex.Explain(dbgout);
        }

    return 0;
    }

void TestDataFile1()
    {
    cout << "\n————————"
         << "\nDataFile Test #1"
         << "\n————————"
         << endl;

    const char * fn = "tsio.dat";
    size_t n;

    //————————————————————————————
    cout << "\nCreating output file object\n";

    DataFileOutput<Record> * ofile =
                        new DataFileOutput<Record>(fn);

    for (n = 0; n < ObjCount; ++n)
```

```
        {
        cout << "Writing record #" << n << " : "
            << TestData[n].Name << " @ "
            << TestData[n].City << endl;


        ofile->Write(TestData[n]);
        }

delete ofile;

//————————————————
cout << "Creating input file object\n";

Record * dataIn = new Record[ObjCount];

if (dataIn == NULL)
    {
    cout << "\acan't allocate input object array!\n";
    exit(EXIT_FAILURE);
    }

DataFileInput<Record> * ifile =
                    new DataFileInput<Record>(fn);


 n = 0;
bool reading = true;

while (reading)
    {
    if (n == 7)
        ifile->Skip();
    else
        {
        try {
            cout << "Reading record #" << n << " : ";
            dataIn[n] = ifile->Read();
            cout << dataIn[n].Name << " @ "
                << dataIn[n].City << endl;
            }
        catch (DataFileEx & ex)
            {
            if (ex.WhatsWrong() == FE_EOF)
                reading = BOOL_FALSE;
```

```
            else
                throw;
            }
        }
    ++n;
    }


  delete ifile;
  delete dataIn;
  }
```

This example shows how I created persistence for a class. `Record` contains two `String` objects—`Name` and `City`—which I then convert to and from `DataBlocks` via `<<=` operators. When the `DataFileOutput<Record>` is created, the template assumes that the conversion functions exist. From a coding perspective, I'm simply telling the file objects to read and write `Record` objects without having to be concerned with `DataBlocks` or other aspects of getting `Records` to and from disk storage. The code looks exactly as you'd expect, with the implementation details hidden.

RANDOM ACCESS FILES

Information is written sequentially to `DataFileOutput` objects and is read sequentially from `DataFileInput` objects. For many applications, sequential file I/O is sufficient. But sequential files have limitations. Once data are stored, they cannot be retrieved, changed, or deleted. The data can be retrieved only in the same order they were written. New data are simply appended to the end of a file.

In an application in which data are referred to by a key, the program will need to locate data by their position within a file. Most applications need the ability to delete and change records, too. Because the two existing file classes don't support these features, a new file class is required.

For the purposes of this discussion, I'll use the term *record* to refer to a distinct piece of data stored at a specific location in a file.

Variable-Length Records

Files can contain fixed-length or variable-length records. *Fixed-length* records are simple; every record has the same length, so moving through the file is merely a matter of incrementing the current file pointer by the size of the record currently being pointed to. The `DataFile` classes automatically handle *variable-length* records, because the `DataBlocks` are stored with length information.

File Pointers and Indexing

A *file pointer* is a value that references a location in a file. Every file has a *current* file pointer that points to the locations where I/O operations will be performed. Each record is located at a specific file pointer. Files that allow records to be read and written in any position are known as *random access* files.

An *index* is a data structure that associates a key value with a file pointer. The file pointer for a record is found by looking up the record's key in the index.

A hash table used for indexing is sometimes referred to as a *scatter table*, or *indirect hash* table. When a record is written to a file, we need to obtain its file pointer within the file. That value, along with a key, is stored in an index so that the key can be used to find the record again.

Record Deletion and Insertion

How should records be deleted from a file? One scheme would be to remove the deleted record from the file, shifting other records to eliminate the now empty space. This approach can be inefficient: Deleting the second record in a 1000-record file would mean moving 998 other records! And moving the records would require regeneration of any index that references the file pointers for those records.

It makes more sense to reuse deleted record space than to remove it. Deleted records can simply be marked as such. When new records are written to the file, a program can check to see whether any of the deleted records is large enough to hold the new record. If so, the new record is written into the same place as a deleted record. Otherwise, the new record is appended to the end of the file. No records move, so indexes for "live" records don't need to change.

A file can use a linked list to keep track of deleted records. In the file's header, it keeps a file pointer to the first deleted record in the list. Each deleted record contains a file pointer to the next deleted record in the list; the last record in the list has a value to indicate that no more deleted records exist. When a record is deleted, it stores the deleted file pointer for the header, and the header contains the file pointer for the newly deleted record. In other words, newly deleted records are inserted at the head of the list. This type of list is called a *deleted list*.

When a new record is inserted into the file, it searches the list of deleted records, looking for a deleted record that it will fit into. The first deleted record that is the same size or larger becomes the new record's home. The deleted record is removed from the linked list. If no records are in the linked list or if the new record is too large to fit into any deleted records, the new record is appended to the file.

Reusing deleted record space has only one drawback: It leaves dead space in the file. Deleted records use space in the file until a new record is written into their location. Because we are using variable-length records, new records must usually be shorter than the deleted records they overwrite, leaving "holes" of various sizes in the file.

Periodically, it makes sense to *compact* the file, removing the wasted space and eliminating deleted records. A file is compacted by simply rewriting the file, record by record, using exact record lengths and ignoring deleted records.

However, when a file is compacted, every record could change positions within the file. For an indexed file, in which a table stores keys and file pointers, a new index will need to be built to reflect the new record positions.

Random Access Data Files

I created a new class, named DataFile, that implements a random access file as just described. This new class is based on the DataFileBase class and provides the capabilities to read, write, and delete records in a file. The class definition is as follows:

```
template <class D>
    class DataFile : public DataFileBase
        {
        public:
            // constructor
            DataFile
                (
                const String & name,
                DataFileMode m = FM_EXISTING
                );

            // write a record
            DataFilePtr Write
                (
                const D & data
                );

            // read a record
            D Read() const;

            // delete a record
            void Delete();

            // remove blanks and wasted space
            void Compact
                (
                void (*func)
                        (
                        DataFilePtr ptr,
                        const D & data
                        ) = NULL
                );

            // move to next record
            bool Skip();
```

```
        // return to beginning of file
        void Rewind();

        // go to  position in file
        DataFilePtr Seek
            (
            DataFilePtr pos
            ) const;

        // get current file position
        DataFilePtr CurrentPtr() const;

protected:
        DataFileHdr Hdr;
    };
```

The `DataFile` file pointer type is defined by `DataFilePtr`. `DataFilePtr` is a `long`, because that is the value defined by ANSI for file pointers. A `long` allows files as large as two billion bytes to be created; this should be large enough for most applications.

```
typedef long DataFilePtr;
```

The deleted list uses `DataFilePtr`s to link deleted records. I also defined this constant:

```
extern const DataFilePtr DFP_NULL;
```

A `DataFile` needs a header record containing the number of the first record in the deleted list. If there are no deleted records, `FirstEmpty` will be set to `DFP_NULL`.

```
struct DataFileHdr
    {
    DataFilePtr FirstEmpty;
    };
```

The records in `DataFileInput` or `DataFileOutput` files have a header that contains a signature and the size of the record. `DataFile` records need two more pieces of header information: the size of the space occupied by the original record and a pointer to the next deleted record.

```
struct IORecordHeader : public RecordHeader
    {
    size_t Size;
    DataFilePtr NextDeleted;
    };
```

The Size value contains the number of bytes in the original record. When a record is written into a new location in the file, Size and RecSize will be the same. When a new record is written into a deleted record, RecSize will contain the size of the new record, and Size will contain the number of bytes in the overwritten record.

A deleted record is indicated by a special Signature value named SIG_DELETED. This is in addition to making the record a part of the deleted list.

```
const Signature SIG_DELETED = 0xFFFFFFFF;
```

The constructor for a DataFile needs to create a header record if the file is new or temporary; otherwise, the constructor needs to read the existing header from disk. A copy of the header record is always kept in the Hdr data member.

```
template <class D>
    DataFile<D>::DataFile
        (
        const String & name,
        DataFileMode m
        )
        : DataFileBase(name,m)
        {
        size_t res;

        if ((m == FM_NEW) || (m == FM_TEMPORARY))
            {
            Hdr.FirstEmpty = DFP_NULL;
```

```
      res = write(DOSHandle,&Hdr,sizeof(DataFileHdr));

      if (res != sizeof(DataFileHdr))
          throw DataFileEx(FEX_NO_WRT_FHDR);
      }
  else
      {
      res = read(DOSHandle,&Hdr,sizeof(DataFileHdr));

      if (res != sizeof(DataFileHdr))
          throw DataFileEx(FEX_NO_RD_FHDR);
      }
  }
```

DataFile doesn't need a destructor; the base class constructor will auto-matically close the file.

The Write function adds new records to the file. Write searches the deleted list for the first deleted record that is large enough to hold the new record:

```
template <class D>
    DataFilePtr DataFile<D>::Write
        (
        const D & data
        )
        {
        // search for first open record that can hold this one
        IORecordHeader rechdr;
        DataFilePtr ptr;
        size_t n;
        long pos;

        DataBlock db;
        db <<= data;

        if (Hdr.FirstEmpty == DFP_NULL)
            {
            // append new data to end of file
            pos = lseek(DOSHandle,0,SEEK_END);

            if (pos == -1L)
                throw DataFileEx(FEX_BAD_SEEK);
```

```
        ptr = tell(DOSHandle);

        rechdr.Size = db.GetSize();
        }
    else
        {
        // start with first empty record
        DataFilePtr prev = DFP_NULL;

        ptr = Hdr.FirstEmpty;

        for (;;)
            {
            // set file pointer
            pos = lseek(DOSHandle,ptr,SEEK_SET);

            if (pos == -1L)
                throw DataFileEx(FEX_BAD_SEEK);

            // read record header
            n = read
                (
                DOSHandle,
                &rechdr,
                sizeof(IORecordHeader)
                );

            if ((n != sizeof(IORecordHeader))
            || (rechdr.RecSig != SIG_DELETED))
                throw DataFileEx(FEX_NO_RD_RHDR);

            // is it big enough?
            if (rechdr.Size >= db.GetSize())
                {
                // go to previous record
                if (prev == DFP_NULL)
                    {
                    // change entry in header
                    Hdr.FirstEmpty = rechdr.NextDeleted;

                    // go to beginning of file
                    pos = lseek(DOSHandle,0,SEEK_SET);

                    if (pos == -1L)
```

```
                    throw DataFileEx(FEX_BAD_SEEK);

            // write new header
            n = write
                (
                DOSHandle,
                &Hdr,
                sizeof(DataFileHdr)
                );

            if (n != sizeof(DataFileHdr))
                throw DataFileEx(FEX_NO_WRT_FHDR);
            }
        else
            {
            // adjust chain by putting next in prev
            pos = lseek(DOSHandle,prev,SEEK_SET);

            if (pos == -1L)
                throw DataFileEx(FEX_BAD_SEEK);

            // read previous record's header
            IORecordHeader prevhdr;

            n = read
                (
                DOSHandle,
                &prevhdr,
                sizeof(IORecordHeader)
                );

            if (n != sizeof(IORecordHeader))
                throw DataFileEx(FEX_NO_RD_RHDR);

            // change next deleted reference
            prevhdr.NextDeleted = rechdr.NextDeleted;

            // rewrite prev. header
            pos = lseek(DOSHandle,prev,SEEK_SET);

            if (pos == -1L)
                throw DataFileEx(FEX_BAD_SEEK);

            // read previous record's header
```

```
                    n = write
                        (
                        DOSHandle,
                        &prevhdr,
                        sizeof(IORecordHeader)
                        );

                if (n != sizeof(IORecordHeader))
                    throw DataFileEx(FEX_NO_WRT_RHDR);
                }

            // set pointer to beginning of ptr record
            pos = lseek(DOSHandle,ptr,SEEK_SET);

            if (pos == -1L)
                throw DataFileEx(FEX_BAD_SEEK);

            break;
            }

        // save pointer
        prev = ptr;

        if (rechdr.NextDeleted == DFP_NULL)
            {
            // append new data to end of file
            pos = lseek(DOSHandle,0,SEEK_END);

            if (pos == -1L)
                throw DataFileEx(FEX_BAD_SEEK);

            ptr = tell(DOSHandle);

            rechdr.Size = db.GetSize();

            break;
            }
        else
            ptr  = rechdr.NextDeleted;
        }
    }

rechdr.RecSig     = db.GetSig();
rechdr.RecSize    = db.GetSize();
```

```
        rechdr.NextDeleted = DFP_NULL;

        // store signature
        n = write(DOSHandle,&rechdr,sizeof(IORecordHeader));

        if (n != sizeof(IORecordHeader))
            throw DataFileEx(FEX_NO_WRT_RHDR);

        // store data
        n = write(DOSHandle,(void *)db,rechdr.RecSize);

     if (n != rechdr.RecSize)
            throw DataFileEx(FEX_NO_WRT_REC);

        // return location data was written to
        return ptr;
        }
```

If Write finds a deleted record in which the new record can be written, it removes that record from the deleted list and writes the new record. If Write can't fit the new record into a deleted slot, it appends the new record to the end of the file.

Reading records is much simpler than writing them. Read assumes that the current file pointer is positioned at the beginning of a record:

```
template <class D>
    D DataFile<D>::Read() const
        {
        size_t n;
        long   pos;
        IORecordHeader rechdr;

        while (1)
            {
            // read record header
            n = read(DOSHandle,&rechdr,sizeof(IORecordHeader));

            if (n == 0) // eof
                throw DataFileEx(FEX_EOF);

            if (n != sizeof(IORecordHeader))
                throw DataFileEx(FEX_NO_RD_RHDR);
```

```
            // we've found an in-use record
            if (rechdr.RecSig != SIG_DELETED)
                break;

            // skip to next record
            pos = lseek(DOSHandle,rechdr.Size,SEEK_CUR);

            if (pos == -1L)
                throw DataFileEx(FEX_BAD_SEEK);
            }

    // allocate buffer to hold data
    DataBlock db(rechdr.RecSig, rechdr.RecSize);

    if (!db.IsNull())
        {
        // read data
        n = read(DOSHandle,(void *)db,rechdr.RecSize);

        if (n != rechdr.RecSize)
            throw DataFileEx(FEX_NO_RD_REC);

        // skip over any "waste" characters
        if (rechdr.RecSize < rechdr.Size)
            {
            pos = lseek(DOSHandle,
                        rechdr.Size - rechdr.RecSize,
                        SEEK_CUR);

            if (pos == -1L)
                throw DataFileEx(FEX_BAD_SEEK);
            }
        }

    D result;
    result <<= db;

    // outta here
    return result;
    }
```

If the record is marked as deleted (by having a Signature of SIG_DELETED), Read skips to the next record. If Read encounters the end of the file or if an error occurs, Read returns DFP_ERROR.

Like `Read`, the `Delete` function assumes that the current file pointer is located at the beginning of a record. `Delete` marks a record as deleted and adds the record's file pointer to the deleted list. `Delete` returns BOOL_TRUE if a record was deleted, and BOOL_FALSE if an error occurred.

```
template <class D>
    void DataFile<D>::Delete()
        {
        size_t n;
        long   pos;
        IORecordHeader rechdr;

        // save this position
        DataFilePtr curptr = tell(DOSHandle);

        // make sure we're not in the header
        if (curptr < sizeof(DataFileHdr))
            throw DataFileEx(FEX_BAD_SEEK);

        // read header
        n = read(DOSHandle,&rechdr,sizeof(IORecordHeader));

        if (n != sizeof(IORecordHeader))
            throw DataFileEx(FEX_NO_RD_RHDR);

        // mark as deleted
        if (rechdr.RecSig != SIG_DELETED)
            {
            // update record header
            rechdr.RecSig      = SIG_DELETED;
            rechdr.NextDeleted = Hdr.FirstEmpty;

            // write record header
            pos = lseek(DOSHandle,curptr,SEEK_SET);

            if (pos == -1L)
                throw DataFileEx(FEX_BAD_SEEK);

            n = write(DOSHandle,&rechdr,sizeof(IORecordHeader));

            if (n != sizeof(IORecordHeader))
                throw DataFileEx(FEX_NO_WRT_RHDR);
```

```
        // modify header
        Hdr.FirstEmpty = curptr;

        pos = lseek(DOSHandle,0,SEEK_SET);

        if (pos == -1L)
            throw DataFileEx(FEX_BAD_SEEK);

        n = write(DOSHandle,&Hdr,sizeof(DataFileHdr));

        if (n != sizeof(DataFileHdr))
            throw DataFileEx(FEX_NO_WRT_FHDR);
        }

    // move back to start of deleted record
    pos = lseek(DOSHandle,curptr,SEEK_SET);

    if (pos == -1L)
        throw DataFileEx(FEX_BAD_SEEK);
    }
```

The `FirstEmpty` member of the `DataFile` header contains the file pointer of the first record in the deleted list. When `Delete` "deletes" a record, it sets the record's `Signature` to `SIG_DELETED`, stores the current value of `Hdr.FirstEmpty` in `NextDeleted`, and sets `Hdr.FirstEmpty` to the file pointer of the record. Thus, as records are deleted they are added to the beginning of the deleted list.

Moving Around the File

The current file pointer is used by the `Read` and `Delete` functions. The `Seek` function sets the current file pointer.

```
template <class D>
    DataFilePtr DataFile<D>::Seek
        (
        DataFilePtr pos
        ) const
```

```
    {
    // make sure position is outside of header
    if (pos < sizeof(DataFileHdr))
        throw DataFileEx(FEX_BAD_SEEK);

    // get current position
    DataFilePtr ptr = tell(DOSHandle);

    // move to new position
    long n = lseek(DOSHandle,pos,SEEK_SET);

    // check for error
    if (n == -1L)
        throw DataFileEx(FEX_BAD_SEEK);

    // done
    return ptr;
    }
```

A program can obtain the current file pointer using the inline CurrentPtr function:

```
template <class D>
    DataFilePtr DataFile<D>::CurrentPtr() const
        {
        return tell(DOSHandle);
        }
```

The Rewind function sets the current file pointer to the beginning of the first record in the file—basically, at the byte directly after the header record:

```
template <class D>
    void DataFile<D>::Rewind()
        {
        long pos = lseek(DOSHandle,sizeof(DataFileHdr),SEEK_SET);

        if (pos == -1L)
            throw DataFileEx(FEX_NO_REWIND);
        }
```

The current file pointer is moved to the beginning of the next record by the Skip function:

```
template <class D>
    bool DataFile<D>::Skip()
        {
        IORecordHeader rechdr;
        long pos;
        size_t n;

        // read record header
        n = read(DOSHandle,&rechdr,sizeof(IORecordHeader));

        if (n == 0)
            return false;

        if (n != sizeof(IORecordHeader))
            throw DataFileEx(FEX_NO_RD_RHDR);

        // skip data
        pos = lseek(DOSHandle,rechdr.Size,SEEK_CUR);

        if (pos == -1L)
            throw DataFileEx(FEX_BAD_SEEK);

        return true;
        }
```

Earlier, I discussed wasted space caused by the deletion and insertion of variable-length records. An active file, in which deletions and insertions are common, will develop significant amounts of wasted space. The Compact function can be used to eliminate dead space in a DataFile:

```
template <class D>
    // remove blanks and wasted space
    void DataFile<D>::Compact
        (
        void (* func)(DataFilePtr ptr, const D & data)
        )
        {
        // generate temporary file name
        char tname[32];
```

```
sprintf(tname,"%lx.TMP",time(NULL));

// open temporary file
int newfile = open(tname,O_BINARY | O_CREAT | O_RDWR,
                         S_IREAD | S_IWRITE);

if (newfile == -1)
    throw DataFileEx(FEX_NO_OPEN_TEMP);

// read and copy header
long pos;
size_t n;

pos = lseek(DOSHandle,0,SEEK_SET);

if (pos == -1L)
    throw DataFileEx(FEX_BAD_SEEK);

n = read(DOSHandle,&Hdr,sizeof(DataFileHdr));

if (n != sizeof(DataFileHdr))
    throw DataFileEx(FEX_NO_RD_FHDR);

n = write(newfile,&Hdr,sizeof(DataFileHdr));

if (n != sizeof(DataFileHdr))
    throw DataFileEx(FEX_NO_WRT_FHDR);


IORecordHeader rechdr;
DataFilePtr ptr;
char * buf;

// read each record
for (;;)
    {
    // read record header
    n = read(DOSHandle,&rechdr,sizeof(IORecordHeader));

    if (n == 0) break;

    if (n != sizeof(IORecordHeader))
        throw DataFileEx(FEX_NO_RD_RHDR);
```

```
        if (rechdr.RecSig == SIG_DELETED)
            {
            // skip deleted records
            pos = lseek(DOSHandle,rechdr.Size,SEEK_CUR);

            if (pos == -1L)
                throw DataFileEx(FEX_BAD_SEEK);
            }
        else
            {
            // allocate buffer to hold data
            buf = new char[rechdr.Size];

            if (buf == NULL)
                throw DataFileEx(FEX_ALLOC);

            // read data
            n = read(DOSHandle,buf,rechdr.Size);

            if (n != rechdr.Size)
                throw DataFileEx(FEX_NO_RD_REC);

            // get output position in new file
            ptr = tell(newfile);

            // write header to new file
            rechdr.Size = rechdr.RecSize;

            n = write(newfile,&rechdr,
                    sizeof(IORecordHeader));

            if (n != sizeof(IORecordHeader))
                throw DataFileEx(FEX_NO_WRT_RHDR);

            // write data to new file
            n = write(newfile,buf,rechdr.Size);

            if (n != rechdr.Size)
                throw DataFileEx(FEX_NO_WRT_REC);

            // call function
            if (func != NULL)
                {
                DataBlock db(rechdr.RecSig,
```

```
                                rechdr.RecSize,buf);
            D data;
            data <<= db;
            func(ptr,data);
            }

        // delete buffer
        delete buf;
        }
    }


// close files
close(newfile);
close(DOSHandle);


// delete old file
if (-1 == remove(FileName))
    throw DataFileEx(FEX_NO_REMOVE);


// rename new file
if (-1 == rename(tname,FileName))
    throw DataFileEx(FEX_NO_RENAME);


// open newly-compacted file
DOSHandle = open(FileName,DOSMode);

if (DOSHandle == -1)
    throw DataFileEx(FEX_NO_OPEN);


// read file header
n = read(DOSHandle,&Hdr,sizeof(DataFileHdr));

if (n != sizeof(DataFileHdr))
    throw DataFileEx(FEX_NO_RD_FHDR);
}
```

Compact begins by calling Commit to ensure that all data have been written to external storage. Then compact generates a temporary file name based on the system time. I don't use the ANSI C tmpnam function, because its file names are not guaranteed to be unique in a multiuser environment. Time-stamped temporary files prevent multiple files from being created with the same name.

The temporary file is opened, and a header record containing a FirstEmpty value of DFP_NULL is created. The DataFile's current pointer is then set to its first record. Records are sequentially read from the DataFile; records that are not marked as deleted are written to the temporary file. For each record written, the function designated by the func parameter is called with the DataBlock and new file pointer. If func is NULL, no call is made. The function type of func is defined by DFCompFunc:

```
typedef void (* DFCompFunc)(DataFilePtr ptr,
                            const DataBlock & db);
```

Once all the records have been written to the temporary file, the old DataFile is closed and deleted. The temporary file is then renamed and is opened as the DataFile.

A Random Access Example

The following function can be plugged into the earlier test program to exercise the DataFile<T> class:

```
void TestDataFile2()
    {
    cout << "\n————"
         << "\nDataFile Test #2"
         << "\n————"
         << endl;

    const char * fn = "tsio2.dat";

    size_t n;

    //————————————————————
    cout << "\nCreating file object\n";

    DataFile<Object> * file = new DataFile<Object>(fn,FM_NEW);

    if (file == NULL)
        {
        cout << fn << "\acould not be opened!\n";
```

```
        exit(EXIT_FAILURE);
        }


DataFilePtr ptr, ptr6, ptr19;

for (n = 0; n < ObjCount; ++n)
    {
    ptr = file->Write(TestData[n]);

    cout << "Writing record #" << n << " : "
         << TestData[n].Name << " @ "
         << TestData[n].City << endl;

    switch (n)
        {
        case 6:
            ptr6 = ptr;
            break;

        case 19:
            ptr19 = ptr;
        }
    }

delete file;


//————————————————————————————
file = new DataFile<Object>(fn, FM_EXISTING);

if (file == NULL)
    {
    cout << fn << "\acould not be reopened!\n";
    exit(EXIT_FAILURE);
    }

Object dataIn;

file->Seek(ptr19);
file->Delete();
file->Seek(ptr6);
file->Delete();
file->Write(TestData[15]);
file->Write(TestData[4]);
file->Rewind();
```

```
    n = 0;

    try
        {
        while (1)
            {
            dataIn = file->Read();

            cout << "Reading record #" << n << " : "
                << dataIn.Name << " @ " << dataIn.City << endl;

            ++n;
            }
        }

    catch (DataFileEx & ex)
        {
        if (ex.WhatsWrong() == FE_EOF)
            cout << "END OF FILE!" << endl;
        else
            throw;
        }

    file->Compact();

    delete file;
    }
```

You'll note that I've developed a technique for handling an end-of-file condition. In general, end-of-file isn't an error, but it is an event that occurs without warning. I embed my calls to Read inside try blocks, with an associated catch (DataFileEx & ex) block that handles FEX_EOF exceptions separately from other errors. The preceding example function shows two different ways of catching the FEX_EOF exception in a loop.

All the data file classes can be found in the files **DataFile.h** and **DataFile.cpp,** located on the accompanying source file diskette.

ONWARD

We need a way to retrieve information from storage by some sort of identifier or key. One of the fastest and simplest indexing tools is the hash table, the subject of the next chapter.

CHAPTER 12

HASH TABLES

Although sequential data storage is useful for many applications, many programs need the ability to store and retrieve data based on a key value. A key identifies a specific piece of data. For example, in an application that handles personnel data it would be useful to be able to access a specific record by the person's name. The name is a key by which personnel records are found.

Computer scientists have invented techniques for associating keys and data. In this book, I'll cover two techniques for handling keyed data: hash tables and trees. I'll begin with hash tables.

HASHING BASICS

A *hash table* contains a fixed number of *buckets*. A bucket contains data associated with a key, or it is empty. To find the data for a key, a bucket number is calculated from the key value by a *hash function*. The hash function always generates the same bucket number for a given key, so that a key always retrieves the same data from the same bucket.

HASH FUNCTIONS

To see how this works, let's examine simple hash tables. A 26-bucket hash table could contain data associated with each letter of the alphabet, using the ordinal value of the letter as a bucket index. The hash function would look like this:

```
int Hash(char ch)
    {
    // return ordinal value of character relative to 'A'
    return (int)ch - 'A';
    }
```

Single letters make simple keys, but they aren't very useful in identifying most real-world information. In many financial applications, information is identified by a number, such as an account number, Social Security number, or ZIP code.

It isn't practical to define a hash table for five-digit ZIP codes where there is a bucket for each code; such a table would have hundreds of thousands of entries! A table with 256 buckets would be manageable; in that case, a ZIP could be converted to a bucket number with a hash function such as this one:

```
int Hash(unsigned long ZIP)
    {
    return (int)(ZIP & 0xFF); // return lowest 8 bits of ZIP
    }
```

Using this function, a ZIP of 80901 (Colorado Springs) would "hash" to bucket number 5. The ZIP 80901 in hexadecimal is 13C05, and the Hash function returns the lowest eight bits, or 05. A ZIP of 10019 (in Manhattan) would Hash to bucket 194.

Collisions and Duplicates

When the number of buckets is smaller than the number of possible keys, two or more keys may hash to the same bucket value. This is known as a *collision*. For example, the ZIP codes 21509 and 80901 hash to the number 5 bucket. When this happens, two choices present themselves: expanding buckets to hold more than one entry or disallowing multiple bucket entries.

Disallowing multiple bucket entries is not a good solution, because it would force us to make very large hash tables to avoid collisions. In most cases, collisions are best handled by allowing each bucket to hold a list of entries that hashed to that location.

The best solution is for each bucket to contain a simple linked list of entries; empty buckets have an empty list, and new entries are appended to the end of the list for their bucket. A simple linear search of the list will find specific keys.

Hash Algorithms

A good hash algorithm distributes data evenly among the buckets, a technique that avoids collisions and limits the number of entries per bucket. The effectiveness of a hash algorithm is affected by the nature of data used as key values. For example, if all your numbers end in the same set of digits or if the data are restricted to a specific range, that hash algorithm must take that into account when distributing keys among buckets.

Where keys are evenly distributed numeric values, the best hashing algorithm is one of the simplest:

```
int Hash(unsigned long ZIP, int buckets)
    {
```

```
    return (int)(ZIP % buckets);
    }
```

The modulus operator returns the remainder of dividing one number by another. In the preceding function, the remainder of dividing the ZIP by the number of buckets generates an index of between 0 and `buckets - 1`. Choosing the number of buckets is important; by the nature of math, a prime number distributes remainders more uniformly than nonprimes do. The number of buckets should be chosen to fit the number of keys stored in the table. Eleven buckets would be too few for a table containing 10,000 keys, because the linked lists would grow very long. In general, use this rough formula to get a feel for the number of buckets you want:

$$buckets = \frac{\textit{\# of keys}}{\textit{desired length of linked lists}}$$

Much of the data manipulated by programs are identified by a string. Fortunately, C++, like C, treats characters as numeric values. Thus, the previous hashing algorithm could be modified to handle strings in a variety of ways:

```
int Hash(const char * key, int buckets)
    {
    unsigned long n = 0;

    for (char * ptr = key; *ptr; ++ptr)
        {
        n <<= 1;
        n += *ptr;
        }

    return (int)(n % buckets);
    }
```

This function sums the characters in the string, shifting itself left one bit before each character is added. The left shift helps distribute keys evenly by lessening the impact of common character sequences.

CLASSES FOR HASH TABLES

These are the components of a hash table:

- A hash table contains a list of buckets.
- A hash function calculates the bucket for data based on a key.
- The hash function should be unique for each type of data.
- Each bucket contains zero or more key/data entries, stored in a linked list.

At this point, I decided to implement my hash table class hierarchy with these core classes:

- `HashEntry`: A template class defining the common features of entries in a bucket's linked list. Each type of entry will contain a key, which can be compared to keys from other similar entries.

- `HashBucket`: A template class defining the bucket type. Each bucket contains a linked list of `HashEntry` pointers. New entries can be added by key, existing entries can be deleted by key, and searches can be performed for specific key values.

- `HashTable`: A template class defining the common characteristics of all hash tables. The hash table contains an array of `HashBuckets`, into which entries are stored. New entries can be added by key, existing entries can be deleted by key, and searches can be performed for specific key values.

HASH TABLE CLASSES

The following class and enumerated type define exceptions thrown by the hash table classes:

```
enum HashError
    {
    HEX_ALLOC,      // fatal:   memory allocation failure
    HEX_ZEROSIZE,   // fatal:   created bucket w/ zero buckets
    HEX_CORRUPTED,  // fatal:   table / list has been corrupted
    HEX_BADTYPES,   // fatal:   mismatched data types
    HEX_TOOSMALL,   // warning: about very small table sizes
    HEX_DUPEKEY,    // warning: about duplicate keys
    HEX_NOTFOUND       // warning: key not found
    };

class HashEx : public ExceptionBase
    {
    public:
        HashEx(HashError err) { Error = err; }
        HashError WhatsWrong() { return Error; }
        void Explain(DiagOutput & out);
    private:
        HashError Error;
    };
void HashEx::Explain(DiagOutput & out)
    {
    switch (Error)
        {
        case HEX_ALLOC:
            out.DisplayMsg
                (
                "memory allocation failure",
                DIAG_ERROR
                );
            break;
        case HEX_ZEROSIZE:
            out.DisplayMsg
                (
                "cannot create zero-size hash table",
                DIAG_ERROR
                );
            break;
        case HEX_CORRUPTED:
            out.DisplayMsg
                (
                "hash table corrupted",
                DIAG_ERROR
                );
            break;
        case HEX_BADTYPES:
            out.DisplayMsg
```

```
                (
                "mismatched types in hash table",
                DIAG_ERROR
                );
            break;
        case HEX_TOOSMALL:
            out.DisplayMsg
                (
                "# of hash buckets is very small",
                DIAG_WARNING
                );
            break;
        case HEX_DUPEKEY:
            out.DisplayMsg
                (
                "duplicate hash key",
                DIAG_WARNING
                );
            break;
        case HEX_NOTFOUND:
            out.DisplayMsg
                (
                "hash record not found",
                DIAG_WARNING
                );
            break;
        default:
            out.DisplayMsg
                (
                "unexpected hash file exception",
                DIAG_FATAL
                );
        }
    }
```

HashEntry

Buckets contain entries stored as a linked list, and each node in the
linked list is a HashEntry structure:

```
template
    <
    class K,
```

```
class D
>
struct HashEntry
    {
    // constructors
    HashEntry();

    HashEntry
        (
        const K & kx,
        const D & dx
        );

    // copy constructor
    HashEntry
        (
        const HashEntry<K,D> & he
        );

    // assignment
    HashEntry<K,D> & operator =
        (
        const HashEntry<K,D> & he
        );

    // comparison functions
    int operator ==
        (
        const HashEntry<K,D> & he
        );

    int operator !=
        (
        const HashEntry<K,D> & he
        );

    // data
    HashEntry<K,D> * Prev;
    HashEntry<K,D> * Next;
    K Key;
    D Data;
    };
```

Why is HashEntry a struct instead of a class? Each HashBucket contains a
linked list of HashEntry objects; as a result, a HashBucket object needs easy

access to the Next and Prev members of a HashEntry. Providing member access functions in HashEntryBase would have complicated the class; making those members public simplifies the program. Note that the object-oriented principle of encapsulation should not be overused; access to structure members should be restricted only when there's a good reason for such protection. HashBucket encapsulates the HashEntry objects it creates; that HashEntry is a public structure does not allow anything outside of a HashBucket to change its component HashEntrys.

A HashEntry object contains two pointers that reference the previous and next entries in the list. I could have used a singly linked list, with each entry pointing only to the next entry in the list. Deleting an entry from the middle of a singly linked list, however, is more complicated that deleting an entry from a doubly linked list. So I opted to trade some data space for algorithmic simplicity. Also, I avoided using a generic, template-based list type (as implemented in Chapter 3), thereby increasing efficiency over a list specifically managed for the needs of a HashBucket.

The constructor is defined inline; it merely assigns NULL values to the Next and Prev pointers. Nearly all the structs in my program include default constructors that automatically initialize the members to a "null" state. It makes programming simpler, and prevents some common errors.

A default constructor creates an "empty" HashEntry used in some HashBucket algorithms. Note that this constructor assumes that the supplied K and D template types implement default constructors.

```
template <class K, class D>
    HashEntry<K,D>::HashEntry()
        {
        Prev = NULL;
        Next = NULL;
        }
```

The primary constructor creates a HashEntry from the supplied key and data objects, assigning NULL to both pointers. The HashBucket owning a HashEntry will set the pointers as needed.

```
template <class K, class D>
    HashEntry<K,D>::HashEntry
```

```
        (
        const K & kx,
        const D & dx
        )
        : Key(kx), Data(dx)
        {
        Prev = NULL;
        Next = NULL;
        }
```

The copy constructor and assignment operator perform a *shallow copy*, meaning that they do not create duplicates of the nodes pointed to by Prev and Next.

```
template <class K, class D>
    HashEntry<K,D>::HashEntry(const HashEntry<K,D> & he)
        : Key(he.Key), Data(he.Data)
        {
        Prev = NULL;
        Next = NULL;
        }


template <class K, class D>
    HashEntry<K,D> & HashEntry<K,D>::operator =
                             (const HashEntry<K,D> & he)
        {
        Prev = NULL;
        Next = NULL;
        Key  = he.Key;
        Data = he.Data;
        return *this;
        }
```

Comparing nodes makes some algorithms easier to implement, as you'll see later; therefore, I created == and != operators for HashEntry.

```
template <class K, class D>
    inline int HashEntry<K,D>::operator ==
                             (const HashEntry<K,D> & he)
        {
        return ((Key == he.Key) && (Data == he.Data));
        }
```

```
template <class K, class D>
    inline int HashEntry<K,D>::operator !=
                              (const HashEntry<K,D> & he)
        {
        return ((Key != he.Key) || (Data != he.Data));
        }
```

HashBucket

A HashBucket contains a list of dynamically allocated HashEntrys; the beginning of the list is pointed to by HashBucket's only data member, First. If First is NULL, the bucket is empty.

```
template <class K, class D>
    class HashBucket
        {
        public:
            // constructors
            HashBucket();

            HashBucket
                (
                const HashBucket<K,D> & hb
                );

            ~HashBucket();

            HashBucket & operator =
                (
                const HashBucket<K,D> & hb
                );

            void AddEntry
                (
                const K & kx, const D & dx
                );

            bool DelEntry
                (
                const K & kx
                );
```

```
        D FindEntry
            (
            const K & kx
            ) const;

        bool Traverse
            (
            bool (*func)(const K & kx, const D & dx)
            );

    protected:
        HashEntry<K,D> * First;

        void Copy(const HashBucket<K,D> & hb);

        void Kill();
    };
```

The constructor simply assigns NULL to First; thus, every new HashBucket is automatically empty:

```
!template <class K, class D>
    inline HashBucket<K,D>::HashBucket()
        {
        First = NULL;
        }
```

The destructor deletes all the entries in the list, if there are any. Once an entry's address has been added to a HashBucket, the HashBucket is responsible for deleting that entry from memory when that entry is no longer required:

```
template <class K, class D>
    inline HashBucket<K,D>::~HashBucket()
        {
        Kill();
        }
```

The Kill function iterates through the list, deleting all entries. It is used by the destructors and the assignment operator to free memory allocated to a HashBucket.

```
template <class K, class D>
    void HashBucket<K,D>::Kill()
        {
        if (First != NULL)
            {
            HashEntry<K,D> * work = First, * next;

            while (work != NULL)
                {
                next = work->Next;
                delete work;
                work = next;
                }

            First = NULL;
            }
        }
```

The Copy function is another utility that performs a deep copy of a linked list of HashEntrys from one HashBucket to another.

```
template <class K, class D>
    void HashBucket<K,D>::Copy(const HashBucket<K,D> & hb)
        {
        if (hb.First == NULL)
            First = NULL;
        else
            {
            First = new HashEntry<K,D>(*(hb.First));

            HashEntry<K,D> * work = First;
            HashEntry<K,D> * src  = hb.First;
            HashEntry<K,D> * last = NULL;

            for (;;)
                {
                if (work == NULL)
                    throw HashEx(HE_ALLOC);

                if (last != NULL)
                    {
                    work->Prev = last;
                    last->Next = work;
                    }
```

```
                    if (src->Next == NULL)
                        break;

                    last = work;
                    src  = src->Next;

                    work = new HashEntry<K,D>(*src);
                    }
                }
            }
```

Combined, the `Kill` and `Copy` functions create the assignment operator:

```
template <class K, class D>
    inline HashBucket<K,D>::HashBucket
        (
        const HashBucket<K,D> & hb
        )
        {
        Copy(hb);
        }


template <class K, class D>
    inline HashBucket<K,D> & HashBucket<K,D>::operator =
        (
        const HashBucket<K,D> & hb
        )
        {
        Kill();
        Copy(hb);
        return *this;
        }
```

The `AddEntry` function adds a `HashEntry` to a `HashBucket`'s list. If the list is empty (`First == NULL`), the entry becomes the head of the list. Otherwise, `AddEntry` appends the entry to the end of the list.

```
template <class K, class D>
    void HashBucket<K,D>::AddEntry
        (
        const K & kx,
        const D & dx
        )
```

```
    {
    HashEntry<K,D> * entry = new HashEntry<K,D>(kx,dx);

    if (First == NULL)
        First = entry;
    else
        {
        HashEntry<K,D> * work = First;

        while (work != NULL)
            {
            if (work->Key == kx)
                {
                delete entry;
                throw HashEx(HE_DUPEKEY);
                }

            if (work->Next == NULL)
                {
                work->Next = entry;
                entry->Prev = work;

                break;
                }

            work = work->Next;
            }
        }
    }
```

The `DelEntry` function deletes an entry from the list. It searches the list for an entry whose key equals the key in the entry given by the parameter `dele`. If the entry is not found or if `dele` is `NULL`, `DelEntry` returns `BOOL_FALSE`. Otherwise, it removes the entry from the linked list and returns `BOOL_TRUE`.

```
template <class K, class D>
    bool HashBucket<K,D>::DelEntry
        (
        const K & kx
        )
        {
        HashEntry<K,D> * work = First;
```

```
        while (work != NULL)
            {
            if (work->Key == kx)
                {
                if (work->Prev == NULL)
                    First = work->Next;
                else
                    work->Prev->Next = work->Next;

                if (work->Next != NULL)
                    work->Next->Prev = work->Prev;

                delete work;

                return true;
                }

            work = work->Next;
            }

        return false;
        }
```

FindEntry is almost identical to IsDupe. Whereas IsDupe returns a true or false value indicating whether a certain key was found among a bucket's entries, FindEntry returns a pointer to the entry in which the key was found. If the key was not found, FindEntry returns NULL.

```
template <class K, class D>
    D HashBucket<K,D>::FindEntry
        (
        const K & kx
        ) const
        {
        HashEntry<K,D> * work = First;

        while (work != NULL)
            {
            if (work->Key == kx)
                return work->Data;

            work = work->Next;
            }
```

```
throw HashEx(HEX_NOTFOUND);

#ifdef _MSC_VER
    // this stupid piece of code will NEVER
    // be executed - it's here to ensure
    // that "all control paths return a
    // value," avoiding error C2202
    return work->Data;
#endif
}
```

The Traverse function passes the address of every entry in a bucket to the function pointed to by func.

```
template <class K, class D>
    bool HashBucket<K,D>::Traverse
        (
        bool (*func)(const K & kx, const D & dx)
        )
        {
        HashEntry<K,D> * work = First;

        while (work != NULL)
            {
            if (!func(work->Key,work->Data))
                return false;

            work = work->Next;
            }

        return true;
        }
```

HashTableBase

The HashTable template class defines the characteristics and functionality of hash tables:

```
template <class K, class D>
    class HashTable
```

```
{
public:
    // constructors
    HashTable
        (
        size_t buckets
        );

    HashTable
        (
        const HashTable<K,D> & ht
        );

    // destructor
    ~HashTable();

    // assignment
    HashTable<K,D> & operator =
        (
        const HashTable<K,D> & ht
        );

    // insert new entry
    void Insert
        (
        const K & kx,
        const D & dx
        );

    // delete an entry by key
    bool Delete
        (
        const K & kx
        );

    // look up data by key
    D LookUp
        (
        const K & kx
        ) const;

    // traverse all entries
    bool Traverse
        (
```

```
        bool (*func)(const K & kx, const D & dx)
        );

protected:
    size_t NoOfBuckets;
    HashBucket<K,D> * Table;

    HashTable(); // only for use by derived classes!

    void Copy(const HashTable<K,D> & ht);

    void Kill();
};
```

A hash table has two data members: a number of buckets, and a dynamically allocated array of pointers to buckets. The constructor allocates Table to have NoOfBuckets elements. If the number of buckets is zero or very small, an error or warning is reported. An error is also reported if the Table cannot be allocated. If the Table was allocated, each element is assigned the address of a dynamically allocated HashBucket. The constructor for HashBucket will ensure that all buckets are empty when the Table is created.

```
template <class K, class D>
    HashTable<K,D>::HashTable
        (
        size_t buckets
        )
        {
        // verify number of buckets
        if (buckets < 9)
            throw HashEx(HEX_TOOSMALL);

// store number of buckets
        NoOfBuckets  = buckets;

// allocate Table
        Table = new HashBucket<K,D> [NoOfBuckets];

if (Table == NULL)
            throw HashEx(HEX_ALLOC);
        }
```

I also created a default constructor that creates an empty HashTable object. The purpose of this constructor will become clear in the next chapter, when I construct a HashTable object from data stored in an external file. Note that I defined this constructor as protected, meaning that it can be used only by derived classes.

```
template <class K, class D>
    HashTable<K,D>::HashTable() // only used by derived classes!
        {
        NoOfBuckets = 0;
        Table = NULL;
        }
```

The destructor's job is to delete the entries in Table before deleting Table iself. To do that, it uses the Kill utility function:

```
HashTableBase::~HashTableBase()
    {
    // delete buckets
    for (size_t b = 0; b < NoOfBuckets; ++b)
        delete Table[b];

    // delete table
    delete[] Table;
    }
```

Kill simply deletes the Table array:

```
template <class K, class D>
    inline void HashTable<K,D>::Kill()
        {
        delete [] Table;
        Table = NULL;
        }
```

The Copy utility function is the basis for the copy constructor and assignment operators:

```
template <class K, class D>
    void HashTable<K,D>::Copy
```

```
        (
        const HashTable<K,D> & ht
        )
        {
        NoOfBuckets = ht.NoOfBuckets;
        Table = new HashBucket<K,D> [NoOfBuckets];

        if (Table == NULL)
            throw HashEx(HEX_ALLOC);

        for (size_t i = 0; i < NoOfBuckets; ++i)
            Table[i] = ht.Table[i];
        }

template <class K, class D>
    inline HashTable<K,D>::HashTable
        (
        const HashTable<K,D> & ht
        )
        {
        Copy(ht);
        }

template <class K, class D>
    inline HashTable<K,D> & HashTable<K,D>::operator =
        (
        const HashTable<K,D> & ht
        )
        {
        Kill();
        Copy(ht);
        return *this;
        }
```

The functions that add, delete, and find entries follow a similar implementation pattern. Each calls a corresponding HashBucket function for an entry in the Table array.

```
template <class K, class D>
    void HashTable<K,D>::Insert(const K & kx, const D & dx)
        {
        Table[Hash(kx,NoOfBuckets)].AddEntry(kx,dx);
        }
```

```
template <class K, class D>
    Boolean HashTable<K,D>::Delete(const K & kx)
        {
        return Table[Hash(kx,NoOfBuckets)].DelEntry(kx);
        }

template <class K, class D>
    D HashTable<K,D>::LookUp(const K & kx) const
        {
        return Table[Hash(kx,NoOfBuckets)].FindEntry(kx);
        }
```

Note that these functions assume the existence of a "Hash" function for the key data type, K. To make this implementation as easy to use as possible, I've defined Hash functions for the common types used as keys:

```
inline size_t Hash(int x, size_t buckets)
    {
    return size_t(x % int(buckets));
    }

inline size_t Hash(unsigned int x, size_t buckets)
    {
    return size_t(x % (unsigned int)(buckets));
    }

inline size_t Hash(long x, size_t buckets)
    {
    return size_t(x % long(buckets));
    }

inline size_t Hash(unsigned long x, size_t buckets)
    {
    return size_t(x % (unsigned long)(buckets));
    }

size_t Hash(const char * x, size_t buckets)
    {
    // assume that character array is null terminated!
    unsigned long n = 0;
    const char * ch = x;

    while (*ch)
```

```
    {
    n <<= 1;
    n += size_t(*ch);
    ++ch;
    }


    return size_t(n % (unsigned long)buckets);
    }


inline size_t Hash(const String & x, size_t buckets)
    {
    return Hash((const char *)(x),buckets);
    }
```

The HashTable::Traverse function calls the HashBucket::Traverse function
for each element of Table.

```
template <class K, class D>
    bool HashTable<K,D>::Traverse
        (
        bool (*func)(const K & kx, const D & dx)
        )
        {
        for (size_t n = 0; n < NoOfBuckets; ++n)
            {
            if (false == Table[n].Traverse(func))
                return false;
            }

        return true;
        }
```

HASH TABLES IN ACTION

All this may seem complicated—and it is! I've developed a half-dozen
table libraries in my career, and the class hierarchy I've described works
wonderfully. By using templates, I have created a single hash table definition for any number of different combinations of keys and data. Here's
an example program to show how the HashTable classes work.

```
struct TestDatum1
    {
    String Name;
    String City;

    TestDatum1(const String & n, const String & c)
        : Name(n), City(c)
        { /* nada */ }
    };

struct TestDatum2
    {
    long Code;
    String Customer;
    };

DiagOutDOS dbgout(cerr);

int main()
    {
    try
        {
        TestHashTable1();
        TestHashTable2();
        }

    catch (ExceptionBase & ex)
        {
        ex.Explain(dbgout);
        }

    return 0;
    }

void TestHashTable1()
    {
    cout << "\n———————-\n"
        << "HashTable Function Test\n"
        << "———————-\n";

    const size_t listlen = 20;

    TestDatum1 keydata[listlen] =
        {
```

```
    {TestDatum1(String("Larry"),       String("Los Angeles"))},
    {TestDatum1(String("John"),        String("San Mateo"))},
    {TestDatum1(String("Cindy"),       String("Boston"))},
    {TestDatum1(String("Fred"),        String("Philadelphia"))},
    {TestDatum1(String("Lucy"),        String("Seattle"))},
    {TestDatum1(String("Jerry"),       String("Newark"))},
    {TestDatum1(String("Adam"),        String("Houston"))},
    {TestDatum1(String("Carmichael"),  String("Lincoln"))},
    {TestDatum1(String("Scott"),       String("Springs"))},
    {TestDatum1(String("Maria"),       String("Springs"))},
    {TestDatum1(String("Rebecca"),     String("Springs"))},
    {TestDatum1(String("Elora"),       String("Springs"))},
    {TestDatum1(String("Rudolph"),     String("North Pole"))},
    {TestDatum1(String("Robert"),      String("Somerset"))},
    {TestDatum1(String("Mary"),        String("Pheonix"))},
    {TestDatum1(String("Abercrombie"), String("Tuscon"))},
    {TestDatum1(String("Eve"),         String("Salt Lake"))},
    {TestDatum1(String("Theodore"),    String("Boise"))},
    {TestDatum1(String("Everett"),     String("Portland"))},
    {TestDatum1(String("Edwin"),       String("Cheyenne"))}
    };

HashTable<String,String> table(13);

//———————————————————
size_t n;

for (n = 0; n < listlen; ++n)
    table.Insert(keydata[n].Name,keydata[n].City);

table.Traverse(ShowThem1);

//———————————————————
String name1("Eve");
String res;

res = table.LookUp(name1);

cout << "Looked for " << name1 << " and FOUND "
    << res << endl;

//———————————————————
if (BOOL_FALSE == table.Delete(name1))
    {
```

```
        cout << "\aCOULD NOT DELETE " << name1 << endl;
        exit(EXIT_FAILURE);
        }

cout << "DELETED: " << name1 << endl;

table.Traverse(ShowThem1);

//————————————————————————————
String name2("Elora");
String name3("Robert");

try
    {
    res = table.LookUp(name1);
    }

catch (HashEx ex)
    {
    if (ex.WhatsWrong() == HE_NOTFOUND)
        cout << "As expected, didn't find " << name1 << endl;
    else
        throw;
    }

res = table.LookUp(name2);
cout << "Looked for " << name2 << " and FOUND "
     << res << endl;

res = table.LookUp(name3);
cout << "Looked for " << name3 << " and FOUND "
     << res << endl;

HashTable<String,String> table2(10), table3(table);

table2 = table;

cout << "All should be equal:" << endl;
table.Traverse(ShowThem1);
cout << endl;
table2.Traverse(ShowThem1);
cout << endl;
table3.Traverse(ShowThem1);
    }
```

```
Boolean ShowThem1(const String & key, const String & str)
    {
    cout << "key = " << key << "\tobj = " << str << endl;
    return BOOL_TRUE;
    }


void TestHashTable2()
    {
    cout << "\n--------------\n"
        << "HashTable Stress Test\n"
        << "--------------\n";

    RandGen gen;
    HashTable<unsigned int, unsigned int> table(101);

    const unsigned int  maxvalue = 1000U;
    const unsigned long testsize = 1000UL;
    unsigned long i;

    for (i = 0; i < testsize; ++i)
        {
        unsigned int n;
        unsigned int p;
        Boolean found;

        n = gen(maxvalue);

        switch (gen(3))
            {
            case 0:
                found = BOOL_TRUE;

                cout << "Lookup: " << n;

                try
                    {
                    p = table.LookUp(n);
                    }

                catch (HashEx & ex)
                    {
                    if (ex.WhatsWrong() == HE_NOTFOUND)
                        {
                        cout << "   (NOT FOUND)" << endl;
```

```
                            found = BOOL_FALSE;
                            }
                    else
                        throw;
                    }

                if (found)
                    cout << "   (" << p << ")" << endl;

                break;
            case 1:
                cout << "Adding: " << n;

                try     {
                    table.Insert(n,n);
                    }

                catch (HashEx & ex)
                    {
                    if (ex.WhatsWrong() == HE_DUPEKEY)
                        cout << "   (DUPE KEY!)";
                    else
                        throw;
                    }

                cout << endl;

                break;
            case 2:
                cout << "Delete: " << n;

                if (table.Delete(n))
                    cout << "   OKAY" << endl;
                else
                    cout << "   FAILED" << endl;
            }
        }

    table.Traverse(ShowThem2);
    }

Boolean ShowThem2(const unsigned int & key,
                  const unsigned int & str)
    {
```

```
cout << "key = " << key << "\tobj = " << str << endl;
return BOOL_TRUE;
}
```

As you can see, the preceding program creates two completely different types of HashTable: one using String keys and objects, and the other using unsigned ints for both data and keys. The StressTest function puts the HashTable through several thousand randomly selected operations, testing the stability of the HashTable classes.

ONWARD

These hash tables have served me well in several applications, but they have the limitation of being memory-resident. As I mentioned in the first part of this chapter, many applications require data to be retrieved from data files based on a key. To do that, I derived a HashTable class that can be stored in a file, and that is the topic of the next chapter.

CHAPTER 13

FILE INDEXING: HASH TABLES

A random access file is most useful when it is used in conjunction with an index that keeps track of which records reside at specific file pointers. An index based on a hash table is an excellent tool for manipulating a database of information, because it allows quick access to records through a key.

In designing my `HashFile` class, I decided that a `HashFile` would be both a `HashTable` and a `DataFile`. I could just as easily have created a `HashFile` class that included `HashTable` and `DataFile` objects; as I've said before, these design decisions are largely a matter of personal taste.

EXCEPTIONS

To handle exceptions for hash files, I paired an enumerated type with a class derived from `ExceptionBase`:

```
enum HashFileError
    {
    HFEX_ENT_ALLOC,
    HFEX_BKT_ALLOC,
    HFEX_INV_HFILE
    };
```

```
class HashFileEx : public ExceptionBase
    {
    public:
        HashFileEx
            (
            HashFileError err
            )
            {
            Error = err;
            }

        HashFileError WhatsWrong()
            {
            return Error;
            }

        void Explain(DiagOutput & out);

    private:
        HashFileError Error;
    };

void HashFileEx::Explain(DiagOutput & out)
    {
    switch(Error)
        {
        case HFEX_ENT_ALLOC:
            out.DisplayMsg
                (
                "can't allocate memory for HashFileEntry",
                DIAG_ERROR
                );
            break;
        case HFEX_BKT_ALLOC:
            out.DisplayMsg
                (
                "can't allocate memory for HashFileBucket",
                DIAG_ERROR
                );
            break;
        case HFEX_INV_HFILE:
            out.DisplayMsg
                (
                "attempt to use invalid hash index file",
                DIAG_ERROR
```

```
                );
            break;
        default:
            out.DisplayMsg
                (
                "unexpected hash file exception",
                DIAG_FATAL
                );
        }
    }
```

HashFileBucket Class

A HashFileBucket is a HashBucket that knows how to store and retrieve
entries from a file:

```
template <class K>
    class HashFileBucket : public HashBucket<K,DataFilePtr>
        {
        public:
            HashFileBucket();

            HashFileBucket
                (
                const HashFileBucket<K> & hb
                );

            HashFileBucket
                (
                const HashBucket<K,DataFilePtr> & hb
                );

            void operator =
                (
                const HashFileBucket<K> & hb
                );

            void Write
                (
                DataFileOutput<DataBlock> & file
                );
```

```
        void Read
            (
            DataFileInput<DataBlock> & file
            );
    };
```

This template class is unusual in that it is derived from another template for which a constant template argument is provided. HashFileBuckets can use any type of key, but the data stored will always be a DataFilePtr, which points to the location of the key's associated data in a DataFile.

The HFTSig Signature identifies a hashbucket stored in a file:

```
const Signature HFTSig = 0xFF746668; // 'hft'
```

The constructors and assignment operator act as shells around inherited base class functions:

```
template <class K>
    inline HashFileBucket<K>::HashFileBucket()
        : HashBucket<K,DataFilePtr>()
        {  }

template <class K>
    inline HashFileBucket<K>::HashFileBucket
        (
        const HashFileBucket<K> & hb
        )
        : HashBucket<K,DataFilePtr>(hb)
        {  }

template <class K>
    inline HashFileBucket<K>::HashFileBucket
        (
        const HashBucket<K,DataFilePtr> & hb
        )
        : HashBucket<K,DataFilePtr>(hb)
        {  }

template <class K>
    inline void HashFileBucket<K>::operator =
        (
```

```
const HashFileBucket<K> & hb
)
{
HashBucket<K,DataFilePtr>::operator = (hb);
}
```

The `Write` function sequentially writes a `HashFileBucket`'s entries to the file specified by the file parameter file. `Write` outputs a short header record, followed by the entries in sequential order; the list is terminated by a `NULL_BLOCK` DataBlock. For each entry, the `Key` is written, followed by the `DataFilePtr`; for the former, a set of `<<=` operators must be defined for conversions to and from `DataBlock`s, whereas the latter uses the unsigned `long` operations predefined in **persist.h**.

```
template <class K>
    void HashFileBucket<K>::Write
        (
        DataFileOutput<DataBlock> & file
        )
        {
        DataBlock db;
        HashEntry<K,DataFilePtr> * e = First;

        while (e != NULL)
            {
            db <<= e->Key;
            file.Write(db);

            db <<= e->Data;
            file.Write(db);

            e = (HashEntry<K,DataFilePtr> *)(e->Next);
            }

        file.Write(NULL_BLOCK);
        }
```

The `Read` function assumes that it can begin reading a list of entries—as formatted by `Write`—from the file specified by `Read`'s `DataFileInput` parameter.

```
template <class K>
    void HashFileBucket<K>::Read
        (
        DataFileInput<DataBlock> & file
        )
        {
        Kill();

        DataBlock db;
        HashEntry<K,DataFilePtr> * e;
        HashEntry<K,DataFilePtr> * prev = NULL;

        for (;;)
            {
            db = file.Read();

            if (db.IsNull()) break;

            e = new HashEntry<K,DataFilePtr>;

            if (e == NULL)
                throw HashEx(HEX_ALLOC);

            e->Key  <<= db;
            e->Data <<= file.Read();
            e->Prev  = prev;

            if (prev != NULL)
                prev->Next = e;
            else
                First = e;

            prev = e;
            }
        }
```

When a `HashFile` is created, empty hash file is constructed. If an existing `HashFile` is opened, the hash table is read from a `DataFileInput`. During the processing of a `HashFile`, the hash table is kept entirely in memory. When the `HashFile` object is destroyed, the buckets are written to a `DataFileOutput`. The actual data records are stored in a separate file.

By keeping the hash table resident in memory, we improve program performance. A `HashFile` does not need to perform any disk reads when looking up a key in the hash table. However, there are two drawbacks to an in-memory hash table. First, the table uses memory; second, the hash table on disk may not be current if the program "crashes" and new records have been written to the data file.

The hash table does not use copious amounts of memory, and it should not significantly affect a program. You can solve the problem with mismatched data and hash files using some simple techniques shown later in the chapter.

HASHFILETABLE CLASS

The `HashTable` class defines a template for hash tables. The `HashFileTable` class provides a derivative of `HashTableBase` that works with any type of key and `DataFilePtr`s, and also has the capability of being written to a file:

```
template <class K>
    class HashFileTable : public HashTable<K,DataFilePtr>
        {
        public:
            // constructor
            HashFileTable
                (
                size_t buckets,
                const String & file
                );

            HashFileTable
                (
                const String & file
                );

            HashFileTable
                (
                const HashFileTable<K> & hft
                );
```

```
            HashFileTable
                (
                const HashTable<K,DataFilePtr> & hft
                );

            ~HashFileTable();

            void operator =
                (
                const HashFileTable<K> & hft
                );

            void Commit();

        protected:
            String FileName;
        };
```

The only data member, `FileName`, holds the name of the file in which this hash file is to be stored.

With one exception, constructors merely call base and member class functions:

```
template <class K>
    inline HashFileTable<K>::HashFileTable
        (
        size_t buckets,
        const String & file
        )
        : HashTable<K,DataFilePtr>(buckets),
          FileName(file)
        {
        // null
        }

template <class K>
    inline HashFileTable<K>::HashFileTable
        (
        const HashFileTable<K> & hft
        )
        : HashTable<K,DataFilePtr>(hft)
        {   }
```

```
template <class K>
    inline HashFileTable<K>::HashFileTable
        (
        const HashTable<K,DataFilePtr> & hft
        )
        : HashTable<K,DataFilePtr>(hft)
        {  }

 template <class K>
    inline void HashFileTable<K>::operator =
        (
        const HashFileTable<K> & hft
        )
        {
        HashTable<K,DataFilePtr>::operator = (hft);
        }
```

The constructor has work to do in opening an existing file on disk to read a hash table. The constructor creates a `DataFileInput` object and reads a header record containing the number of hash buckets to be read. The constructor also allocates the `Table` array and then calls `Read` for each of its elements.

```
template <class K>
    HashFileTable<K>::HashFileTable
        (
        const String & file
        )
        : FileName(file)
        {
        // open data file
        DataFileInput<DataBlock> input(FileName);

        // read header w/ # of buckets
        DataBlock db = input.Read();

        if ((HFTSig != db.GetSig())
        || (sizeof(size_t) != db.GetSize()))
            throw HashFileEx(HFEX_INV_HFILE);

        NoOfBuckets = *((size_t *)((void *)db));

        // allocate Table
```

```
Table = new HashFileBucket<K> [NoOfBuckets];

if (Table == NULL)
    throw HashEx(HEX_ALLOC);

HashFileBucket<K> *tptr = (HashFileBucket<K>*)Table;

// read buckets
for (size_t n = 0; n < NoOfBuckets; ++n)
    {
    tptr->Read(input);
    ++tptr;
    }
}
```

To insert, delete, or look up values in a HashFileTable, use the functions HashFileTable inherits from its HashTable base class. The only specific functions defined by HashFileTable are its destructor and the function Commit, which writes all the buckets into a file.

```
template <class K>
    inline HashFileTable<K>::~HashFileTable()
        {
        Commit();
        }

template <class K>
    void HashFileTable<K>::Commit()
        {
        if (Table != NULL)
            {
            // open data file
            DataFileOutput<DataBlock> output(FileName);

            // write header w/ # of buckets
            DataBlock hdr
                (
                HFTSig,
                sizeof(size_t),
                &NoOfBuckets
                );

            output.Write(hdr);
```

```
            // write buckets
            HashFileBucket<K> * bucket =
                            (HashFileBucket<K> *)Table;

            for (size_t n = 0; n < NoOfBuckets; ++n)
                {
                bucket->Write(output);
                ++bucket;
                }
            }
        }
```

Commit performs the reverse of the constructor by writing a header followed by a call to Write for each HashFileBucket in Table.

HASHFILE CLASS

Now we get to the goal of this entire discussion: the creation of a DataFile that is indexed by a HashTable. The HashFile class is derived from two base classes: DataFile and HashFileTable.

```
template <class K, class D>
    class HashFile : private HashFileTable<K>,
                     private DataFile<D>
        {
        public:
            // existing hash file
            HashFile
                (
                const String & basename
                );

            // new hash file
            HashFile
                (
                size_t buckets,
                const String & basename
                );

            // create hash index from existing DataFile
```

```
        HashFile
            (
            size_t buckets,
            const String & basename,
            const String & srcname,
            K (* getkey)(const D & data)
            );

        // copy constructor
        HashFile
            (
            const HashFile & hfile
            );

        // assignment operator
        HashFile & operator =
            (
            const HashFile & hfile
            );

        // write a record
        void Write
            (
            const K & key, const D & data
            );

        // read a record
        D Read
            (
            const K & key
            );

        // delete a record
        bool Delete
            (
            const K & key
            );

        // write all data to disk!
        void Commit();
    };
```

I wanted all access to a `HashFile` to occur through the functions it explicitly defines; therefore, I defined the base classes as `private`. Allowing a user to call the DataFile version of Write, for example, would result in a hash index that lacked a key for the stored information.

Base class and object member constructor calls occur between the time a constructor is called and the first executable line of constructor code. The only parameters that can be passed to base class constructors are the arguments passed to the constructor. This arrangement presents a difficult problem when the constructor parameters need processing before the base classes are initialized.

The file containing the hash index has a header record that contains the number of buckets in the hash table. This header record has a Signature value of HashHdrSig:

```
const Signature HFTSig = 0xFF746668; // 'hft'
```

The HashFile class defines three constructors. The first constructor creates a new HashFile with an empty DataFile and HashFileTable. The second constructor creates a HashFile that uses an existing hash table (in an external file) and DataFile. The third constructor builds a HashFile from an existing DataFile by building a new HashFileTable. All three constructors must call constructors to initialize the base class DataFile and TableFile objects. The three constructors also initialize the HashFileName data member.

The DataFile base class requires a file name, but the HashFile constructors are passed only the base file name sans extension. The actual DataFile name is constructed by appending DataFileExt to basename. Similarly, the HashFileName data member also needs to be initialized with a file name made from concatenating basename and HashFileExt.

HashFile objects generate two external files: one for the hash table and the other for data records. These two files have the same one-to eight-character file name but different extensions. The extensions for these files are defined by the HashFileExt and DataFileExt static class members:

```
const String HashFileExt(".HFH");
const String DataFileExt(".HFD");
```

The name of the file containing the hash index is generated when the `HashFile` object is created. I created a private utility function named `MakeFileName`, which returns the result of appending an extension to a base file name. I include an embedded call to `MakeFileName` when constructing the `DataFile` and `HashFileName` base class objects:

```
String MakeFileName
    (
    const String & basename,
    const String & ext
    )
    {
    String name;

    if (basename.Length() < 8)
        name = basename;
    else
        name = basename.CutHead(8);

    name += ext;

    return name;
    }
```

The first constructor has only two parameters: a number of buckets and the base file name. The constructor uses `MakeFileName` to create names for the `DataFile` and `HashFileName`, and creates an empty hash table by passing buckets to the `HashFileTable` constructor:

```
template <class K, class D>
    HashFile<K,D>::HashFile
        (
        const String & basename
        )
        : DataFile<D>
            (
            MakeFileName(basename,DataFileExt),
            FM_EXISTING
            ),
          HashFileTable<K>
            (
            MakeFileName(basename,HashFileExt)
```

```
        )
    {
    // empty
    }
```

Another constructor opens an existing `HashFile` and creates the internal hash file by reading data from the hash file stored in an external file:

```
template <class K, class D>
    HashFile<K,D>::HashFile
        (
        size_t buckets,
        const String & basename
        )
    : DataFile<D>
        (
        MakeFileName(basename,DataFileExt),
        FM_NEW
        ),
      HashFileTable<K>
        (
        buckets,
        MakeFileName(basename,HashFileExt)
        )
    {
    // empty
    }
```

The third constructor creates a `HashFile` from a `DataFile`. For each `data-block` in the `DataFile`, the constructor calls `getkey` to obtain a key value used to generate hash table entries. The `getkey` function returns a `K` object based on the data item for which it is called.

```
template <class K, class D>
    HashFile<K,D>::HashFile
        (
        size_t buckets,
        const String & basename,
        const String & srcname,
        K (* getkey)(const D & data)
        )
        : DataFile<D>
            (
```

```
            MakeFileName(basename,DataFileExt),
            FM_NEW
            ),
        HashFileTable<K>
            (
            buckets,
            MakeFileName(basename,HashFileExt)
            )
    {
    DataFile<D> input(srcname);

    D rec;
    bool reading = true;

    while (reading)
        {
        try {
            rec = input.Read();
            Write(getkey(rec),rec);
            }
        catch (DataFileEx & ex)
            {
            if (ex.WhatsWrong() == FEX_EOF)
                reading = false;
            else
                throw;
            }
        }

    Commit();
    }
```

If the external hash file ceases to match its associated data file (such as when a program crashes before the external hash file is generated), this constructor can be used to generate a new hash table.

The HashFile class doesn't define a destructor, but the destructors for DataFile and HashFileTable will be called automatically to close those files when a program destroys the HashFile object.

The Write function writes an object to disk via the DataFile base class, obtaining a record pointer that is stored in the hash table.

```
template <class K, class D>
    void HashFile<K,D>::Write
        (
        const K & key,
        const D & data
        )
        {
        // store data
        DataFilePtr ptr = DataFile<D>::Write(data);

        // add key and pointer to hash table
        HashFileTable<K>::Insert(key,ptr);
        }
```

The Read function looks up a key value in the hash table, receiving a file pointer that Read uses to retrieve a record from the DataFile:

```
template <class K, class D>
    D HashFile<K,D>::Read
        (
        const K & key
        )
        {
        // get pointer to record via key in hash table
        DataFilePtr ptr = HashFileTable<K>::LookUp(key);

        // set file pointer
        DataFile<D>::Seek(ptr);

        // read record at pointer
        return DataFile<D>::Read();
        }
```

Assuming that a record identified by key exists, the Delete function removes the key entry from the hash table and deletes the associated record from the DataFile:

```
template <class K, class D>
    bool HashFile<K,D>::Delete
        (
```

```
         const K & key
         )
         {
         // get pointer to record via key lookup in hash table
         DataFilePtr ptr;
         try {
             ptr = HashFileTable<K>::LookUp(key);
             }
         catch (HashEx & ex)
             {
             if (ex.WhatsWrong() == HEX_NOTFOUND)
                 return false;
             else
                 throw;
             }

         // set pointer to record
         DataFile<D>::Seek(ptr);

         // delete record
         DataFile<D>::Delete();

         // delete key from hash table
         HashFileTable<K>::Delete(key);

         // done
         return true;
         }
```

Because I define the base classes as `private`, I created a `HashFile::Commit` function that simply calls the `Commit` functions for both base classes:

```
template <class K, class D>
    inline void HashFile<K,D>::Commit()
        {
        HashFileTable<K>::Commit();
        DataFile<D>::Commit();
        }
```

USING HASHFILES

The following short program uses a `HashFile` to store and retrieve objects identified by a `key`.

```
struct HashObj
    {
    String Name;
    String City;

    HashObj(const char * n = NULL, const char * c = NULL)
        : Name(n), City(c)
        { /* nada */ }

    HashObj(const HashObj & obj)
        : Name(obj.Name), City(obj.City)
        { /* nada */ }

    void operator = (const HashObj & obj)
        {
        Name = obj.Name;
        City = obj.City;
        }

    static const Signature Sig;
    };

const Signature HashObj::Sig = 0x4444414C;

static void operator <<=
    (
    DataBlock & dest,
    const HashObj & src
    )
    {
    size_t sz = src.Name.Length() + src.City.Length() + 2;

    DataBlock db(HashObj::Sig,sz);

    char * blk = (char *)((void *)db);

    strcpy(blk,src.Name);
    strcpy(blk + src.Name.Length() + 1,src.City);

    dest = db;
    }

static void operator <<=
```

```
    (
    HashObj & dest,
    const DataBlock & src
    )
    {
    if (HashObj::Sig != src.GetSig())
        throw DataFileEx(FEX_BAD_SIG);

    const char * ptr = (const char *)((const void *)src);
    dest.Name = ptr;
    ptr += dest.Name.Length() + 1;
    dest.City = ptr;
    }

static String GetHashObjKey(const HashObj & rec)
    {
    return rec.Name;
    }


static const size_t KDlen = 20;

static HashObj KeyData[KDlen] =
    {
    {HashObj("Larry",    "Los Angeles")},
    {HashObj("John",     "San Mateo")},
    {HashObj("Cindy",    "Boston")},
    {HashObj("Fred",     "Philadelphia")},
    {HashObj("Lucy",     "Seattle")},
    {HashObj("Jerry",    "Newark")},
    {HashObj("Adam",     "Houston")},
    {HashObj("Carmen",   "San Diego")},
    {HashObj("Scott",    "Colorado Springs")},
    {HashObj("Maria",    "Colorado Springs")},
    {HashObj("Rebecca",  "Colorado Springs")},
    {HashObj("Elora",    "Colorado Springs")},
    {HashObj("Rudolph",  "North Pole")},
    {HashObj("Robert",   "Somerset")},
    {HashObj("Mary",     "Pheonix")},
    {HashObj("Albert",   "Tuscon")},
    {HashObj("Eve",      "Salt Lake City")},
    {HashObj("Theodore", "Boise")},
    {HashObj("Everett",  "Portland")},
    {HashObj("Edwin",    "Cheyenne")}
    };
```

```
static void DoHashFiles
    (
    strstream & buffer
    );

static DiagOutWin dbgout("Hash File Test");

void TestHashFiles
    (
    strstream & buffer
    )
    {
    try
        {
        DoHashFiles(buffer);
        }

    catch (ExceptionBase & ex)
        {
        ex.Explain(dbgout);
        }

    catch (...)
        {
        buffer << "What the hell was that?\r\n";
        }
    }

static void DoHashFiles
    (
    strstream & buffer
    )
    {
    buffer << "\r\nHashFile test"
           << "\r\n————\r\n";

    const String fn("hftest");
    size_t n;
    HashFile<String,HashObj> * file;
    HashObj rec;

    //————————————————
    file = new HashFile<String,HashObj>(23,fn);
```

```
if (file == NULL)
    {
    buffer << "alloc new file failed\r\n";
    return;
    }

buffer << "OPENED\r\n";

delete file;
buffer << "CLOSED\r\n";

//————————————————————
file = new HashFile<String,HashObj>(fn);

if (file == NULL)
    {
    buffer << "alloc new file failed\r\n";
    return;
    }

buffer << "OPENED\r\n";

for (n = 0; n < KDlen; ++n)
    {
    file->Write(KeyData[n].Name,KeyData[n]);

    buffer << "WRITTEN: " << KeyData[n].Name
              << " @ " << KeyData[n].City
                        << "\r\n";
    }

String key1("Edwin");
String key2("Mary");

file->Commit();

rec = file->Read(key1);
buffer << "FOUND: (" << rec.Name
    << "," << rec.City
    << ") with key " << key1 << "\r\n";

rec = file->Read(key2);
buffer << "FOUND: (" << rec.Name
```

```
        << "," << rec.City
        << ") with key " << key1 << "\r\n";

file->Delete(key1);
buffer << "DELETED: " << key1 << "\r\n";


file->Delete(key2);
buffer << "DELETED: " << key2 << "\r\n";


// new HashObjs
HashObj new1("Vincent", "New York City");
HashObj new2("Sandy",    "Pittsburg");


file->Write(new1.Name,new1);
file->Write(new2.Name,new2);


// close file
delete file;
buffer << "CLOSED\r\n";


//————————————————————————
// open file
file = new HashFile<String,HashObj>(fn);

if (file == NULL)
    {
    buffer << "alloc new file failed\r\n";
    return;
    }


buffer << "OPENED\r\n";


try    {
    rec = file->Read("Edwin");
    }
catch (HashEx & ex)
    {
    if (ex.WhatsWrong() == HEX_NOTFOUND)
        buffer << "CORRECT: Edwin has been deleted\r\n";
    else
        throw;
    }


file->Delete("Scott");
```

```
buffer << "DELETED: Scott\r\n";

delete file;
buffer << "CLOSED\r\n";


//————————————————

HashFile<String,HashObj> newfile
                        (
                         17,
                         "hftest2",
                         "hftest.hfd",
                         GetHashObjKey
                         );

if (file == NULL)
    {
    buffer << "alloc new file failed\r\n";
    return;
    }

for (n = 0; n < KDlen; ++n)
    {
    try {
        rec = newfile.Read(KeyData[n].Name);

        buffer << "FOUND: ("    << rec.Name
               << ","           << rec.City
               << ") with key " << KeyData[n].Name
               << "\r\n";
        }
    catch (HashEx & ex)
        {
        if (ex.WhatsWrong() == HEX_NOTFOUND)
            buffer << "Didn't find: "
                   << KeyData[n].Name
                   << "\r\n";
        else
            throw;
        }
    }
}
```

The `HashFile` classes are defined in the files **HashFile.h** and **HashFile.cpp**, located on the accompanying source diskette.

ONWARD

Hash-indexed files have their uses, but they don't allow data to be retrieved sequentially in a sorted order. A tree structure automatically sorts information by key. In the next chapter, I introduce tree structures; Chapter 15 shows how to attach tree structures to files.

CHAPTER 14

TREE STRUCTURES

Applications often require that data be accessed in a sequence, such as alphabetical order. A tree structure may be the perfect choice when your program must automatically store data in sorted order.

BINARY TREES

All trees consist of *nodes* that contain keys. Nodes have *links* to other nodes, and the type of tree being constructed defines the structure of the links between nodes. Links are one-way; they connect *parent* nodes to *child* nodes. All trees have a single *root* node, to which all other nodes are linked. Any node lacking links is known as a *leaf* node. These definitions will become clearer when you view the figures that follow.

A *binary tree* is the simplest type of tree structure. Each node in a binary tree contains a key and two links; one link connects to all nodes with lesser keys, and the other link connects to all nodes with greater keys. If there are no lesser or greater nodes, the link contains a sentinel value marking it as a *null link*.

Searching

I employ Figures in which nodes are boxes containing their key value. For simplicity, the examples use single-letter keys. Links are shown by lines connecting the lower-left and lower-right corners of a parent node to the center top of a child node. Lesser nodes are linked on the left, and greater nodes are linked on the right.

Figure 14.1 shows an example of a binary tree. K is the root of the tree, and it is the parent of G and M. Notice that a node can be both a parent and a child; G is a child of K and the parent of D and H. The nodes containing the A, E, H, N, and S keys are leaf nodes.

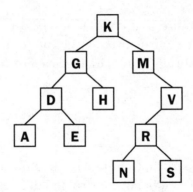

FIGURE 14.1 BINARY TREE

The algorithm for finding a key in a binary tree begins by comparing the search key to the key stored in the root node. If the keys don't match, the algorithm follows the links to other nodes in the tree based on the relationship between the search key and the keys in the nodes. For example, if the search key is less than the root key, we follow the left link to the next node; if the search key is greater than the root key, we follow the right link. The newly selected node is now treated just as the root was, by comparing the search key against the node key and selecting the next search node. If the link to be followed does not connect to a child node, the search key is not in the tree.

Figure 14.2 uses arrows to show the links followed in searching for the key E in the example binary tree. E is less than the root node key K, so we follow the left link. E is less than G, so again we follow the left link. E is greater than D, and we follow the right link to the node that contains E.

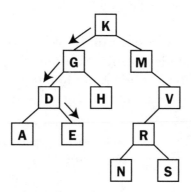

FIGURE 14.2 SEARCHING FOR E IN A BINARY TREE

Figure 14.3 shows the procedure followed when you're searching for the key T. The search begins at the root and travels down through the tree until it reaches the S node. T would be connected to the right of S—if T were in the tree! When a null link is found, the search key is not resident in the tree.

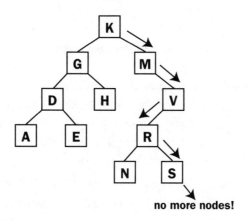

FIGURE 14.3 SEARCHING FOR A KEY THAT IS NOT IN THE TREE

You probably noticed that a binary tree search is recursive. Start at the root node, compare keys, and select another node. Compare keys, select another node, and so on until a null link is reached or the key is found.

Insertion

The first node inserted into a binary tree becomes the root node. Inserting subsequent nodes involves searching the tree for the proper location. If the key being inserted is not found, the search ends at a null link. When a null link is encountered, a new leaf node is constructed and linked to that part of the tree.

Figure 14.4 assumes that insertion begins with an empty tree and shows the results of inserting each of the keys C, A, R, K, D, and U, in that order.

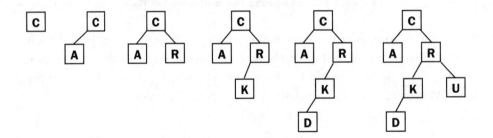

FIGURE 14.4 BINARY TREE INSERTION

The first key inserted, C, becomes the root node. A is less than C, so it is attached to the left of C; R is greater than C, so it links to C's right side. K is greater than C but less than R, placing it left of R. D is greater than C and less than R and K, so it is attached to K's left link. The U is greater than C and R, and it is linked to R's right side.

Figure 14.5 shows the tree after adding the keys P, B, E, N, X, Z, and S. You may notice that more nodes are greater than the root, giving the tree a lopsided appearance. For now, we'll ignore this problem; I'll address it later in the chapter.

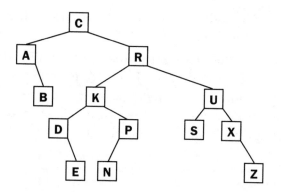

FIGURE 14.5 THE RESULT OF INSERTING MORE NODES

Deletion

Deleting a node from a tree requires that we handle one of three situations. The node will be childless, or it will have one or two links to child nodes; the algorithm must adjust the tree's nodes to ensure that all remaining keys have the proper, in-order connections.

Figure 14.6 shows the deletion of the H node. Because H is a leaf node, it is deleted simply by setting the link from its parent to null. Deleting a leaf node does not require us to change the organization of other nodes.

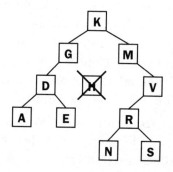

FIGURE 14.6 DELETING A LEAF NODE

When a parent node is deleted from a binary tree, all its child nodes must be relinked to the tree.

Figure 14.7 shows how a parent with a single child is deleted from a binary tree. The deleted node is replaced by its child; in this case, G is replaced by D. All children of a node have the same relationship to the node's parent as does the node, so replacing a deleted node with its child maintains the integrity of the tree's organization.

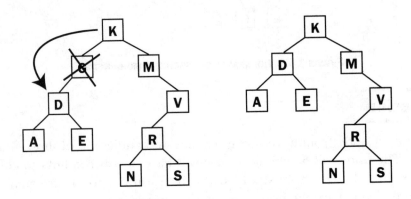

FIGURE 14.7 DELETING A PARENT NODE WITH ONE CHILD

When deleting a two-child node from the tree, we need to use a more complicated algorithm, as shown in Figure 14.8. The deleted node is replaced by its immediate successor, which is defined as the node that immediately follows the deleted node in sequence. In Figure 14.8, N immediately follows M and is therefore its successor. The data stored in N—such as the key value—are transferred to the deleted node (M). All of M's links remain intact. Once the successor node has replaced the deleted node, the algorithm deletes the original successor node from the tree. The relationship of the keys remains intact.

Implementing binary trees with a C++ class is not as complicated as you might expect. By using templates, I've defined a set of classes that allow any type of data to be stored in binary trees. The BinaryTree class is defined with a single template class parameter that identifies the data type being stored. The type must support comparison operators, assignment, and default (no argument) construction.

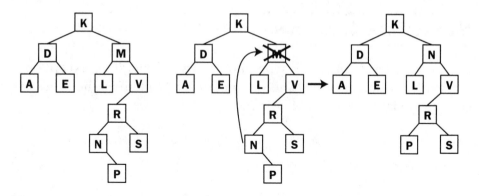

FIGURE 14.8 DELETING A PARENT NODE WITH TWO CHILDREN

Iterators

An *iterator* is an object through which you can examine the contents of another object. A pointer to the elements of an array is one type of iterator that's built into C++. An iterator class is usually a `friend` of the container class, and it usually acts as a pointer to some element of the container it is associated with. More than one iterator can exist contemporaneously, allowing different sections of a program to examine the same container in different ways.

For a binary tree, an iterator would point to some node in the tree. I define the dereferencing operator * to return the data pointed to by a node. Increment and decrement operators "move" the iterator to the next or previous element of the tree, and other functions set an iterator to the first or last tree element. This approach allows an iterator to traverse the tree from end to end, in order and in reverse order.

A problem will arise if an iterator references a node that is changed by some manipulation—insertion or deletion, for example—of the tree. To prevent that problem, I've incorporated the theory of "locks" into my binary trees. The creation of an iterator object increments the lock count; when an iterator is destroyed, the lock count is decremented. If the lock count is greater than zero, a binary tree throws an exception for an operation that might potentially affect an iterator. Thus, while iterators exist, items cannot be inserted or deleted from a binary tree.

BINARY TREE EXCEPTIONS

I've defined an enumerated type and a class for handling exceptions thrown from binary trees. The enumerated type defines the types of error that might occur in a binary tree:

```
enum TreeError
    {
    BTX_ALLOC,
    BTX_NOTFOUND,
    BTX_LOCKVIOLATION,
    BTX_LOCKMAX,
    BTX_LOCKZERO
    };
```

The class `TreeEx` defines an exception object to be thrown whenever a problem occurs. When creating a new `TreeEx` object, you provide a `TreeError` value to indicate the type of error:

```
class TreeEx : public ExceptionBase
    {
    public:
        TreeEx
            (
            TreeError err
            )
            {
            Error = err;
            }

        TreeError WhatsWrong()
            {
            return Error;
            }

        virtual void Explain
            (
            DiagOutput & out
            );

    private:
        TreeError Error;
    };
```

`WhatsWrong` reports the error type, and `Explain` is the polymorphic function that displays the error message:

```
void TreeEx::Explain(DiagOutput & out)
    {
    switch (Error)
        {
        case BTX_ALLOC:
            out.DisplayMsg("Can't alloc memory for tree",
                           DIAG_ERROR);
            break;
        case BTX_NOTFOUND:
            out.DisplayMsg("Tree look-up failed",
                           DIAG_WARNING);
            break;
        case BTX_LOCKVIOLATION:
            out.DisplayMsg("Attempt change in locked tree",
                           DIAG_WARNING);
            break;
        case BTX_LOCKMAX:
            out.DisplayMsg("Too many lock increments for tree",
                           DIAG_WARNING);
            break;
        case BTX_LOCKZERO:
            out.DisplayMsg("Too many lock decrements for tree",
                           DIAG_WARNING);
            break;
        default:
            out.DisplayMsg("Unknown tree exception",
                           DIAG_FATAL);
        }
    }
```

NODE STRUCTURE

A template defines the appropriate structure for nodes in a binary tree:

```
template <class D>
    struct TreeNode
        {
        // links
        TreeNode<D> * Less;
        TreeNode<D> * More;
```

```
    TreeNode<D> * Parent;

    // contents
    D Data;

    // constructor
    TreeNode
        (
        const D & item,
        TreeNode<D> * sentinel
        );

    TreeNode(); // creates a sentinel node

    // copy constructor
    TreeNode
        (
        const TreeNode<D> & node
        );

    // assignment operator
    void operator =
        (
        const TreeNode<D> & node
        );
    };
```

The Less member points to a child node containing a lesser key; the More member points to a child node containing a greater key. The Parent pointer is a backward link to the node's parent. Deletion of nodes from the tree is greatly simplified when a link provides the address of the parent node. Key identifies the information stored in Data.

Null nodes are indicated by Less or More pointers set to a special node called a *sentinel*. The sentinel could be NULL, which is the way most binary trees indicate empty nodes. In the case of more-advanced binary tree types, such as the red-black trees shown later in this chapter, the sentinel is actually a special node that points to itself. As you'll see later, using a sentinel node can simplify the implementation of red-black trees.

The default TreeNode constructor creates a sentinel node that points to itself. For a sentinel, the data element is meaningless. Because Data is static, it must be initialized through a constructor call; for a `sentinel` node, `Data` is generated through a default constructor. This arrangement requires the data type stored in a node to support a default (no argument) constructor. Standard arrays also require a default constructor; in general, it is good practice to define a default constructor for any class.

```
template <class D>
    TreeNode<D>::TreeNode()
        : Data()
        {
        Parent = this;
        Less   = this;
        More   = this;
        }
```

The default `TreeNode` constructor is used only to create a `sentinel` node; `BinaryTree` generates all other nodes with a constructor that requires a data parameter and a `sentinel` pointer.

```
template <class D>
    TreeNode<D>::TreeNode
        (
        const D & item,
        TreeNode<D> * sentinel
        )
        : Data(item)
        {
        Parent = sentinel;
        Less   = sentinel;
        More   = sentinel;
        }
```

The `TreeNode` copy constructor duplicates an existing node, and the assignment operator copies one `TreeNode` to another:

```
template <class D>
    TreeNode<D>::TreeNode
        (
        const TreeNode<D> & node
        )
        : Data(node.Data)
```

```
        {
        Parent = node.Parent;
        Less   = node.Less;
        More   = node.More;
        }

template <class D>
    void TreeNode<D>::operator =
        (
        const TreeNode<D> & node
        )
        {
        Parent = node.Parent;
        Less   = node.Less;
        More   = node.More;
        Data   = node.Data;
        }
```

The binary tree class manages TreeNodes directly, creating them dynamically and managing their pointers and internal data.

BINARYTREE CLASS

The BinaryTree class defines three data members: the Root pointer to the root node, a Sentinel node, and a function pointer named WalkFunc that's used in listing the entries in a tree. The function pointer locates a function that has a type D parameter, matching the parameter passed to the Walk member function.

```
template <class D>
    class BinaryTree

        {

        friend

            class BinaryTreeIterator<D>;

        public:
```

```
        // constructor
        BinaryTree();

        BinaryTree
            (
            const BinaryTree<D> & tree
            );

        // destructor
        ~BinaryTree();

        // assignment opeartor
        void operator =
            (
            const BinaryTree<D> & tree
            );

        // store an item
        void Insert
            (
            const D & item
            );

        // delete an item
        Bool Delete
            (
            const D & item
            );

        // walk entire tree, calling function for nodes
        void Walk
            (
            void (* func)(const D & item)
            );

        // examine lock count
        unsigned int  GetLockCount();

        // retrieve pointer to sentinel
        const TreeNode<D> * GetSentinel();

protected:
    TreeNode<D> * Root;     // root node
    TreeNode<D> * Sentinel; // sentinel node
```

```
unsigned int LockCount; // number of iterator locks

// function called during traverse
void (*WalkFunc)(const D & item);

// function to create and delete nodes
TreeNode<D> * CreateNode
    (
    const D & item
    );

void DeleteNode
    (
    TreeNode<D> * node
    );

// internal insert function
TreeNode<D> * InternalInsert
    (
    const D & item
    );

// recursive copy function
void RecursiveCopy
    (
    TreeNode<D> * node
    );

// recursive traversal function
void RecurseWalk
    (
    TreeNode<D> * node
    );

// recursive deletion function
void RecursiveDelete
    (
    TreeNode<D> * node
    );

// find minimum node
TreeNode<D> * Minimum
    (
    TreeNode<D> * node
    );
```

```
        // find maximum node
        TreeNode<D> * Maximum
            (
            TreeNode<D> * node
            );

        // find successor node
        TreeNode<D> * Successor
            (
            TreeNode<D> * node
            );

        // find predecessor node
        TreeNode<D> * Predecessor
            (
            TreeNode<D> * node
            );

        // find node containing specific item
        TreeNode<D> * Search
            (
            const D & item
            );
    };
```

LockCount tracks the number of iterators created; functions such as Delete throw an exception if they are called for a BinaryTree with a LockCount greater than zero. LockCount is changed only by the BinaryTreeIterator class.

Utility Functions

A dozen protected utility functions provide basic services for a BinaryTree.

I placed the creation and deletion of nodes in the functions CreateNode and DeleteNode, rather than embed calls to new and delete in various functions. This technique places exception handling for memory allocation in a single location.

```
template <class D>
    TreeNode<D> * BinaryTree<D>::CreateNode
        (
```

```
        const D & item
        )
        {
        TreeNode<D> * z = new TreeNode<D>(item, Sentinel);

        if (z == NULL)
            throw TreeEx(BTX_ALLOC);

        return z;
        }

template <class D>
    void BinaryTree<D>::DeleteNode
        (
        TreeNode<D> * node
        )
        {
        delete node;
        }
```

The three utility functions discussed next are recursive; they process all nodes in a given subtree by passing the Less and Greater pointers to themselves. To process the entire tree, pass these functions the Root node.

RecursiveCopy duplicates a tree. The copy constructor and assignment operator call RecursiveCopy with the Root node of a tree that is being duplicated. The function then adds those nodes recursively to the destination tree:

```
template <class D>
    void BinaryTree<D>::RecursiveCopy
        (
        TreeNode<D> * node
        )
        {
        if (node != Sentinel)
            {
            Insert(node->Data);
            RecursiveCopy(node->Less);
            RecursiveCopy(node->More);
            }
        }
```

The destructor calls `RecursiveDelete` with the `Root` node. `RecursiveDelete` recursively deletes the subtrees before deleting the node itself:

```
template <class D>
    void BinaryTree<D>::RecursiveDelete
        (
        TreeNode<D> * node
        )
        {
        if (node != Sentinel)
            {
            RecursiveDelete(node->Less);
            RecursiveDelete(node->More);
            DeleteNode(node);
            }
        }
```

`Walk` assigns its function pointer parameter to the `WalkFunc` data member; then it calls `RecurseWalk` with the `Root` node. `RecurseWalk` first recursively processes the `Less` subtree; then `RecurseWalk` calls `WalkFunc` for the current node, followed by a call to itself for the `More` subtree.

```
template <class D>
    void BinaryTree<D>::Walk
        (
        void (* func)(const D & item)
        )
        {
        WalkFunc = func;
        RecurseWalk(Root);
        }

template <class D>
    void BinaryTree<D>::RecurseWalk
        (
        TreeNode<D> * node
        )
        {
        if (node != Sentinel)
            {
            RecurseWalk(node->Less);
```

```
        WalkFunc(node->Data);
        RecurseWalk(node->More);
        }
    }
```

The `Minimum`, `Maximum`, `Predecessor`, and `Successor` utility functions find, respectively, the first, last, previous, and next items in a binary tree by following the links between nodes:

```
// find minimum node
template <class D>
    TreeNode<D> * BinaryTree<D>::Minimum
        (
        TreeNode<D> * node
        )
        {
        while (node->Less != Sentinel)
            node = node->Less;

        return node;
        }


// find maximum node
template <class D>
    TreeNode<D> * BinaryTree<D>::Maximum
        (
        TreeNode<D> * node
        )
        {
        while (node->More != Sentinel)
            node = node->More;

        return node;
        }

// find successor node
template <class D>
    TreeNode<D> * BinaryTree<D>::Successor
        (
        TreeNode<D> * node
        )
        {
```

```
        TreeNode<D> * x, * y;

        if (node->More != Sentinel)
            return Minimum(node->More);
        else
            {
            x = node;
            y = node->Parent;

            while ((y != Sentinel) && (x == y->More))
                {
                x = y;
                y = y->Parent;
                }
            }

        return y;
        }


// find predecessor node
template <class D>
    TreeNode<D> * BinaryTree<D>::Predecessor
        (
        TreeNode<D> * node
        )
        {
        TreeNode<D> * x, * y;

        if (node->Less != Sentinel)
            return Maximum(node->Less);
        else
            {
            x = node;
            y = node->Parent;

            while ((y != Sentinel) && (x == y->Less))
                {
                x = y;
                y = y->Parent;
                }
            }

        return y;
        }
```

Finally, the Search utility function finds the node that contains a specific data item. Beginning at the root, Search follows the node links by comparing the requested item against node contents. If Search finds a Sentinel node, it has reached the end of the tree; it then returns Sentinel to indicate that the item was not found.

```
template <class D>
    TreeNode<D> * BinaryTree<D>::Search
        (
        const D & item
        )
        {
        TreeNode<D> * n = Root;

        while ((n != Sentinel) && (n->Data != item))
            {
            if (item < n->Data)
                n = n->Less;
            else
                n = n->More;
            }

        return n;
        }
```

Constructors and Destructors

The default constructor creates a Sentinel node and creates an empty tree by setting Count to 0 and Root to Sentinel.

```
template <class D>
    BinaryTree<D>::BinaryTree()
        {
        Sentinel  = new TreeNode<D>;

        if (Sentinel == NULL)
            throw TreeEx(BTX_ALLOC);

        Root      = Sentinel;
        LockCount = 0;
        }
```

The destructor calls RecursiveDelete to destroy all nodes and the Sentinel.

```
template <class D>
    BinaryTree<D>::~BinaryTree()
        {
        if (LockCount > 0)
            throw TreeEx(BTX_LOCKVIOLATION);

        RecursiveDelete(Root);
        }
```

The copy constructor and assignment operator duplicate the members of an existing tree using the RecursiveCopy utility.

```
template <class D>
    BinaryTree<D>::BinaryTree
        (
        const BinaryTree<D> & tree
        )
        {
        Sentinel = new TreeNode<D>(*(tree.Sentinel));

        if (Sentinel == NULL)
            throw TreeEx(BTX_ALLOC);

        Root       = Sentinel;
        LockCount = 0;

        RecursiveCopy(tree.Root);
        }

template <class D>
    void BinaryTree<D>::operator =
        (
        const BinaryTree<D> & tree
        )
        {
        if (LockCount > 0)
            throw TreeEx(BTX_LOCKVIOLATION);

        Sentinel = new TreeNode<D>(*(tree.Sentinel));
```

```
        if (Sentinel == NULL)
            throw TreeEx(BTX_ALLOC);

        RecursiveDelete(Root);
        Root = Sentinel;
        RecursiveCopy(tree.Root);

        delete Sentinel;
        }
```

Each tree creates a unique `Sentinel` to prevent conflicts with other trees. A conflict could arise if two separate threads of a program contained `BinaryTree`s that manipulate a common `Sentinel`. To the greatest extent possible, objects should be independent and self-contained.

Insertion and Deletion

The `InternalInsert` function performs a standard binary tree insertion and returns the address of the new node. The basic `BinaryTree` class can insert a new node simply by calling `InternalInsert` and ignoring the return value; red-black trees, however, perform operations to rebalance a tree after each new node is inserted.

After it creates a node, `InternalInsert` searches the tree for the data value. If a match is found, the new node replaces the existing one using the original links and parent. Otherwise, the search ends at a `sentinel` where the new node is added.

```
template <class D>
    TreeNode<D> * BinaryTree<D>::InternalInsert
        (
        const D & item
        )
        {
        if (LockCount > 0)
            throw TreeEx(BTX_LOCKVIOLATION);

        TreeNode<D> * z = CreateNode(item);
        TreeNode<D> * y = Sentinel;
        TreeNode<D> * x = Root;
```

```
        while (x != Sentinel)
            {
            y = x;

            if (z->Data < x->Data)
                x = x->Less;
            else
                x = x->More;
            }

        z->Parent = y;

        if (y == Sentinel)
            Root = z;
        else
            {
            if (z->Data < y->Data)
                y->Less = z;
            else
                y->More = z;
            }

        return z;
        }
```

The inline `Insert` function calls `InternalInsert` and returns, ignoring the returned node pointer.

```
template <class D>
    void BinaryTree<D>::Insert
        (
        const D & item
        )
        {
        InternalInsert(item);
        }
```

Deleting an item involves the removal of nodes having zero, one, or two links. Subtle differences in deletion algorithms prevented me from creating an efficient "internal delete" function that works for all binary trees.

```
template <class D>
    Bool BinaryTree<D>::Delete
```

```
(
const D & item
)
{
if (LockCount > 0)
    throw TreeEx(BTX_LOCKVIOLATION);

// find node
TreeNode<D> * z = Search(item);

if (z == Sentinel)
    return FALSE;

TreeNode<D> * y, * x;

// find node to splice out
if ((z->Less == Sentinel) || (z->More == Sentinel))
    y = z;
else
    y = Successor(z);

// find child with which to replace y
if (y->Less != Sentinel)
    x = y->Less;
else
    x = y->More;

// splice child onto parent
if (x != Sentinel)
    x->Parent = y->Parent;

if (y->Parent == Sentinel)
    Root = x; // replace root
else
    {
    // splice in child node
    if (y == y->Parent->Less)
        y->Parent->Less = x;
    else
        y->Parent->More = x;
    }

// if needed, save y data
if (y != z)
```

```
        z->Data = y->Data;

    // free memory
    DeleteNode(y);

    return TRUE;
    }
```

Delete begins by searching for the key. If the key isn't found, Delete returns FALSE, indicating that it didn't perform any deletions. Otherwise, node is deleted and the tree is adjusted. If the deleted node is the only node, Delete leaves an empty tree. If the node has only one child, that child replaces the deleted node, becoming the new root if the root node is being deleted. Otherwise, the node has two children and is swapped with its immediate successor.

Interrogators

Two interrogation functions return, respectively, a BinaryTree's lock count and the sentinel pointer:

```
template <class D>
    inline size_t BinaryTree<D>::GetLockCount()
        {
        return LockCount;
        }

template <class D>
    inline const TreeNode<D> * BinaryTree<D>::GetSentinel()
        {
        return Sentinel;
        }
```

ITERATORS

The BinaryTreeIterator class is defined largely in terms of functions provided by BinaryTree.

```
template <class D>
    class BinaryTreeIterator
        {
        public:
            BinaryTreeIterator
                (
                BinaryTree<D> & bt
                );

            BinaryTreeIterator
                (
                BinaryTreeIterator<D> & iter
                );

            ~BinaryTreeIterator();

            void operator =
                (
                BinaryTreeIterator<D> & iter
                );

            void Smallest();
            void Largest();

            void operator ++ ();
            void operator - ();

            D operator * ();

        protected:
            BinaryTree<D> & Tree;
            TreeNode<D>    * Node;
        };
```

Each iterator contains a reference, Tree, to the tree it is traversing and a pointer, Node, to the currently selected node.

In creating a new BinaryTreeIterator, a program must provide a reference to a BinaryTree. The constructor increments the tree's lock count and sets the Node pointer to the smallest element in the tree.

```
template <class D>
    BinaryTreeIterator<D>::BinaryTreeIterator
```

```
    (
    BinaryTree<D> & bt
    )
    : Tree(bt)
    {
    if (Tree.LockCount == UINT_MAX)
        throw TreeEx(BTX_LOCKMAX);

    ++Tree.LockCount;

    Smallest();
    }
```

The copy constructor and assignment operator duplicate the contents of an existing iterator.

```
template <class D>
    BinaryTreeIterator<D>::BinaryTreeIterator
        (
        BinaryTreeIterator<D> & iter
        )
        : Tree(iter.Tree)
        {
        if (Tree.LockCount == UINT_MAX)
            throw TreeEx(BTX_LOCKMAX);

        ++Tree.LockCount;

        Node = iter.Node;
        }

template <class D>
    void BinaryTreeIterator<D>::operator =
        (
        BinaryTreeIterator<D> & iter
        )
        {
        Tree = iter.Tree;

        if (Tree.LockCount == 0)
            throw TreeEx(BTX_LOCKZERO);

        —Tree.LockCount;
```

```
        if (Tree.LockCount == UINT_MAX)
            throw TreeEx(BTX_LOCKMAX);

        ++Tree.LockCount;

        Node = iter.Node;
        }
```

The destructor ensures that Tree's lock count is decremented when the program destroys an iterator.

```
template <class D>
    BinaryTreeIterator<D>::~BinaryTreeIterator()
        {
        if (Tree.LockCount == 0)
            throw TreeEx(BTX_LOCKZERO);

        —Tree.LockCount;
        }
```

The remaining functions move Node through Tree's elements using the private functions built into BinaryTree.

```
template <class D>
    void BinaryTreeIterator<D>::Smallest()
        {
        Node = Tree.Minimum(Tree.Root);
        }

template <class D>
    void BinaryTreeIterator<D>::Largest()
        {
        Node = Tree.Maximum(Tree.Root);
        }

template <class D>
    void BinaryTreeIterator<D>::operator ++ ()
```

```
        {
        Node = Tree.Successor(Node);
        }

template <class D>
    void BinaryTreeIterator<D>::operator − ()
        {
        Node = Tree.Predecessor(Node);
        }
```

In keeping with the nomenclature of pointers, I use the increment and decrement operators to move an iterator forward and backward, respectively, in the tree. The * operator returns the data contained in Node.

```
template <class D>
    D BinaryTreeIterator<D>::operator * ()
        {
        if (Node == Tree.GetSentinel())
            throw TreeEx(BTX_NOTFOUND);
        else
            return Node->Data;
        }
```

BINARY TREE LIMITATIONS

Binary trees sort information as it is inserted, making them very useful for applications in which dynamic information must be organized. Binary trees, however, have deficiencies.

Figure 14.9 shows a tree constructed from the keys C, A, R, K, D, U, P, B, E, N, X, Z, and S, inserted in that order. The tree has two nodes left of the root and 10 nodes to its right. Searching for a key greater than C can require as many as five comparisons, a number that is certainly less than optimal.

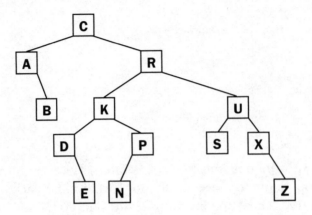

FIGURE 14.9 AN UNBALANCED BINARY TREE

A tree is balanced when it has equal numbers of nodes on both sides of its root. For example, inserting the same set of keys in a different order will result in a perfectly balanced tree.

Figure 14.10 shows the keys inserted in the order NCUBADEKRP-SXZ. N is a good root value, because it is near the median value of all keys. C was a bad root value, because it tended toward one end of the range of values.

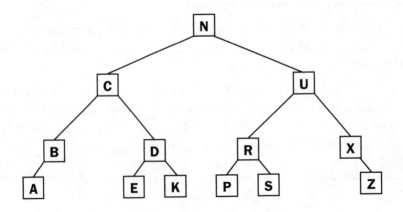

FIGURE 14.10 A BALANCED BINARY TREE

Figure 14.11 shows a binary tree generated from the keys A, B, C, D, E, and F. Because each subsequent node is greater than its predecessor, the binary tree degenerates into a linked list. A search on a linked list is very inefficient, and all benefits of a binary tree are lost.

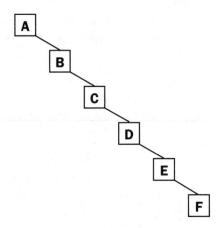

FIGURE 14.11 A DEGENERATE BINARY TREE

Sorted and almost-sorted data are common, and, as with QuickSort, computer scientists have developed several schemes for lessening the impact of sorted data. Balancing and nearly balancing binary trees require sophisticated rearrangement of the tree as nodes are added and deleted.

RED-BLACK TREES

Red-black trees use a marking technique to ensure that portions of the tree do not become massively unbalanced with other parts of the tree. Each red-black tree node contains a color marker, which can be either "red" or "black." All red-black nodes follow this set of rules:

1. Every node is either red or black.

2. Every leaf (sentinel) node is considered black.

3. If a node is red, its children are black.

4. All paths from a node to descendent leaves will contain the same number of black nodes.

The number of black nodes in any path is that path's *black height*. The preceding rules ensure that a red-black tree is approximately balanced; no path through the tree can be more than twice as long as its sibling path.

For the most part, red-black trees operate exactly like standard binary trees; only insertion and deletion change substantially, because they need to maintain the four color rules I specified. Red-black trees, then, should be derived from BinaryTrees.

Red-black nodes contain a color indicator not found in standard binary nodes. The most effective way I've found to do this is to create a template for an auxiliary data structure, RBData, that combines a data item and a color indicator.

```
enum RBColor { BLACK, RED };

template <class D>
    struct RBData
        {
        RBColor Color;
        D       RealData;

        RBData()
            : RealData()
            {
            Color = BLACK;
            }

        RBData
            (
            const D & item
            )
            {
            RealData = item;
            Color = BLACK;
            }
```

```
int operator <
    (
    const RBData & rbd
    )
    const
    {
    return (RealData < rbd.RealData);
    }

int operator >
    (
    const RBData & rbd
    )
    const
    {
    return (RealData > rbd.RealData);
    }

int operator ==
    (
    const RBData & rbd
    )
    const
    {
    return (RealData == rbd.RealData);
    }

int operator !=
    (
    const RBData & rbd
    )
    const
    {
    return (RealData == rbd.RealData);
    }
};
```

At first glance, this implementation may seem a bit strange. Why didn't I derive a new "red black node" class from TreeNode? In fact, my original implementation did just that, creating a RedBlackNode class that added a color value to TreeNode. This method, however, didn't solve a rather nasty problem: TreeNode defines the Less, More, and Parent members as pointers to TreeNode<D>. in the RedBlackTree functions, I needed to constantly cast those pointers to RedBlackNode<D> pointers. Not only was this approach messy, but it was also error-prone. By using the RBData structure, I extended TreeNode without having to create a new type.

RED-BLACK TREE CLASS

I then derive the RedBlackTree class from BinaryTree < RBData<D> >:

```
template <class D>
    class RedBlackTree : public BinaryTree< RBData<D> >
        {
        public:
            // constructor
            RedBlackTree();

            RedBlackTree
                (
                const RedBlackTree<D> & tree
                );

            // assignment operator
            void operator =
                (
                const RedBlackTree<D> & tree
                );

            // store an item
            void Insert
                (
                const D & item
                );

            // delete an item
            Bool Delete
                (
                const D & item
                );

        protected:
            // tree adjustment utilities
            void RotateLeft
                (
```

```
                  TreeNode< RBData<D> > * node
                  );

           void RotateRight
                  (
                  TreeNode< RBData<D> > * node
                  );

           void DeleteFixup
                  (
                  TreeNode< RBData<D> > * node
                  );
     };
```

`RedBlackTree` adds to `BinaryTree` those functions needed to handle the organization of the tree.

Constructors and Destructors

The constructors, destructors, and assignment operators simply provide shells for calling their `BinaryTree` equivalents.

```
template <class D>
     inline RedBlackTree<D>::RedBlackTree()
          : BinaryTree< RBData<D> >()
          {
          // placeholder
          }

template <class D>
     inline RedBlackTree<D>::RedBlackTree
          (
          const RedBlackTree<D> & tree
          )
          : BinaryTree< RBData<D> >(tree)
          {
          // placeholder
          }

template <class D>
     void RedBlackTree<D>::operator =
          (
```

```
          const RedBlackTree<D> & tree
          )
          {
          BinaryTree< RBData<D> >::operator = (tree);
          }
```

Utility Functions

RotateLeft and RotateRight exchange (in opposite directions) the two
subtrees of a node.

```
template <class D>
    void RedBlackTree<D>::RotateLeft
        (
        TreeNode< RBData<D> > * node
        )
        {
        TreeNode< RBData<D> > * y = node->More;

        // turn y's left subtree into node's right subtree
        node->More = y->Less;

        if (y->Less != Sentinel)
            y->Less->Parent = node;

        // link node's parent to y
        y->Parent = node->Parent;

        if (node->Parent == Sentinel)
            Root = y;
        else
            {
            if (node == node->Parent->Less)
                node->Parent->Less = y;
            else
                node->Parent->More = y;
            }

        // put node on y's left
        y->Less = node;
        node->Parent = y;
```

```
        }

template <class D>
    void RedBlackTree<D>::RotateRight
        (
        TreeNode< RBData<D> > * node
        )
        {
        TreeNode< RBData<D> > * y = node->Less;

        // turn y's right subtree into node's left subtree
        node->Less = y->More;

        if (y->More != Sentinel)
            y->More->Parent = node;

        // link node's parent to y
        y->Parent = node->Parent;

        if (node->Parent == Sentinel)
            Root = y;
        else
            {
            if (node == node->Parent->More)
                node->Parent->More = y;
            else
                node->Parent->Less = y;
            }

        // put node on y's right
        y->More = node;
        node->Parent = y;
        }
```

DeleteFixup adjusts the tree after a node has been deleted. In essence, DeleteFixup travels down through the tree, rotating nodes until the red-black tree conditions are met.

```
template <class D>
    void RedBlackTree<D>::DeleteFixup
        (
        TreeNode< RBData<D> > * node
        )
```

```
        {
TreeNode< RBData<D> > * w, * x = node;

while ((x != Root) && (x->Data.Color == BLACK))
      {
    if (x == x->Parent->Less)
        {
        w = x->Parent->More;

        if (w->Data.Color == RED)
            {
            w->Data.Color = BLACK;
            x->Parent->Data.Color = RED;
            RotateLeft(x->Parent);
            w = x->Parent->More;
            }

        if ((w->Less->Data.Color == BLACK)
        &&  (w->More->Data.Color == BLACK))
            {
            w->Data.Color = RED;
            x = x->Parent;
            }
        else
            {
            if (w->More->Data.Color == BLACK)
                {
                w->Less->Data.Color = BLACK;
                w->Data.Color = RED;
                RotateRight(w);
                w = x->Parent->More;
                }

            w->Data.Color = x->Parent->Data.Color;
            x->Parent->Data.Color = BLACK;
            w->More->Data.Color = BLACK;
            RotateLeft(x->Parent);
            x = Root;
            }
        }
    else
        {
        w = x->Parent->Less;

        if (w->Data.Color == RED)
```

```
          {
          w->Data.Color = BLACK;
          x->Parent->Data.Color = RED;
          RotateRight(x->Parent);
          w = x->Parent->Less;
          }

     if ((w->More->Data.Color == BLACK)
     &&  (w->Less->Data.Color == BLACK))
          {
          w->Data.Color = RED;
          x = x->Parent;
          }
     else
          {
          if (w->Less->Data.Color == BLACK)
              {
              w->More->Data.Color = BLACK;
              w->Data.Color = RED;
              RotateLeft(w);
              w = x->Parent->Less;
              }

          w->Data.Color = x->Parent->Data.Color;
          x->Parent->Data.Color = BLACK;
          w->Less->Data.Color = BLACK;
          RotateRight(x->Parent);
          x = Root;
          }
     }
 }


x->Data.Color = BLACK;
}
```

When a black node is deleted from the tree, it causes any path containing the removed node to have one fewer black node, thus possibly violating the red-black tree conditions. The problem is corrected by pretending that an extra "black" node is connected to x; this artificial "blackness" is moved toward the root until a red node is found or the root is encountered. If a red node is found, it is colored black; if the loop reaches the root, the blackness is simply discarded.

Insertion and Deletion

The `Insert` function begins by calling `InternalInsert` to insert a new node into the tree. Then the `Insert` function moves up the tree, rotating subtrees to restore the red-black tree conditions:

```
template <class D>
    void RedBlackTree<D>::Insert
        (
        const D & item
        )
        {
        RBData<D> rbitem(item);

        TreeNode< RBData<D> > * x = InternalInsert(rbitem);
        TreeNode< RBData<D> > * y;

        x->Data.Color = RED;

        while ((x != Root) && (x->Parent->Data.Color == RED))
            {
            if (x->Parent == x->Parent->Parent->Less)
                {
                y = x->Parent->Parent->More;

                if (y->Data.Color == RED)
                    {
                    x->Parent->Data.Color = BLACK;
                    y->Data.Color = BLACK;
                    x->Parent->Parent->Data.Color = RED;
                    x = x->Parent->Parent;
                    }
                else
                    {
                    if (x == x->Parent->More)
                        {
                        x = x->Parent;
                        RotateLeft(x);
                        }

                    x->Parent->Data.Color = BLACK;
                    x->Parent->Parent->Data.Color = RED;
                    RotateRight(x->Parent->Parent);
```

```
                  }
              }
         else
              {
              y = x->Parent->Parent->Less;

              if (y->Data.Color == RED)
                  {
                  x->Parent->Data.Color = BLACK;
                  y->Data.Color = BLACK;
                  x->Parent->Parent->Data.Color = RED;
                  x = x->Parent->Parent;
                  }
              else
                  {
                  if (x == x->Parent->Less)
                      {
                      x = x->Parent;
                      RotateRight(x);
                      }

                  x->Parent->Data.Color = BLACK;
                  x->Parent->Parent->Data.Color = RED;
                  RotateLeft(x->Parent->Parent);
                  }
              }
          }

     Root->Data.Color = BLACK;
     }
```

Delete is almost—but not quite—identical to the BinaryTree::Delete function. The assignment of y's parent as x's parent is automatic; if x points to Sentinel, Sentinel's parent pointer now points to y's parent. If y is black, a call to DeleteFixup adjusts the tree based on x. At that call, x is the node that was y's sole child before y was spliced out of the tree—or x is the Sentinel if y had no children. In any case, x's parent pointer will reference the parent of y, allowing DeleteFixup to treat x in a generic fashion.

```
template <class D>
    Bool RedBlackTree<D>::Delete
        (
        const D & item
```

```
)
{
if (LockCount > 0)
    throw TreeEx(BTX_LOCKVIOLATION);

// find node
TreeNode< RBData<D> > * z = Search(item);

if (z == Sentinel)
    return FALSE;

TreeNode< RBData<D> > * y, * x;

// find node to splice out
if ((z->Less == Sentinel) || (z->More == Sentinel))
    y = z;
else
    y = Successor(z);

// find child with which to replace y
if (y->Less != Sentinel)
    x = y->Less;
else
    x = y->More;

// splice child onto parent
x->Parent = y->Parent;

if (y->Parent == Sentinel)
    Root = x; // replace root
else
    {
    // splice in child node
    if (y == y->Parent->Less)
        y->Parent->Less = x;
    else
        y->Parent->More = x;
    }

// if needed, save y data
if (y != z)
    z->Data = y->Data;

// adjust tree under red-black rules
```

```
    if (y->Data.Color == BLACK)
        DeleteFixup(x);

    // free memory
    DeleteNode(y);

    return TRUE;
    }
```

Why didn't I implement Insert and Delete as virtual functions, thus making BinaryTree and RedBlackTree polymorphic? It wasn't possible! Because the underlying parent BinaryTree has used an RBData<D> type for its item type, its Insert(RBData<D>) and Delete(RBData<D>) functions do not match the Insert(D) and Delete(D) functions in RedBlackTree.

RED-BLACK TREE ITERATORS

Because the data elements in a RedBlackTree reside within RBData structures, I created a new type of iterator to add the required extra level of indirection to BinaryTreeIterator:

```
template <class D>
    class RBTreeIterator : public BinaryTreeIterator< RBData<D> >
        {
        public:
            RBTreeIterator
                (
                RedBlackTree<D> & bt
                );

            RBTreeIterator
                (
                RBTreeIterator<D> & iter
                );

            void operator =
                (
                RBTreeIterator<D> & iter
                );
```

471

```
            D operator * ();
        };

template <class D>
    RBTreeIterator<D>::RBTreeIterator
        (
        RedBlackTree<D> & bt
        )
        : BinaryTreeIterator< RBData<D> >(bt)
        {
        // placeholder
        }

template <class D>
    RBTreeIterator<D>::RBTreeIterator
        (
        RBTreeIterator<D> & iter
        )
        : BinaryTreeIterator< RBData<D> >(iter)
        {
        // placeholder
        }

template <class D>
    void RBTreeIterator<D>::operator =
        (
        RBTreeIterator<D> & iter
        )
        {
        BinaryTreeIterator< RBData<D> >::operator = (iter);
        }

template <class D>
    D RBTreeIterator<D>::operator * ()
        {
        if (Node == Tree.GetSentinel())
            throw TreeEx(BTX_NOTFOUND);
        else
            return Node->Data.RealData;
        }
```

You'll find the binary tree classes in **BinTree.h**, and the exception types
in **Treex.h** and **Treex.cpp**. I implemented the red-black tree classes in

the file **RBTree.h**. Look in the **TBTree.cpp** module for examples of working with both binary and red-black trees.

ONWARD

The goal of this chapter is to introduce tree structures for file handling. In the context, binary trees are not a good choice because they include too many levels. The number of times data must be read from an external file determines the efficiency of any file-indexing scheme. The goal is to minimize the number of records that must be read from the index file while searching for a key.

A balanced binary tree containing 1000 keys will have 10 levels; a tree containing 10,000 nodes will contain 14 levels. Unbalanced trees will be even "deeper." Nodes could be stored as individual records, but several records would need to be read during a key search. Paging schemes that store more than one node per record work well—until you change the tree and need to move nodes between pages.

Keeping the binary tree in memory would eliminate the need to read key data from an external file; this was the solution I used with the hash file classes in the last chapter. The drawback of keeping the tree in memory is just that: It uses memory. Ideally, an index should be stored in a file on disk, where it avoids using internal memory. The file would be organized so that reading would be kept to a minimum.

When you're using a tree as an index, what you need is a structure that keeps itself balanced, holds more than one key per page, and is easy to reorganize. A brilliant algorithm for manipulating just this type of tree was invented in 1972 by R. Bayer and E. McCreight. These structures, known as BTrees, have become the foundation of nearly every database product on the market today. Chapter 15 culminates this book by discussing BTrees as they apply to file indexing.

CHAPTER 15

FILE INDEXES: BTREES

Binary trees, the subject of the previous chapter, are useful in many contexts. However, they fail to provide a solution to indexing files. Binary trees can easily become unbalanced, and even a balanced binary tree is too "high" for practical use on large files. Balancing techniques and paged binary files improve the situation, but only slightly.

What we need is a tree structure that stores many keys in a few records and automatically maintains its balance. That type of tree is known as a BTree.

PROPERTIES OF BTREES

BTrees were invented and introduced by R. Bayer and E. McCreight in a 1972 paper titled "Organization and Maintenance of Larger Order Indexes." Within a few years, BTrees were synonymous with file handling; nearly every major database system, from ISAM to dBASE, uses BTrees.

As I discussed at the end of Chapter 13, a binary tree's problems stem from the way it is constructed. We begin with a root and build downward from there; if the root key is a bad one, so that most subsequent keys are greater or less than the root, the tree will become unbalanced. Various algorithms can then come into play to rebalance the tree—in other words, fixing the problem after it's occurred.

Pages and Keys

Bayer and McCreight solved the binary tree's problems by looking at the problem from a new perspective. They decided to build a tree structure from the bottom up, letting the root emerge as keys are added. To reduce the number of nodes in the tree, they decided to store more than one key per node. Bayer and McCreight apparently named their creation a BTree because it sounded appropriate.

Figure 15-1 shows a BTree node, known as a *page*. Each page contains a set of keys and a set of pointers (also called *links*) to other pages. The keys are stored in an ordered sequential list. There is always one more pointer than there are keys, and the maximum number of pointers in a page is known as the BTree's *order*. Figure 15.1 shows a BTree page of order 6. The pointer to the left of a key points to a subtree that contains all lesser keys. The key to the right points to a subtree containing all greater keys.

FIGURE 15.1 A BTREE PAGE

Figure 15.2 shows a BTree of order 5, in which the single-letter keys CAKRMGOTDXSLJZNPW have been inserted.

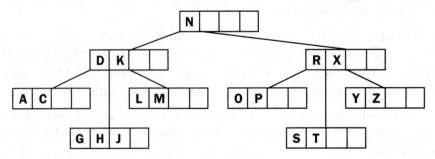

FIGURE 15.2 AN ORDER-5 BTREE CONTAINING 17 KEYS

BTrees follow these rules:

1. A BTree consists of pages that contain order links and order - 1 keys.
2. The keys are stored in sequential lists.
3. Every page has a maximum of order descendents.
4. All leaf pages are the same number of links away from the root.
5. With the exception of the root and leaf pages, every page has at least order / 2 links.
6. The root has at least one key (and thus two links) unless it is also a leaf page.
7. A leaf page has at least order / 2 - 1 keys.
8. New keys are added only to leaf pages.

The construction of this tree will be described later in this chapter. First, let's look at searching a BTree for a given key.

Searching

To describe searching, I'll use these terms: The *search key* is the key being sought, and the *page key* is a key in a page. The search key is compared against page keys until a match is found or the end of the tree is reached.

Searching a page consists of sequentially comparing page keys with the search key. The algorithm's action depends on the relationship of the search key and page key:

1. If a match is found, the search has been successful.
2. If the page key is less than the search key, we move to the next key in the page. If the algorithm has reached the last key in the page, it follows the rightmost link to a page that contains greater keys.
3. If the page key is greater than the search key, we can move to a new page by following the link to a page containing keys less than the page key.

4. In cases 2 and 3, the algorithm may find that the link it wishes to follow does not connect to another page, indicating that the search is in a leaf page. When this happens, the algorithm has failed to find the search key, because there are no more pages to search.

To search the entire tree, begin by examining the first key in the root page. The search routine can be called recursively when the algorithm moves to a new page.

Figure 15.3 shows the process followed in looking for some keys in the BTree shown in Figure 15.2. Here are the steps involved in looking for the key S:

1. We begin at the root page. S is greater than the first root key, N. N is the only key in the root page, so we follow the link to the pages that contain keys greater than N.

2. The next page contains the keys R and X. S is between R and X, so we follow the middle link to the next page.

3. The first key in the page matches S, and we're finished.

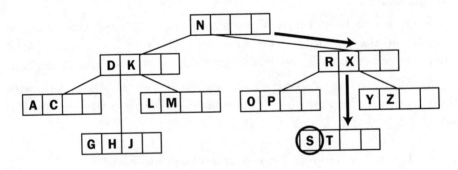

FIGURE 15.3 SEARCHING FOR S

Figure 15.4 shows how looking for the B leads us down a different path:

1. B is less than the root key N, so we move to the page that contains keys less than N.

2. B is less than D, so we move to a new page.

3. B is between A and C—but this is a leaf page, so we can't go any farther. B was not found.

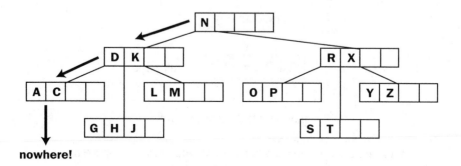

FIGURE 15.4 SEARCHING FOR B

Insertion

To demonstrate key insertion, I'll use an order 5 BTree. Each page can contain as many as five links and four keys.

Inserting the first key into a BTree is simple: It becomes the only key in a new root page. Note that the root page begins existence as a leaf page. Figure 15.5 shows a new root containing a single key, C.

FIGURE 15.5 A NEW ROOT PAGE, WITH ONE KEY

The root page is full after inserting the three keys AKR. Figure 15.6 shows the full root page.

FIGURE 15.6 A FULL ROOT PAGE

Inserting the next key, M, forces changes in the tree structure (see Figure 15.7). Were there enough key slots in the page, M would be inserted between K and R. Because there isn't an open slot, we need to add pages to the tree.

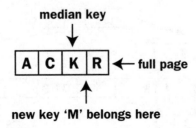

FIGURE 15.7 IDENTIFYING THE COMPONENTS WHEN A PAGE SPLITS

For the purpose of making the algorithm simpler, let's assume that we can "squeeze" M between K and R. We then *split* the page by creating a new page and distributing the keys between it and the original page. The keys A and C remain in the original page, and the keys M and R move into the new page. The median (middle) key, K, is then *promoted* to separate the original page and its new sibling. Because the original page was the root, K becomes the sole key in a new root, increasing the height of the tree by one level. Figure 15.8 shows the result of this process.

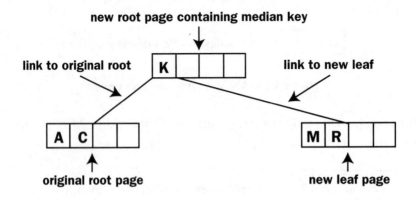

FIGURE 15.8 SPLITTING AND PROMOTION

After adding the keys MGDT, both leaf pages are full. Figure 15.9 shows the tree just before the key H is inserted.

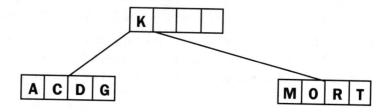

FIGURE 15.9 ADDING A FEW MORE KEYS

When a non-root page is split, it promotes its median key into its parent. Thus, the page containing ACDG splits, creating two pages with the keys AC and GH, respectively. The median key D is promoted into the parent page (which is also the root). Figure 15.10 shows the result of this split and promotion.

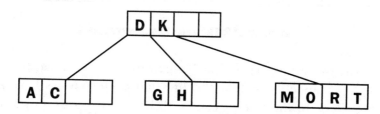

FIGURE 15.10 SPLITTING AND PROMOTING A KEY INTO A PARENT PAGE

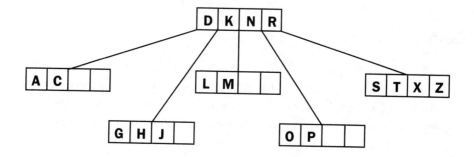

FIGURE 15.11 A FULL ROOT PAGE

When a key is promoted, it causes a full parent page to split and promote, too. This chain reaction broadens the base of the tree by splitting and pushes the root up by promotion. Figure 15.11 shows that after adding the keys OXSLJZNP to the tree, the root page has become full through promotions.

Adding the key Z splits a leaf node and promotes the key X into the root. Because the root is full, it, too, splits. A new root is generated, and the height of the tree is uniformly increased by one level (see Figure 15.12).

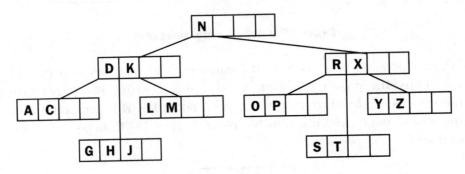

FIGURE 15.12 THE TREE AFTER INSERTING Z

This algorithm guarantees that insertions do not cause the tree to become unbalanced and that the internal nodes always have at least order / 2 keys. In the tree in Figure 15.12, 17 keys were stored in nine pages. Assuming that each page is stored as a record in a file, no more than three records must be read from the file to find any key.

Deletion

When I embarked upon the journey to create my own BTree class library, I encountered a significant problem: a general lack of documentation on the *deletion* of keys. Most references explain insertion and searching in depth—but when they come to deletion, they give vague excuses about complexity. The implementation of BTree key deletion is often given as a "reader exercise."

Deleting a key isn't very difficult once you realize that it involves three major actions that are implemented for a variety of tree configurations. When deleting a key, you must maintain the rules of a BTree as set forth previously. This involves the following steps:

1. Search the tree for the key to be deleted. We'll presume that the key is found.

2. If the key is in the root or an internal page, replace the key with its immediate successor, deleting the successor from the leaf. If the key is found in a leaf page, simply remove the key.

3. A page has now shrunk by one key entry. This action may reduce the number of keys in the page below `order / 2`. If so, we must reorganize the tree.

4. If the leaf page has a sibling with more than `order / 2` keys, we simply redistribute keys among the sibling, its parent, and the leaf page.

5. If the page's siblings have only `order / 2` keys, then we concatenate the page and a sibling. The key in the parent page that separates the deletion page and its sibling is demoted into the combined page. If demoting a key from the parent reduces the parent below `order / 2` keys, we process the parent page beginning at step 4. This recursive process continues until we reach a parent node that has more than `order / 2` keys or until we can redistribute rather than concatenate.

It is possible that the concatenations and demotions will remove the only key from a single-key node, thus reducing the height of the tree by one level.

In essence, deleting a key from the tree involves the reverse of an insertion. Whereas insertion splits nodes and promotes keys, deletion concatenates nodes and demotes keys. Whereas insertions can increase the height of the tree by splitting the root page, deletion can reduce the height of the tree by concatenating two sibling pages and demoting the only key from the root page.

I couldn't draw any Figures that made the deletion process easier to visualize. Review the code that follows; it should clarify how the deletion process works.

Implementation Issues

A compromise must be struck between the size of a tree's pages and its height. The larger the order, the shorter the tree, thereby reducing the number of pages that must be read to find a key. However, larger pages require longer sequential searches for keys in each page. A tree with order 500, for example, will store 1,000,000 keys in three levels, and a tree with order 10 will require six levels of pages. In general, because reading data from disk is vastly slower than sequentially searching a list of in-memory keys, the page size should be made as large as possible.

To use a BTree as an index, each key must be associated with a pointer to a data record. I decided to implement a BTree-indexed file using two physical disk files. One file contains the BTree pages, and the other file contains the data records. After I write a record to the data file, I pass its key and file pointer to the routine that inserts the information into the BTree.

Until now, the file types described in this book have stored variable-length records. A list of deleted records is kept, and, when a new record is written to the file, the empty records are scanned to see whether any of them is large enough to contain the new record. When a variable-length record is changed, it may become larger, and it may not be written into the same position it originally occupied. This scheme works well for data records, because they often vary a great deal in length.

A file that contains BTree pages has different requirements. Because pages have links to other pages, it makes algorithms simpler to implement if pages are treated as fixed-length records stored in a fixed location. This technique requires a file that contains fixed-length records and that stores a modified record in the same location it was read from. Because pages are sometimes deleted from the tree when keys are deleted, the page file will need to keep a list of deleted records for use by newly generated pages.

484

BTREE UTILITY CLASSES

When I began implementing the page file class, I ran into another problem: Assuming that the pages were fixed in length meant that the keys themselves had to have a fixed length, too.

This assumption isn't a problem when you're using elementary data types, such as `long`s or `float`s, but it did mean that I couldn't use a variable-length type such as a `char` array or `String`. Because most databases are indexed via a text key, I needed to create a fixed-length string-type key.

Fixed-Length String Keys

I used a template to create a class named `StringKey`, which contains a fixed-length array of characters:

```
template <size_t L = 32>
    class StringKey
        {
        public:
            // constructors
            StringKey();

            StringKey
                (
                const String & str
                );

            StringKey
                (
                const char * str
                );

            StringKey
                (
                const StringKey<L> & sk
                );

            void operator =
                (
```

```
                const StringKey<L> & sk
                );

           bool operator <
                (
                const StringKey<L> & sk
                ) const;

           bool operator ==
                (
                const StringKey<L> & sk
                ) const;

           bool operator >
                (
                const StringKey<L> & sk
                ) const;

           operator String() const;

      protected:
           char Text[L];
      };
```

I've seen very little code that uses template arguments as does StringKey. This much-overlooked technique defines, at compile time, the specific size attributes of a data type. In the case of StringKey, I can create a specific type with a fixed-length buffer, thus avoiding the need to dynamically allocate memory. In this case, I've supplied a default StringKey size of 32, which, in my experience, is the average length of a database string key.

The StringKey functions allow StringKeys to interact with Strings (and, through automatic conversions, with char arrays). Note that the constructor converts the incoming data to uppercase so that string comparisons are unaffected by the case of the original information.

```
template <size_t L>
    StringKey<L>::StringKey()
        {
        memset(Text,0,L);
        }
```

```
template <size_t L>
    StringKey<L>::StringKey
        (
        const String & str
        )
        {
        memset(Text,0,L);
        const char * ch = (const char *)str;

        for (size_t n = 0; (*ch) && (n < (L - 1)); ++n)
            {
            Text[n] = toupper(*ch);
            ++ch;
            }
        }

template <size_t L>
    StringKey<L>::StringKey
        (
        const char * str
        )
        {
        memset(Text,0,L);

        const char * ch = str;

        for (size_t n = 0; (*ch) && (n < (L - 1)); ++n)
            {
            Text[n] = toupper(*ch);
            ++ch;
            }
        }

template <size_t L>
    StringKey<L>::StringKey
        (
        const StringKey<L> & sk
        )
        {
        for (size_t n = 0; n < L; ++n)
            Text[n] = sk.Text[n];
        }

template <size_t L>
    void StringKey<L>::operator =
```

```
        (
        const StringKey<L> & sk
        )
        {
        for (size_t n = 0; n < L; ++n)
            Text[n] = sk.Text[n];
        }

template <size_t L>
    inline StringKey<L>::operator String() const
        {
        return String(Text);
        }
```

The BTree algorithms require that keys support the basic equality, less-than, and greater-than operations, which I have defined for StringKey using the standard library function strcmp.

```
template <size_t L>
    inline bool StringKey<L>::operator <
        (
        const StringKey<L> & sk
        ) const
        {
        return (strcmp(Text,sk.Text) < 0);
        }

template <size_t L>
    inline bool StringKey<L>::operator ==
        (
        const StringKey<L> & sk
        ) const
        {
        return (!strcmp(Text,sk.Text));
        }

template <size_t L>
    inline bool StringKey<L>::operator >
        (
        const StringKey<L> & sk
        ) const
        {
        return (strcmp(Text,sk.Text) > 0);
        }
```

Exceptions

The BTreeEx class implements the same system of exception handling that I introduced in earlier chapters.

```
enum BTreeError
    {
    BTEX_ALLOC,        // fatal: memory allocation failure
    BTEX_TOOSMALL,     // fatal: created bucket w/ zero buckets
    BTEX_INV_PAGE,     // invalid page encountered
    BTEX_NO_PG_HDR,    // no page file header
    BTEX_BAD_SEEK,     // seek failed
    BTEX_BAD_WRITE,    // write failed
    BTEX_BAD_READ,     // read failed
    BTEX_LOCKED,       // attempt to change while locked
    BTEX_NOTFOUND,     // record not found
    BTEX_CORRUPTED     // fatal: table / list has been corrupted
    };


class BTreeEx : public ExceptionBase
    {
    public:
        BTreeEx(BTreeError err) { Error = err; }
        BTreeError WhatsWrong() { return Error; }
        void Explain(DiagOutput & out);
    private:
        BTreeError Error;
    };


void BTreeEx::Explain
    (
    DiagOutput & out
    )
    {
    switch (Error)
        {
        case BTEX_ALLOC:
            out.DisplayMsg
                (
                "BTree memory allocation failure",
                DIAG_ERROR
                );
            break;
        case BTEX_TOOSMALL:
```

```
            out.DisplayMsg
                (
                "cannot create zero-size BTree",
                DIAG_ERROR
                );
            break;
        case BTEX_INV_PAGE:
            out.DisplayMsg
                (
                "invalid Page for this BTree",
                DIAG_ERROR
                );
            break;
        case BTEX_NO_PG_HDR:
            out.DisplayMsg
                (
                "cannot find Page File header",
                DIAG_ERROR
                );
            break;
        case BTEX_BAD_SEEK:
            out.DisplayMsg
                (
                "Page file seek failed",
                DIAG_ERROR
                );
            break;
        case BTEX_BAD_WRITE:
            out.DisplayMsg
                (
                "Page file write failed",
                DIAG_ERROR
                );
            break;
        case BTEX_BAD_READ:
            out.DisplayMsg
                (
                "Page file read failed",
                DIAG_ERROR
                );
            break;
        case BTEX_LOCKED:
            out.DisplayMsg
                (
                "attempted operation on locked BTree",
                DIAG_ERROR
                );
```

```
                break;
        case BTEX_NOTFOUND:
            out.DisplayMsg
                (
                "BTree record not found",
                DIAG_ERROR
                );
            break;
        case BTEX_CORRUPTED:
            out.DisplayMsg
                (
                "BTree corrupted",
                DIAG_ERROR
                );
            break;
        default:
            out.DisplayMsg
                (
                "unexpected BTree exception",
                DIAG_ERROR
                );
        }
    }
```

BTREE PAGE CLASS

The Page structure defines a single page in a BTree. I defined it as a structure to simplify manipulation of its contents. Implementing Page as a
class, with its data members private, would have required a mass of functions that allowed changes to those members—eliminating any value in
making them private in the first place.

```
template <class K>
    struct Page
        {
        PageHeader Hdr;    // header information
        K * Key;           // key array [MaxKeys]
        DataFilePtr * Ptr; // rec  index array [MaxKeys]
        DataFilePtr * Lnk; // page index array [Order]

        Page(size_t ord);
        Page(const Page & p);
```

```
        ~Page();
        void operator = (const Page & page);
        };
```

The parameters that define the `Page` are contained in a header. The `Hdr` record simplifies writing the page to a file, as you'll see in the implementation of the `PageFile` class.

```
struct PageHeader
    {
    DataFilePtr FilePtr;    // ptr to location in PageFile
    DataFilePtr ParentPtr; // ptr to parent in PageFile

    size_t Order;     // maximum # of page  links in page
    size_t MaxKeys;   // maximum # of keys  in page
    size_t MinKeys;   // minimum # of keys  in page
    size_t NoOfKeys;  // actual  # of keys  in page
    size_t KeySize;   // maximum # of bytes in a key
    };
```

In the header, `Order` is the order of the tree, `KeySize` is the maximum length of the keys the tree contains, `NoOfKeys` is the number of keys currently stored in a `Page`, `MaxKeys` is the maximum number of keys the `Page` can hold, and `MinKeys` is the minimum number of keys allowed in an internal `Page`. The file pointer of a `Page`'s parent is stored in its `ParentPtr` member, and `FilePtr` contains the location in the `PageFile` where a `Page` is stored.

In `Page`, the `Key`, `Ptr`, and `Lnk` members point to dynamically allocated arrays of keys and `DataFilePtr`s.

The constructor's parameters define the order and key size for a new `Page`. Other header values are calculated from the order. A new `Page` is always empty; it has no parent and no children and does not contain any keys or links.

```
template <class K>
    Page<K>::Page(size_t ord)
        {
        size_t n;
```

```
      Hdr.FilePtr   = DFP_NULL;
Hdr.ParentPtr = DFP_NULL;
Hdr.Order     = ord;
Hdr.MaxKeys   = ord - 1;
Hdr.MinKeys   = ord / 2;
Hdr.NoOfKeys  = 0;
Hdr.KeySize   = sizeof(K);

if (Hdr.Order == 0)
    {
    Key = NULL;
    Ptr = NULL;
    Lnk = NULL;


    return;
    }

// allocate key array
Key = new K [Hdr.MaxKeys];

if (Key == NULL)
    throw BTreeEx(BTEX_ALLOC);


memset(Key,0,Hdr.MaxKeys * sizeof(K));

// allocate record pointer array
Ptr = new DataFilePtr [Hdr.MaxKeys];

if (Ptr == NULL)
    throw BTreeEx(BTEX_ALLOC);

// set pointers to nothing
for (n = 0; n < Hdr.MaxKeys; ++n)
    Ptr[n] = DFP_NULL;

// allocate page pointer array
Lnk = new DataFilePtr [Hdr.Order];

if (Lnk == NULL)
    throw BTreeEx(BTEX_ALLOC);

/// fill page indexes with "empty" values
for (n = 0; n < Hdr.Order; ++n)
```

```
        Lnk[n] = DFP_NULL;
    }
```

The copy constructor creates a new Page from an existing one.

```
template <class K>
    Page<K>::Page(const Page<K> & pg)
        {
        Hdr = pg.Hdr;

        // allocate key array
        Key = new K [Hdr.MaxKeys];

        if (Key == NULL)
            throw BTreeEx(BTEX_ALLOC);

        for (size_t n = 0; n < Hdr.MaxKeys; ++n)
            Key[n] = pg.Key[n];

        // allocate record pointer array
        Ptr = new DataFilePtr [Hdr.MaxKeys];

        if (Ptr == NULL)
            throw BTreeEx(BTEX_ALLOC);

        memcpy(Ptr,pg.Ptr,Hdr.MaxKeys * sizeof(DataFilePtr));

        // allocate page pointer array
        Lnk = new DataFilePtr [Hdr.Order];

        if (Lnk == NULL)
            throw BTreeEx(BTEX_ALLOC);

        memcpy(Lnk,pg.Lnk,Hdr.Order * sizeof(DataFilePtr));
        }
```

The destructor deletes the Key, Ptr, and Lnk arrays when a Page object is destroyed.

```
template <class K>
    Page<K>::~Page()
```

```
        {
        // delete old buffers
        delete [] Key;
        delete [] Ptr;
        delete [] Lnk;
        }
```

The assignment operator copies the contents of one Page to another. It copies the source Page's header, deletes the existing buffers (if they have been allocated), allocates new buffers, and copies the contents of the source buffers.

```
template <class K>
    void Page<K>::operator = (const Page<K> & pg)
        {
        if (Hdr.Order != pg.Hdr.Order)
            {
            // allocate key array
            if (Key != NULL)
                delete [] Key;

            Key = new K [pg.Hdr.MaxKeys];

            if (Key == NULL)
                throw BTreeEx(BTEX_ALLOC);

            // allocate record pointer array
            if (Ptr != NULL)
                delete [] Ptr;

            Ptr = new DataFilePtr [pg.Hdr.MaxKeys];

            if (Ptr == NULL)
                throw BTreeEx(BTEX_ALLOC);

            // allocate page pointer array
            if (Lnk != NULL)
                delete [] Lnk;

            Lnk = new DataFilePtr [pg.Hdr.Order];

            if (Lnk == NULL)
```

```
            throw BTreeEx(BTEX_ALLOC);
    }

    Hdr = pg.Hdr;

    for (size_t n = 0; n < Hdr.MaxKeys; ++n)
        Key[n] = pg.Key[n];

    memcpy(Ptr,pg.Ptr,Hdr.MaxKeys * sizeof(DataFilePtr));
    memcpy(Lnk,pg.Lnk,Hdr.Order * sizeof(DataFilePtr));
    }
```

PAGEFILE CLASS

A PageFile is a file type that's specifically optimized for storing BTree Page objects. PageFile is based on the DataFileBase class, and it has some similarities to the DataFile class implemented in Chapter 9.

```
template <class K>
    class PageFile : public DataFileBase
        {
        public:
            PageFile
                (
                const String & name
                );

            PageFile
                (
                const String & name, size_t ord
                );

            ~PageFile();

            void ReadRoot
                (
                Page<K> & pg
                );

            void WriteRoot
```

```
                    (
                    Page<K> & pg
                    );

            void Write
                    (
                    Page<K> & pg,
                    bool root = false
                    );

            void Read
                    (
                    DataFilePtr ptr,
                    Page<K> & pg
                    );

            void Delete
                    (
                    DataFilePtr ptr
                    );

            void Commit();

    private:
            PageFileHdr Hdr;
    };
```

A `PageFile` defines a single data member, `Hdr`, which is a file header containing format information. `Hdr` is a `PageFileHdr` structure.

```
struct PageFileHdr
    {
    size_t KeySize;
    size_t Order;

    DataFilePtr RootPtr;
    DataFilePtr FirstDead;
    };
```

The `PageFile` header stores the order of pages stored in the file, the maximum size of a key, a file pointer to the root page, and a file pointer to the first deleted record. All pages stored in a given `PageFile` have the same order and page size, allowing a `PageFile` to treat `Page`s as fixed-length records.

`PageFile`s maintain a list of deleted records using the techniques demonstrated by the `DataFile` class in Chapter 12. When a `Page` is deleted, it is placed at the head of the list by storing the current `Hdr.FirstDead` value in the record and placing the file pointer of the deleted record in `Hdr.FirstDead`.

A new `PageFile` is constructed by providing a file name and an order:

```
template <class K>
    PageFile<K>::PageFile
        (
        const String & name,
        size_t ord
        )
        : DataFileBase(name,FM_NEW)
        {
        Hdr.Order     = ord;
        Hdr.KeySize   = sizeof(K);
        Hdr.RootPtr   = DFP_NULL;
        Hdr.FirstDead = DFP_NULL;

        size_t n = write
                    (
                    DOSHandle,
                    &Hdr,
                    sizeof(PageFileHdr)
                    );

        if (n != sizeof(PageFileHdr))
            throw BTreeEx(BTEX_NO_PG_HDR);

        // create Root page
        Page<K> root(Hdr.Order);

        // store root
        Write(root);

        // save root address
        Hdr.RootPtr = root.Hdr.FilePtr;
        }
```

An existing `PageFile` can be opened by simply contructing a `PageFile` object with a name. The order and key size information is retrieved from the file header:

```
template <class K>
    PageFile<K>::PageFile
        (
        const String & name
        )
        : DataFileBase(name,FM_EXISTING)
        {
        size_t n;

        n = read(DOSHandle,&Hdr,sizeof(PageFileHdr));

        if (n != sizeof(PageFileHdr))
            throw BTreeEx(BTEX_NO_PG_HDR);
        }
```

The destructor simply calls `Commit` to make certain that the header record has been updated before the `PageFile` is closed:

```
template <class K>
    inline PageFile<K>::~PageFile()
        {
        Commit();
        }
```

A `Page` is the only type of data that can be stored in a `PageFile`. The `Write` function has two parameters: `pg`, a reference to a page being written, and `root`, a `Boolean` value indicating that a new root page is being written. The default value of `root` is `BOOL_FALSE`; a program does not generate new roots as often as it creates internal and leaf pages.

```
template <class K>
    void PageFile<K>::Write
        (
        Page<K> & pg,
        bool root
        )
```

```
    {
size_t n;
long    pos;

// confirm that this page belongs in this file
if ((Hdr.Order    != pg.Hdr.Order)
||  (Hdr.KeySize != pg.Hdr.KeySize))
    throw BTreeEx(BTEX_INV_PAGE);

// if page has never been written
//    find a spot to write it
if (pg.Hdr.FilePtr == DFP_NULL)
    {
    if (Hdr.FirstDead != DFP_NULL)
        {
        // write this record to 1st dead entry
        pg.Hdr.FilePtr = Hdr.FirstDead;

        // find record to write new page in
        pos = lseek
                (
                DOSHandle,
                Hdr.FirstDead,
                SEEK_SET
                );

        if (pos == -1L)
            throw BTreeEx(BTEX_BAD_SEEK);

        // set first dead to next dead record
        n = read
                (
                DOSHandle,
                &Hdr.FirstDead,
                sizeof(DataFilePtr)
                );

        if (n != sizeof(DataFilePtr))
            throw BTreeEx(BTEX_BAD_READ);
        }
    else // append to end of file!
        {
        // look for end of file
        pos = lseek(DOSHandle,0,SEEK_END);
```

```
        if (pos == -1L)
            throw BTreeEx(BTEX_BAD_SEEK);

        // and get a pointer to it
        pg.Hdr.FilePtr = tell(DOSHandle);
        }
    }

// construct block of memory
size_t keysize = pg.Hdr.MaxKeys
                    * Hdr.KeySize;

size_t ptrsize = pg.Hdr.MaxKeys
                    * sizeof(DataFilePtr);

size_t lnksize = pg.Hdr.Order
                    * sizeof(DataFilePtr);

size_t bufsize = sizeof(PageHeader)
                    + keysize
                    + ptrsize
                    + lnksize;

char * buffer  = new char [bufsize];

if (buffer == NULL)
        throw BTreeEx(BTEX_ALLOC);

char * bufptr = buffer;

// copy page header to buffer
memcpy(bufptr,&pg.Hdr,sizeof(PageHeader));
bufptr += sizeof(PageHeader);

// copy keys
memcpy(bufptr,pg.Key,keysize);
bufptr += keysize;

// copy data file pointers
memcpy(bufptr,pg.Ptr,ptrsize);
bufptr += ptrsize;

// copy page links
```

```
    memcpy(bufptr,pg.Lnk,lnksize);

    // write buffer to file
    pos = lseek(DOSHandle,pg.Hdr.FilePtr,SEEK_SET);

        if (pos == -1L)
            throw BTreeEx(BTEX_BAD_SEEK);

    n = write(DOSHandle,buffer,bufsize);

    if (n != bufsize)
            throw BTreeEx(BTEX_BAD_WRITE);

    // delete buffer
    delete [] buffer;

    // update root pointer in header, if this is a new root
    if (root)
        Hdr.RootPtr = pg.Hdr.FilePtr;

    // make sure header is current
    Commit();
    }
```

Write begins by comparing the order and key size stored in its header with the order and key size of the page being written. If these values don't match, the page is rejected and Write throws an exception. This approach ensures that the PageFile will only contain pages having identical orders and key sizes.

If the Page being written has an assigned file pointer in its Hdr.FilePtr member, Write stores the Page in its original location. If Hdr.FilePtr is empty (indicated by a PFP_NULL value), Write checks the deleted list to see whether any "dead" records are available. If the list of deleted records contains an entry, the new Page is written into the first deleted record. Otherwise, the new Page is appended to the file. If the Page has an Hdr.FilePtr value of DFP_NULL, Hdr.FilePtr is set to the location where the Page was written before it is stored.

I store `Pages` using a simple technique. The `Page Hdr` value is written first, followed by the keys written as a fixed-length block. Then the arrays pointed to by `Ptr` and `Lnk` are written.

The `Read` function differs in many respects from the `Read` function in `DataFile`. Whereas `DataFile::Read` reads a `DataBlock` from the current position in a file, the `PageFile::Read` function obtains a `Page` from a file location specified by the parameter `ptr`. `PageFile` does not implement a `Seek` function. Each page contains explicit links to other pages, and the algorithms directly process pages via those links.

```
template <class K>
    void PageFile<K>::Read
        (
        DataFilePtr ptr,
        Page<K> & pg
        )
        {
        long pos;
        size_t n;

        // locate requested record
        pos = lseek(DOSHandle,ptr,SEEK_SET);

            if (pos == -1L)
                throw BTreeEx(BTEX_BAD_SEEK);

        // create a blank page
        Page<K> temp(Hdr.Order);

        n = read(DOSHandle,&temp.Hdr,sizeof(PageHeader));

        // be sure that this header matches expected values
        if ((n != sizeof(PageHeader))
        || (temp.Hdr.Order    != Hdr.Order)
        || (temp.Hdr.KeySize != Hdr.KeySize)
        || (temp.Hdr.FilePtr != ptr))
            throw BTreeEx(BTEX_CORRUPTED);

        // allocate a buffer to hold incoming keys
```

```
        size_t keysize = temp.Hdr.KeySize
                        * temp.Hdr.MaxKeys;

        size_t ptrsize = temp.Hdr.MaxKeys
                        * sizeof(DataFilePtr);

        size_t lnksize = temp.Hdr.Order
                        * sizeof(DataFilePtr);

        size_t recsize = keysize + ptrsize + lnksize;

        char * buffer = new char [recsize];

        if (buffer == NULL)
            throw BTreeEx(BTEX_ALLOC);

        // read keys from file
        n = read(DOSHandle,buffer,recsize);

        if (n != recsize)
            throw BTreeEx(BTEX_BAD_READ);

        char * bufptr = buffer;

        // move keys into page
        memcpy(temp.Key,bufptr,keysize);
        bufptr += keysize;

        // read data record pointers and page links
        memcpy(temp.Ptr,bufptr,ptrsize);
        bufptr += ptrsize;

        memcpy(temp.Lnk,bufptr,lnksize);

        pg = temp;

        delete [] buffer;
    }
```

Read checks the data read from the file to be sure that the Order and
KeySize values in the Page's header match the corresponding values in
the PageFile's header.

To read the root record, use the `ReadRoot` function. This simple inline function returns the result of calling `Read` with an argument of `Hdr.RootPtr`.

```
template <class K>
    inline void PageFile<K>::ReadRoot
        (
        Page<K> & pg
        )
        {
        Read(Hdr.RootPtr, pg);
        }
```

`Delete` removes a `Page` from a `PageFile` by marking its record as deleted. The location of the newly deleted record in the file becomes the `FirstDead` value in the header, and the previous value of `FirstDead` is stored in the first few bytes of the deleted record. This method maintains a linked list of deleted records that can be reused by the `Write` function.

```
template <class K>
    void PageFile<K>::Delete
        (
        DataFilePtr ptr
        )
        {
        // locate record to be deleted
        long pos = lseek(DOSHandle,ptr,SEEK_SET);

            if (pos == -1L)
                throw BTreeEx(BTEX_BAD_SEEK);

        // store the previous head of the deleted list
        size_t n = write
                (
                DOSHandle,
                &Hdr.FirstDead,
                sizeof(DataFilePtr)
                );

        if (n != sizeof(DataFilePtr))
                throw BTreeEx(BTEX_BAD_WRITE);

        // update header
```

```
        Hdr.FirstDead = ptr;

        Commit();
        }
```

Commit updates the file header on disk from the Hdr data member.

```
template <class K>
    void PageFile<K>::Commit()
        {
        // rewrite header
        long pos = lseek(DOSHandle,0,SEEK_SET);

        if (pos == -1L)
            throw BTreeEx(BTEX_BAD_SEEK);

        size_t n = write
                    (
                    DOSHandle,
                    &Hdr,
                    sizeof(PageFileHdr)
                    );

        if (n != sizeof(PageFileHdr))
                throw BTreeEx(BTEX_BAD_WRITE);
        }
```

BTreeFile Class

Now we get to the meat: the BTreeFile template class. A BTreeFile has a PageFile object for storing Pages, and a DataFile object for storing DataBlocks. When data are stored in a BTreeFile, they are associated with a key in the PageFile. To find a record, a key is used to retrieve the DataFilePtr of its associated data from a Page in the PageFile.

```
template <class K, class D>
    class BTreeFile
        {
```

```
public:
    // construct new BTree file
    BTreeFile
        (
        const String & basename,
        size_t ord
        );

    // construct from existing BTree file
    BTreeFile
        (
        const String & basename
        );

    ~BTreeFile();

    void Write
        (
        const K & key,
        const D & data
        );

    D Read
        (
        const K & key
        );

    void Delete
        (
        const K & key
        );

    void InOrder
        (
        void (*func)(const K & key, const D & data)
        );

private:
    // data members
    DataFile<D> * Data; // file w/ DataBlocks
    PageFile<K> * Tree; // file w/ tree pages

    bool     Locked; // set True during InOrder
    Page<K>  Root;   // root page
    String   TreeFileName;
```

```
String      DataFileName;

// pointer used by Traverse
void (*TravFunc)(const K & key,const D & data);

// search for a node
bool Search
    (
    const Page<K> & pg,
    const K & searchkey,
    Page<K> & keypage,
    size_t & pos
    );

// insert node into leaf
void InsertKey
    (
    const K & inskey,
    DataFilePtr dataptr
    );

// promote a key into a parent node
void PromoteInternal
    (
    Page<K> & pg,
    const K & inskey,
    DataFilePtr dataptr,
    DataFilePtr pagelnk
    );

// promote a key by creating a new root
void PromoteRoot
    (
    const K & inskey,
    DataFilePtr dataptr,
    Page<K> & lesspage,
    Page<K> & grtrpage
    );

// adjust tree if leaf has shrunk in size
void AdjustTree
    (
    Page<K> & leafpg
    );
```

```
// redistribute keys among siblings and parent
void Redistribute
    (
    size_t keypos,
    Page<K> & lesspage,
    Page<K> & parpage,
    Page<K> & grtrpage
    );

// concatenate sibling pages
void Concatenate
    (
    size_t keypos,
    Page<K> & lesspage,
    Page<K> & parpage,
    Page<K> & grtrpage
    );

// recursive traversal function used by InOrder
void RecurseTraverse
    (
    const Page<K> & pg
    );
};
```

The data members `Data` and `Tree` are dynamically allocated file objects that contain the BTree's `DataBlock`s and `Page`s, respectively. I implemented these objects as pointers and allocated `DataFile` and `PageFile` objects during `BTreeFile` construction. I could have derived `BTreeFile` from `DataFile` and `PageFile`, as I derived `HashFile` from `HashFileTable` and `DataFile`. The difference in designs serves to illustrate different approaches to solving similar problems.

The data items `DataFileExt` and `HashFileExt`, defined outside the class, provide extensions that are appended to the base file name by the private `MakeBTreeName` function. The `HashFile` class uses a similar convention.

```
const String TreeFileExt(".BTK");
const String TreeDataExt(".BTD");

String MakeBTreeName(const String & basename, const String & ext)
    {
```

```
String name;

if (basename.Length() < 8)
    name = basename;
else
    name = basename.CutHead(8);

name += ext;

return name;
}
```

In the BTreeFile class, `Root` contains the current root `Page` of the BTree; keeping the root resident in memory speeds most operations. The `Locked` member is set to `BOOL_TRUE` when the `InOrder` function is called; otherwise, it is `BOOL_FALSE`. When `Locked` is `BOOL_TRUE`, the `Write` and `Delete` functions generate an exception, preventing changes in the files while a search is under way. This mechanism could be extended for multiuser environments to create record and file locking.

Constructors

A new `BTreeFile` is constructed by providing a base file name and an order. The constructor begins by calling constructors to assign values to the file names `DataFileName` and `PageFileName`. Then the constructor creates `DataFile` and `PageFile` objects that generate new files on disk. The constructor finishes by reading the blank root page from `Page`.

```
template <class K, class D>
    BTreeFile<K,D>::BTreeFile
        (
        const String & basename,
        size_t ord
        )
        : DataFileName
            (
            MakeBTreeName(basename,TreeDataExt)
            ),
          TreeFileName
```

```
    (
    MakeBTreeName(basename,TreeFileExt)
    ),
  Root(0)
{
// create data file object
Data = new DataFile<D>(DataFileName,FM_NEW);

if (Data == NULL)
    throw BTreeEx(BTEX_ALLOC);

// create tree file object
Tree = new PageFile<K>(TreeFileName,ord);

if (Tree == NULL)
    throw BTreeEx(BTEX_ALLOC);

Tree->ReadRoot(Root);

Locked = false;
}
```

To open an existing `BTreeFile`, only the base file name is specified. The file names are constructed, `DataFile` and `PageFile` objects are created to open and access the existing information, and the root page is read;

```
template <class K, class D>
    BTreeFile<K,D>::BTreeFile
        (
        const String & basename
        )
        : DataFileName
            (
            MakeBTreeName(basename,TreeDataExt)
            ),
          TreeFileName
            (
            MakeBTreeName(basename,TreeFileExt)
            ),
          Root(0)
        {
        // create data file object
        Data = new DataFile<D>(DataFileName,FM_EXISTING);
```

```
    if (Data == NULL)
        throw BTreeEx(BTEX_ALLOC);

    // create tree file object
    Tree = new PageFile<K>(TreeFileName);

    if (Tree == NULL)
        throw BTreeEx(BTEX_ALLOC);

    // create root page
    Tree->ReadRoot(Root);

    Locked = false;
    }
```

The destructor automatically deletes the allocated file objects when a BTreeFile object is destroyed. The data and pages, of course, remain in the files on disk and are automatically saved when their associated objects are destroyed.

```
template <class K, class D>
    BTreeFile<K,D>::~BTreeFile()
        {
        // delete files
        delete Data;
        delete Tree;
        }
```

Writing Records

To write a record in a BTreeFile, both a key and data must be provided. The Write function stores the data object in the Data file, which returns a DataFilePtr indicating the location of the DataBlock in the file. That pointer and the key are then passed to the InsertKey function, which updates the BTree.

```
template <class K, class D>
    void BTreeFile<K,D>::Write
        (
        const K & key, const D & db
```

```
)
{
if (Locked)
    throw BTreeEx(BTEX_LOCKED);

// write the data record
DataFilePtr dataptr = Data->Write(db);

// store the key in a page
InsertKey(key,dataptr);
}
```

The Search function is a private member function. Search is recursive; it is
called initially with the root page of the tree, and it moves down the tree,
following links, by calling itself. If Search finds the search key, keypage is
assigned to the page in which the key was found and pos is set to the key's
location within that page. If the key was not found, Search returns
BOOL_FALSE, sets keypage to the leaf page where the search key should be
inserted, and sets pos to the position in that page where the key belongs.
The Read, Write, and Delete functions use Search to find keys or the leaf
into which a key should be inserted.

```
template <class K, class D>
    bool BTreeFile<K,D>::Search
        (
        const Page<K> & pg,
        const K & searchkey,
        Page<K> & keypage,
        size_t & pos
        )
        {
        bool result;
        pos = 0;

        for (;;)
          {
            if (pos == pg.Hdr.NoOfKeys)
                goto getpage;

            if (pg.Key[pos] == searchkey)
                {
                keypage = pg;
```

```
            result = true;
            break;
            }
        else
            {
        if (pg.Key[pos] < searchkey)
            ++pos;
        else
            {
            // You don't see this label <grin>
            getpage:

            // if in a leaf page, key wasn't found
            if (pg.Lnk[pos] == DFP_NULL)
                {
                keypage = pg;
                result  = false;
                }
            else
                {
                Page<K> nextpg(pg.Hdr.Order);

                Tree->Read(pg.Lnk[pos],nextpg);

                result = Search(nextpg,searchkey,
                                    keypage,pos);
                }

            break;
            }
            }
        }

    return result;
    }
```

InsertKey is a private member function; it is called only by the Write function. InsertKey begins by calling the Search function. If the key was
found, InsertKey deletes the data record associated with its entry in the
Page and then sets the Page to point to the new record referenced by dat-
aptr. Thus, duplicate keys cause a new data record to replace the old data
associated with a key.

```
template <class K, class D>
    void BTreeFile<K,D>::InsertKey
        (
        const K & inskey,
        DataFilePtr dataptr
        )
        {
        Page<K> inspage(0);
        size_t inspos;

        if (Search(Root,inskey,inspage,inspos))
            {
            // delete old data record
            Data->Seek(inspage.Ptr[inspos]);
            Data->Delete();

            // store new data record pointer
            inspage.Ptr[inspos] = dataptr;

            // rewrite modified page
            Tree->Write(inspage);
            }
        else
            {
            if (inspage.Hdr.NoOfKeys == inspage.Hdr.MaxKeys)
                {
                // temporary arrays
                K * tempkeys = new K[inspage.Hdr.MaxKeys+1];

                DataFilePtr * tempptrs =
                    new DataFilePtr[inspage.Hdr.MaxKeys+1];

                // copy entries from inspage to temporaries
                size_t nt = 0; // index into temporaries
                size_t ni = 0; // index into inspage

                tempkeys[inspos] = inskey;
                tempptrs[inspos] = dataptr;

                while (ni < inspage.Hdr.MaxKeys)
                    {
                    if (ni == inspos)
                        ++nt;
```

```
                        tempkeys[nt] = inspage.Key[ni];
                        tempptrs[nt] = inspage.Ptr[ni];


                        ++ni;
                        ++nt;
                        }


                // generate a new leaf node
                Page<K> sibpage(inspage.Hdr.Order);
                sibpage.Hdr.ParentPtr =
                                inspage.Hdr.ParentPtr;


                // clear # of keys in pages
                inspage.Hdr.NoOfKeys = 0;
                sibpage.Hdr.NoOfKeys = 0;


                // copy approp. keys from temp to pages
                for (ni=0; ni < inspage.Hdr.MinKeys; ++ni)
                        {
                        inspage.Key[ni] = tempkeys[ni];
                        inspage.Ptr[ni] = tempptrs[ni];


                        ++inspage.Hdr.NoOfKeys;
                        }


                for (
                        ni  = inspage.Hdr.MinKeys + 1;
                        ni <= inspage.Hdr.MaxKeys;
                        ++ni
                        )
                        {
                        sibpage.Key[ni-1-inspage.Hdr.MinKeys] =
                                        tempkeys[ni];


                        sibpage.Ptr[ni-1-inspage.Hdr.MinKeys] =
                                        tempptrs[ni];


                        ++sibpage.Hdr.NoOfKeys;
                        }


                // Fill remaining entries in inspage with null
                // Sibpage is initialized to null values by
                // the constructor.
```

```
for (
    ni = inspage.Hdr.MinKeys;
    ni < inspage.Hdr.MaxKeys;
    ++ni
    )
    {
    inspage.Key[ni] = K();
    inspage.Ptr[ni] = DFP_NULL;
    }

// write pages
Tree->Write(inspage);
Tree->Write(sibpage);

// promote key and pointer
if (inspage.Hdr.ParentPtr == DFP_NULL)
    {
    // we need to create a new root
    PromoteRoot
        (
        tempkeys[inspage.Hdr.MinKeys],
        tempptrs[inspage.Hdr.MinKeys],
        inspage,
        sibpage
        );
    }
else
    {
    Page<K> parpage(0);

    Tree->Read
            (
            inspage.Hdr.ParentPtr,
            parpage
            );

    // promote into parent
    PromoteInternal
        (
        parpage,
        tempkeys[inspage.Hdr.MinKeys],
        tempptrs[inspage.Hdr.MinKeys],
        sibpage.Hdr.FilePtr
        );
    }
```

```
                delete [] tempkeys;
                delete [] tempptrs;
                }
        else // simply insert new key and data ptr
            {
            for (
                size_t n = inspage.Hdr.NoOfKeys;
                n > inspos;
                —n
                )
                {
                inspage.Key[n] = inspage.Key[n - 1];
                inspage.Ptr[n] = inspage.Ptr[n - 1];
                }

            inspage.Key[inspos] = inskey;
            inspage.Ptr[inspos] = dataptr;

            ++inspage.Hdr.NoOfKeys;

            Tree->Write(inspage);
            }
        }

    // refresh root in memory
    Tree->ReadRoot(Root);
    }
```

If the key was not found, Search returns the leaf page in inspage where the key should be inserted at inspos. If inspage is not full, the key is inserted by shifting keys to the left and placing the new key and its data record pointer in the opened position.

When inspage is full, it needs to be split and the median key is promoted. The split is accomplished by creating a temporary list of keys and data record pointers, in which the new key and its data pointer are located in their correct relationship to other keys. The first half of these keys is copied back into inspage, and the second half is copied into the sibling page. The median key is then promoted. If inspage has a parent, InsertKey calls PromoteKey to promote the median key into the parent page; otherwise, PromoteRoot is called to generate a new root page.

The private `PromoteInternal` function inserts a key promoted by splitting into a parent page.

```
template <class K, class D>
    void BTreeFile<K,D>::PromoteInternal
        (
        Page<K> & inspage,
        const K & inskey,
        DataFilePtr dataptr,
        DataFilePtr pagelnk
        )
        {
        if (inspage.Hdr.NoOfKeys == inspage.Hdr.MaxKeys)
            {
            // temporary arrays
            K * tempkeys = new K[inspage.Hdr.MaxKeys + 1];

            DataFilePtr * tempptrs =
                new DataFilePtr[inspage.Hdr.MaxKeys + 1];

            DataFilePtr * templnks =
                new DataFilePtr[inspage.Hdr.Order   + 1];

            // copy entries from inspage to temporaries
            size_t nt = 0; // index into temporaries
            size_t ni = 0; // index into inspage

            templnks[0] = inspage.Lnk[0];

            size_t inspos = 0;

            // find insertion position
            while ((inspos < inspage.Hdr.MaxKeys)
               && (inspage.Key[inspos] < inskey))
                            ++inspos;

            // store new info
            tempkeys[inspos]    = inskey;
            tempptrs[inspos]    = dataptr;
            templnks[inspos + 1] = pagelnk;

            // copy existing keys
            while (ni < inspage.Hdr.MaxKeys)
```

```
        {
        if (ni == inspos)
            ++nt;

        tempkeys[nt]     = inspage.Key[ni];
        tempptrs[nt]     = inspage.Ptr[ni];
        templnks[nt + 1] = inspage.Lnk[ni + 1];

        ++ni;
        ++nt;
        }

// generate a new leaf node
Page<K> sibpage(inspage.Hdr.Order);

sibpage.Hdr.ParentPtr = inspage.Hdr.ParentPtr;

// clear # of keys in pages
inspage.Hdr.NoOfKeys = 0;
sibpage.Hdr.NoOfKeys = 0;

inspage.Lnk[0] = templnks[0];

// copy appropriate keys from temp to pages
for (ni = 0; ni < inspage.Hdr.MinKeys; ++ni)
        {
        inspage.Key[ni]     = tempkeys[ni];
        inspage.Ptr[ni]     = tempptrs[ni];
        inspage.Lnk[ni + 1] = templnks[ni + 1];

        ++inspage.Hdr.NoOfKeys;
        }

sibpage.Lnk[0] = templnks[inspage.Hdr.MinKeys+1];

for (
    ni = inspage.Hdr.MinKeys + 1;
    ni <= inspage.Hdr.MaxKeys;
    ++ni
    )
    {
    sibpage.Key[ni - 1 - inspage.Hdr.MinKeys] =
                    tempkeys[ni];
```

```
        sibpage.Ptr[ni - 1 - inspage.Hdr.MinKeys] =
                    tempptrs[ni];

        sibpage.Lnk[ni - inspage.Hdr.MinKeys] =
                    templnks[ni + 1];

        ++sibpage.Hdr.NoOfKeys;
        }

// Fill any remaining entries in inspage with null.
// Note that sibpage is initialized to null values
// by the constructor.

for (
    ni = inspage.Hdr.MinKeys;
    ni < inspage.Hdr.MaxKeys;
    ++ni
    )
    {
    inspage.Key[ni]     = K();
    inspage.Ptr[ni]     = DFP_NULL;
    inspage.Lnk[ni + 1] = DFP_NULL;
    }

// write pages
Tree->Write(inspage);
Tree->Write(sibpage);

// update child parent links
Page<K> child(0);

for (ni = 0; ni <= sibpage.Hdr.NoOfKeys; ++ni)
    {
    Tree->Read(sibpage.Lnk[ni],child);

    child.Hdr.ParentPtr = sibpage.Hdr.FilePtr;
    Tree->Write(child);
    }

// promote key and pointer
if (inspage.Hdr.ParentPtr == DFP_NULL)
    {
    // we need to create a new root
    PromoteRoot
```

```
                    (
                    tempkeys[inspage.Hdr.MinKeys],
                    tempptrs[inspage.Hdr.MinKeys],
                    inspage,
                    sibpage
                    );
            }
        else
            {
            Page<K> parpage(0);

            Tree->Read(inspage.Hdr.ParentPtr,parpage);

            // promote into parent
            PromoteInternal
                (
                parpage,
                tempkeys[inspage.Hdr.MinKeys],
                tempptrs[inspage.Hdr.MinKeys],
                sibpage.Hdr.FilePtr
                );
            }


        delete [] tempkeys;
        delete [] tempptrs;
        delete [] templnks;
        }
    else // simply insert new key and data ptr
        {
        size_t inspos = 0;

        // find insertion position
        while ((inspos < inspage.Hdr.NoOfKeys)
          && (inspage.Key[inspos] < inskey))
                    ++inspos;

        // shift any keys right
        for (
            size_t n = inspage.Hdr.NoOfKeys;
            n > inspos;
            —n
            )
            {
            inspage.Key[n]     = inspage.Key[n - 1];
            inspage.Ptr[n]     = inspage.Ptr[n - 1];
```

```
            inspage.Lnk[n + 1] = inspage.Lnk[n];
            }

        // store new info
        inspage.Key[inspos]       = inskey;
        inspage.Ptr[inspos]       = dataptr;
        inspage.Lnk[inspos + 1] = pagelnk;


        ++inspage.Hdr.NoOfKeys;

        Tree->Write(inspage);
        }
    }
```

When the root node is split by `InsertKey` or `PromoteKey`, the `PromoteRoot` function is called to generate a new root that contains a single key.

```
template <class K, class D>
    void BTreeFile<K,D>::PromoteRoot
        (
        const K & inskey,
        DataFilePtr dataptr,
        Page<K> & lesspage,
        Page<K> & grtrpage
        )
        {
        // create new root page
        Page<K> newroot(Root.Hdr.Order);

        // insert key into new root
        newroot.Key[0] = inskey;
        newroot.Ptr[0] = dataptr;

        newroot.Lnk[0] = lesspage.Hdr.FilePtr;
        newroot.Lnk[1] = grtrpage.Hdr.FilePtr;

        newroot.Hdr.NoOfKeys = 1;

        // write new root to tree file
        Tree->Write(newroot,true);

        lesspage.Hdr.ParentPtr = newroot.Hdr.FilePtr;
        grtrpage.Hdr.ParentPtr = newroot.Hdr.FilePtr;
```

```
// rewrite pages
Tree->Write(lesspage);
Tree->Write(grtrpage);
}
```

Reading Records

Reading a record from the file is simple: Search for the key in the BTree page files, and, if it is found, read the DataFile record identified by that key's Ptr value. If the record isn't found, Read throws a BTE_NOTFOUND exception.

```
template <class K, class D>
    D BTreeFile<K,D>::Read
        (
        const K & key
        )
        {
        if (Locked)
            throw BTreeEx(BTEX_LOCKED);

        Page<K> inspage(0);
        size_t  inspos;

        if (Search(Root,key,inspage,inspos))
            {
            // seek data record
            Data->Seek(inspage.Ptr[inspos]);

            // read data record
            return Data->Read();
            }
        else
            throw BTreeEx(BTEX_NOTFOUND);

        #ifdef _MSC_VER
            // another kludge to avoid error
            //   "all paths must return value"
            // line will NEVER be executed!
            return Data->Read();
        #endif
        }
```

Deleting Records

And now we come to deletion. The `Delete` function performs the first stage of deletion, which involves removing a key from a leaf page.

```
template <class K, class D>
    void BTreeFile<K,D>::Delete
        (
        const K & delkey
        )
        {
        if (Locked)
            throw BTreeEx(BTEX_LOCKED);

        Page<K> delpage(0);
        size_t  delpos, n;

        if (!Search(Root,delkey,delpage,delpos))
            throw BTreeEx(BTEX_NOTFOUND);

        // delete data record associated with deleted key
        Data->Seek(delpage.Ptr[delpos]);
        Data->Delete();

        if (delpage.Lnk[0] == DFP_NULL) // is this leaf page?
            {
            // remove key from leaf
            —delpage.Hdr.NoOfKeys;

            for (n = delpos; n < delpage.Hdr.NoOfKeys; ++n)
                {
                delpage.Key[n] = delpage.Key[n + 1];
                delpage.Ptr[n] = delpage.Ptr[n + 1];
                }

            delpage.Key[delpage.Hdr.NoOfKeys] = K();
            delpage.Ptr[delpage.Hdr.NoOfKeys] = DFP_NULL;

            // write page to disk
            Tree->Write(delpage);
```

```
        // adjust tree
        if (delpage.Hdr.NoOfKeys < delpage.Hdr.MinKeys)
            AdjustTree(delpage);
    }
else // delpage is internal
    {
    // replace deleted key with immediate successor
    Page<K> sucpage(0);

    // find successor
    Tree->Read(delpage.Lnk[delpos + 1],sucpage);

    while (sucpage.Lnk[0] != DFP_NULL)
        Tree->Read(sucpage.Lnk[0],sucpage);

    // first key is the "swappee"
    delpage.Key[delpos] = sucpage.Key[0];
    delpage.Ptr[delpos] = sucpage.Ptr[0];

    // deleted swapped key from sucpage
    —sucpage.Hdr.NoOfKeys;

    for (n = 0; n < sucpage.Hdr.NoOfKeys; ++n)
        {
        sucpage.Key[n] = sucpage.Key[n + 1];
        sucpage.Ptr[n] = sucpage.Ptr[n + 1];
        sucpage.Lnk[n + 1] = sucpage.Lnk[n + 2];
        }

    sucpage.Key[sucpage.Hdr.NoOfKeys] = K();
    sucpage.Ptr[sucpage.Hdr.NoOfKeys] = DFP_NULL;
    sucpage.Lnk[sucpage.Hdr.NoOfKeys + 1] = DFP_NULL;

    // write pages to disk
    Tree->Write(delpage);
    Tree->Write(sucpage);

    // adjust tree for leaf node
    if (sucpage.Hdr.NoOfKeys < sucpage.Hdr.MinKeys)
        AdjustTree(sucpage);
    }
}
```

The Delete function begins by calling Search to find the key in the tree. If the key was not found, the function throws a BTEX_NOTFOUND exception, because it can't delete a key that isn't there!

Delete checks the page where the key was found; if the page is a leaf, Delete simply removes the key. If the page has children, it is an internal (possibly root) page. For an internal node, Delete searches through the tree, finding the key that immediately succeeds the deleted key. The successor key is found by looking at the subtree containing keys greater than the deleted key, traveling down the tree until a leaf is found. The first key in that leaf is the successor, and its values replace those of the deleted key. Then the successor key is deleted from the leaf. If the leaf contains less than Hdr.MinKeys keys, Delete calls the AdjustTree function.

```
template <class K, class D>
    void BTreeFile<K,D>::AdjustTree
        (
        Page<K> & pg
        )
        {
        if (pg.Hdr.ParentPtr == DFP_NULL)
            return;

        Page<K> parpage(0);
        Page<K> sibless(0);
        Page<K> sibgrtr(0);

        // get parent page
        Tree->Read(pg.Hdr.ParentPtr,parpage);

        // find pointer to pg in parent
        for (
            size_t n = 0;
            parpage.Lnk[n] != pg.Hdr.FilePtr;
            ++n
            )
            ;

        // read sibling pages
        if (n < parpage.Hdr.NoOfKeys)
```

```
        Tree->Read(parpage.Lnk[n + 1],sibgrtr);

    if (n > 0)
        Tree->Read(parpage.Lnk[n - 1],sibless);

    // decide to redistribute or concatenate
    if (sibless.Hdr.NoOfKeys > sibgrtr.Hdr.NoOfKeys)
        {
        —n;

        if (sibless.Hdr.NoOfKeys > sibless.Hdr.MinKeys)
            Redistribute(n,sibless,parpage,pg);
        else
            Concatenate(n,sibless,parpage,pg);
        }
    else
        {
        if (sibgrtr.Hdr.NoOfKeys > sibgrtr.Hdr.MinKeys)
            Redistribute(n,pg,parpage,sibgrtr);
        else
            Concatenate(n,pg,parpage,sibgrtr);
        }
    }
```

The parameter pg references a page that contains order / 2 - 1 keys; when AdjustTree is called by Delete, pg references the leaf page from which a key was deleted. AdjustTree finds the sibling nodes of pg. Note that pg will have at least one sibling, and it may have two. If a pg has only one sibling, the other (nonexistent) sibling is assumed to contain zero keys for comparison purposes. AdjustTree also reads pg's parent page.

AdjustTree calls the Concatenate function to combine pg with a sibling, or the Redistribute function to redistribute keys among pg, its parent page, and a sibling page. Redistribute is called if one of pg's siblings has more than MinKeys keys; otherwise, Concatenate is called. A comparison is made to redistribute or concatenate with the sibling that has the most keys; thus, pg may be the page to the right of the parent's separation key, or it may be to the left, depending on the number of keys in the sibling with which it is processed. Calls to both Concatenate and Redistribute include the index of the key in the parent page that separates pg and its sibling; this key is hereafter called the separation key.

```
template <class K, class D>
    void BTreeFile<K,D>::Redistribute
        (
        size_t keypos,
        Page<K> & lesspage,
        Page<K> & parpage,
        Page<K> & grtrpage
        )
        {
        // this function is ONLY called for leaf nodes!
        size_t n;

        if (lesspage.Lnk[0] == DFP_NULL)
            {
            // working with leaves
            if (lesspage.Hdr.NoOfKeys > grtrpage.Hdr.NoOfKeys)
                {
                // slide a key from lesser to greater
                // move keys in greater page to the left by one
                for (n = grtrpage.Hdr.NoOfKeys; n > 0; —n)
                    {
                    grtrpage.Key[n] = grtrpage.Key[n - 1];
                    grtrpage.Ptr[n] = grtrpage.Ptr[n - 1];
                    }

                // store parent separator key in > page
                grtrpage.Key[0] = parpage.Key[keypos];
                grtrpage.Ptr[0] = parpage.Ptr[keypos];

                // increment greater page's key count
                ++grtrpage.Hdr.NoOfKeys;

                // decrement lesser page's key count
                —lesspage.Hdr.NoOfKeys;

                // move last key in lesser page to parent
                // as separator
                parpage.Key[keypos] =
                    lesspage.Key[lesspage.Hdr.NoOfKeys];

                parpage.Ptr[keypos] =
                    lesspage.Ptr[lesspage.Hdr.NoOfKeys];

                // clear last key in lesser page
                lesspage.Key[lesspage.Hdr.NoOfKeys] = K();
```

```
                lesspage.Ptr[lesspage.Hdr.NoOfKeys] =
                                        DFP_NULL;
            }
        else
            {
            // slide a key from greater to lesser
            // add parent key to lesser page
            lesspage.Key[lesspage.Hdr.NoOfKeys] =
                parpage.Key[keypos];

            lesspage.Ptr[lesspage.Hdr.NoOfKeys] =
                parpage.Ptr[keypos];

            // increment lesser page's key count
            ++lesspage.Hdr.NoOfKeys;

            // insert in parent the lowest key in > page
            parpage.Key[keypos] = grtrpage.Key[0];
            parpage.Ptr[keypos] = grtrpage.Ptr[0];

            // decrement # of keys in greater page
            —grtrpage.Hdr.NoOfKeys;

            // move keys in greater page to left
            for (n = 0; n < grtrpage.Hdr.NoOfKeys; ++n)
                {
                grtrpage.Key[n] = grtrpage.Key[n + 1];
                grtrpage.Ptr[n] = grtrpage.Ptr[n + 1];
                }

            // make last key blank
            grtrpage.Key[n]    = K();
            grtrpage.Ptr[n]    = DFP_NULL;
            }
        }
    else
        {
        if (lesspage.Hdr.NoOfKeys > grtrpage.Hdr.NoOfKeys)
            {
            // slide a key from lesser to greater
            // move keys in greater page to the left by one
            for (n = grtrpage.Hdr.NoOfKeys; n > 0; —n)
                {
                grtrpage.Key[n] = grtrpage.Key[n - 1];
                grtrpage.Ptr[n] = grtrpage.Ptr[n - 1];
```

```
    grtrpage.Lnk[n + 1] = grtrpage.Lnk[n];
    }

grtrpage.Lnk[1] = grtrpage.Lnk[0];

// store parent separator key in greater page
grtrpage.Key[0] = parpage.Key[keypos];
grtrpage.Ptr[0] = parpage.Ptr[keypos];
grtrpage.Lnk[0] =
    lesspage.Lnk[lesspage.Hdr.NoOfKeys];

// update child link
Page<K> child(0);

Tree->Read(grtrpage.Lnk[0],child);

child.Hdr.ParentPtr = grtrpage.Hdr.FilePtr;

Tree->Write(child);

// increment greater page's key count
++grtrpage.Hdr.NoOfKeys;

// decrement lesser page's key count
—lesspage.Hdr.NoOfKeys;

// move last key in lesser page to
// parent as separator
parpage.Key[keypos] =
    lesspage.Key[lesspage.Hdr.NoOfKeys];

parpage.Ptr[keypos] =
    lesspage.Ptr[lesspage.Hdr.NoOfKeys];

// clear last key in less page
lesspage.Key[lesspage.Hdr.NoOfKeys] = K();

lesspage.Ptr[lesspage.Hdr.NoOfKeys] =
                                DFP_NULL;

lesspage.Lnk[lesspage.Hdr.NoOfKeys + 1] =
                                DFP_NULL;
}
```

```
else
    {
    // slide a key from greater to lesser
    // add parent key to lesser page
    lesspage.Key[lesspage.Hdr.NoOfKeys] =
        parpage.Key[keypos];

    lesspage.Ptr[lesspage.Hdr.NoOfKeys] =
        parpage.Ptr[keypos];

    lesspage.Lnk[lesspage.Hdr.NoOfKeys + 1] =
        grtrpage.Lnk[0];

    // update child link
    Page<K> child(0);

    Tree->Read(grtrpage.Lnk[0],child);

    child.Hdr.ParentPtr = lesspage.Hdr.FilePtr;

    Tree->Write(child);

    // increment lesser page's key count
    ++lesspage.Hdr.NoOfKeys;

    // insert in parent the lowest key in > page
    parpage.Key[keypos] = grtrpage.Key[0];
    parpage.Ptr[keypos] = grtrpage.Ptr[0];

    // decrement # of keys in greater page
    -grtrpage.Hdr.NoOfKeys;

    // move keys in greater page to left
    for (n = 0; n < grtrpage.Hdr.NoOfKeys; ++n)
        {
        grtrpage.Key[n] = grtrpage.Key[n + 1];
        grtrpage.Ptr[n] = grtrpage.Ptr[n + 1];
        grtrpage.Lnk[n] = grtrpage.Lnk[n + 1];
        }

    grtrpage.Lnk[n] = grtrpage.Lnk[n + 1];

    // make last key blank
```

```
              grtrpage.Key[n]     = K();
              grtrpage.Ptr[n]     = DFP_NULL;
              grtrpage.Lnk[n + 1] = DFP_NULL;
              }
        }


    // write pages
    Tree->Write(lesspage);
    Tree->Write(parpage);
    Tree->Write(grtrpage);


    if (parpage.Hdr.ParentPtr == DFP_NULL)
        Root = parpage;
    }
```

Redistribute looks long and complicated, but it is actually one process implemented for special cases. Redistribution occurs either from lesspage to grtrpage or from grtrpage to lesspage; when redistributing keys among internal nodes, links must also be changed, whereas leaf nodes can have their keys redistributed without worrying about links. This arrangement gives us four cases. In each case, the separator key is moved from the parent into the page that lacks a key. The page that has extra keys provides a new separator key. No further adjustments in the tree are required, because no page is reduced below MinKeys keys.

Concatenate begins by appending the separation key to lesspage; the separation key is then removed from the parent page. The keys from the grtrpage are sequentially added to lesspage, and grtrpage is deleted. Concatenate updates the parent links in all moved nodes so that they point back to lesspage. If the parent page now contains zero keys, it is deleted and lesspage becomes the new root. And, if the parent page has been reduced to fewer than MinKeys, Concatenate calls AdjustTree. This process is, of course, recursive, because AdjustTree calls Concatenate.

```
template <class K, class D>
    void BTreeFile<K,D>::Concatenate
        (
        size_t keypos,
        Page<K> & lesspage,
        Page<K> & parpage,
```

```
Page<K> & grtrpage
)
{
size_t n, ng;

// move separator key from parent into lesspage
lesspage.Key[lesspage.Hdr.NoOfKeys] =
    parpage.Key[keypos];

lesspage.Ptr[lesspage.Hdr.NoOfKeys] =
    parpage.Ptr[keypos];

lesspage.Lnk[lesspage.Hdr.NoOfKeys + 1] =
    grtrpage.Lnk[0];

++lesspage.Hdr.NoOfKeys;

// delete separator from parent
—parpage.Hdr.NoOfKeys;

for (n = keypos; n < parpage.Hdr.NoOfKeys; ++n)
    {
    parpage.Key[n] = parpage.Key[n + 1];
    parpage.Ptr[n] = parpage.Ptr[n + 1];
    parpage.Lnk[n + 1] = parpage.Lnk[n + 2];
    }

// clear unused key in parent
parpage.Key[n]     = K();
parpage.Ptr[n]     = DFP_NULL;
parpage.Lnk[n + 1] = DFP_NULL;

// copy keys from grtrpage to lesspage
ng = 0;
n  = lesspage.Hdr.NoOfKeys;

while (ng < grtrpage.Hdr.NoOfKeys)
    {
    ++lesspage.Hdr.NoOfKeys;

    lesspage.Key[n] = grtrpage.Key[ng];
    lesspage.Ptr[n] = grtrpage.Ptr[ng];
    lesspage.Lnk[n + 1] = grtrpage.Lnk[ng + 1];
```

```
        ++ng;
        ++n;
        }


// delete greater page
Tree->Delete(grtrpage.Hdr.FilePtr);


// is this a leaf page?
if (lesspage.Lnk[0] != DFP_NULL)
    {
    // adjust child pointers to point to lesspage
    Page<K> child(0);

    for (n = 0; n <= lesspage.Hdr.NoOfKeys; ++n)
        {
        Tree->Read(lesspage.Lnk[n],child);

        child.Hdr.ParentPtr = lesspage.Hdr.FilePtr;

        Tree->Write(child);
        }
    }


// write less page and parent
if (parpage.Hdr.NoOfKeys == 0)
    {
    // only root page can ever be deleted to 0 keys
    Tree->Delete(parpage.Hdr.FilePtr);

    lesspage.Hdr.ParentPtr = DFP_NULL;

    Tree->Write(lesspage,true);

    Root = lesspage;
    }
else
    {
    Tree->Write(lesspage);
    Tree->Write(parpage);

    // reset root page, if necessary
    if (parpage.Hdr.ParentPtr == DFP_NULL)
        Root = parpage;
```

```
        // if parent is too small, adjust tree!
        if (parpage.Hdr.NoOfKeys < parpage.Hdr.MinKeys)
            AdjustTree(parpage);
        }
    }
```

Sorted Retrieval

The greatest advantage of BTree indexes over hash indexes is that BTrees allow sequential access to the data records. To examine all the records in a BTreeFile in alphabetical order, call the InOrder member.

```
template <class K, class D>
    void BTreeFile<K,D>::InOrder
        (
        void (* func)(const K & key, const D & data)
        )
        {
        // lock the file so changes can't be made
        Locked = true;

        // save the address of the function to call
        TravFunc = func;

        // recurse the tree
        RecurseTraverse(Root);

        // unlock the file
        Locked = false;
        }
```

InOrder stores the func value in the data member TravFunc and calls the private recursive function RecurseTraverse. RecurseTraverse alternates between calling itself for page links and calling TravFunc with keys and DataBlocks.

```
template <class K, class D>
    void BTreeFile<K,D>::RecurseTraverse
        (
        const Page<K> & pg
        )
```

```
{
size_t n;
Page<K> * p = new Page<K>(0);
D * db = new D;

// sequence through keys in page
//    by recursively processing links
for (n = 0; n < pg.Hdr.NoOfKeys; ++n)
    {
    // follow each link before processing page
    if (pg.Lnk[n] != DFP_NULL)
        {
        Tree->Read(pg.Lnk[n],*p);
        RecurseTraverse(*p);
        }


    // if ptr does not point to anything
    //      don't read a record!
    if (pg.Ptr[n] != DFP_NULL)
        {
        Data->Seek(pg.Ptr[n]);
        *db = Data->Read();
        TravFunc(pg.Key[n],*db);
        }
    }

// handle greatest subtree link
if (pg.Lnk[n] != DFP_NULL)
    {
    Tree->Read(pg.Lnk[n],*p);
    RecurseTraverse(*p);
    }

// delete temporaries
delete p;
delete db;
}
```

USING BTREE FILES

The following program illustrates how to use a BTree file. The
TestBTreeFile function stores, deletes, and retrieves Objects from a file
indexed by StringKey<16> objects. The StressTest function works the

BTree system by writing and reading thousands of small records that are indexed by unsigned ints.

```
strstream * Buffer;

struct BTObj
    {
    String Name;
    String City;

    BTObj(const char * n = NULL, const char * c = NULL)
        : Name(n), City(c)
        { /* nada */ }

    BTObj(const BTObj & obj)
        : Name(obj.Name), City(obj.City)
        { /* nada */ }

    void operator = (const BTObj & obj)
        {
        Name = obj.Name;
        City = obj.City;
        }

    static const Signature Sig;
    };

String GetBTObjKey(const BTObj & rec)
    {
    return rec.Name;
    }

const Signature BTObj::Sig = 0x4444414CuL;

static const size_t KDlen = 20;

static BTObj KeyData[KDlen] =
    {
    {BTObj("Larry",    "Los Angeles")},
    {BTObj("John",     "San Mateo")},
    {BTObj("Cindy",    "Boston")},
    {BTObj("Fred",     "Philadelphia")},
    {BTObj("Lucy",     "Seattle")},
```

```
    {BTObj("Jerry",    "Newark")},
    {BTObj("Adam",     "Houston")},
    {BTObj("Carmen",   "San Diego")},
    {BTObj("Scott",    "Colorado Springs")},
    {BTObj("Maria",    "Colorado Springs")},
    {BTObj("Rebecca",  "Colorado Springs")},
    {BTObj("Elora",    "Colorado Springs")},
    {BTObj("Rudolph",  "North Pole")},
    {BTObj("Robert",   "Somerset")},
    {BTObj("Mary",     "Pheonix")},
    {BTObj("Albert",   "Tuscon")},
    {BTObj("Eve",      "Salt Lake City")},
    {BTObj("Theodore", "Boise")},
    {BTObj("Everett",  "Portland")},
    {BTObj("Edwin",    "Cheyenne")}
    };

void operator <<= (DataBlock & dest, const BTObj & src)
    {
    size_t sz = src.Name.Length() + src.City.Length() + 2;

    DataBlock db(BTObj::Sig,sz);

    char * blk = (char *)((void *)db);

    strcpy(blk,src.Name);
    strcpy(blk + src.Name.Length() + 1,src.City);

    dest = db;
    }

void operator <<= (BTObj & dest, const DataBlock & src)
    {
    if (BTObj::Sig != src.GetSig())
        throw DataFileEx(FEX_BAD_SIG);

    const char * ptr = (const char *)((const void *)src);
    dest.Name = ptr;
    ptr += dest.Name.Length() + 1;
    dest.City = ptr;
    }

static void TestBTree(strstream & buffer);
static void StressTest(strstream & buffer);
```

```
static void ShowBTObj(const StringKey<16> & key, const BTObj & rec);
static void ShowInts(const unsigned int & key, const unsigned int & rec);

static DiagOutWin dbgout("BTree File Test");

void TestBTreeFiles
    (
    strstream & buffer
    )
    {
    Buffer = &buffer;
    try
        {
        TestBTree(buffer);
        StressTest(buffer);
        }
    catch (ExceptionBase & ex)
        {
        ex.Explain(dbgout);
        }
    catch (...)
        {
        buffer << "What the hell was that?\r\n";
        }
    }

static void TestBTree
    (
    strstream & buffer
    )
    {
    buffer << "\r\n————-"
        << "\r\nBTree file test"
        << "\r\n————-\r\n\r\n";

    size_t n;
    BTObj rec;
    BTreeFile<StringKey<16>,BTObj> tree("btree1",7);

    buffer << "BTree file created...\r\n";

    for (n = 0; n < KDlen; ++n)
        {
        tree.Write(StringKey<16>(KeyData[n].Name),KeyData[n]);
        buffer << "wrote: " << KeyData[n].Name << " @ " <<
KeyData[n].City << "\r\n";
```

```
        }

    StringKey<16> key1("Edwin");
    StringKey<16> key2("Mary");


    rec = tree.Read(key1);
    buffer << " read: (" << rec.Name << "," << rec.City << ") with key
" << key1 << "\r\n";


    rec = tree.Read(key2);
    buffer << " read: (" << rec.Name << "," << rec.City << ") with key
" << key2 << "\r\n";


    tree.Delete(key1);
    buffer << "deleted: " << key1 << "\r\n";


    tree.Delete(key2);
    buffer << "deleted: " << key2 << "\r\n";


    BTObj new1("Vincent", "New York City");
    BTObj new2("Sandy", "Pittsburg");


    tree.Write(StringKey<16>(new1.Name),new1);
    buffer << "stored: " << new1.Name << " @ " << new1.City << "\r\n";


    tree.Write(StringKey<16>(new2.Name),new2);
    buffer << "stored: " << new2.Name << " @ " << new2.City << "\r\n";


    tree.InOrder(ShowBTObj);
    }


static void StressTest
    (
    strstream & buffer
    )
    {
    const size_t maxtest = 1000u;
    const size_t maxval  = 1000u;
    size_t n, val;
    RandDev gen;
    BTreeFile<unsigned int, unsigned int> tree("btree2",31);


    for (n = 0; n < maxtest; ++n)
        {
```

```
        val = gen(maxval);

        if ((n > 200) && (gen(10) < 2))
            {
            buffer << "d " << n << " = " << val;

            try {
                tree.Delete(val);
                }

            catch (BTreeEx & ex)
                {
                if (ex.WhatsWrong() == BTEX_NOTFOUND)
                    buffer << " !";
                else
                    throw;
                }

            buffer << "\r\n";
            }
        else
            {
            buffer << "i " << n << " = " << val << "\r\n";
            tree.Write(val,val);
            }
        }

    tree.InOrder(ShowInts);
    }

static void ShowBTObj(const StringKey<16> & key, const BTObj & rec)
    {
    (*Buffer) << "traverse: " << String(key) << " @ " << rec.City <<
"\r\n";
    }

static void ShowInts(const unsigned int & key, const unsigned int &
rec)
    {
    (*Buffer) << "traverse: " << key << " = " << rec << "\r\n";
    }
```

CONCLUSION

This book has focused on many topics, ranging from sorting and statistics to hash tables and strings. I hope you've found the code useful and my descriptions informative. Good luck!

APPENDIX A

TESTBED APPLICATION

Four years ago, when I wrote the first edition of this book, I was writing applications for MS-DOS. Today, everything I do is in Windows. Whereas the first two editions of this book contained code tested under MS-DOS, everything in this edition was developed using a Windows application. Although the code still works with MS-DOS, UNIX, and OS/2, the actual creative process happened with my machine running Windows 95.

When I test code for algorithms and basic processes, I don't want to spend much time playing with interfaces; I just want to know that the code *works*. In an MS-DOS test program, I simply display output to the screen or capture it in a text file. One of my great frustrations was the apparent complexity of writing even the most basic Windows program—until it dawned on me that Windows was no more complicated and obscure than other environments. It was just *different*. Once I had vaulted that intellectual barrier, I created a basic framework application for testing classes.

Testbed is a simple Windows application written to work directly with the Windows 95 API. I do not use MFC, OWL, or any of the other application frameworks; my experience with those giant class hierarchies is that they make programs more difficult to understand while doing little to hide the details of Windows programming.

Testbed has a main window containing a read-only edit control. Test modules write to a `strstream` object, which I then load into the edit control for review. The menu has built-in commands for copying the contents of the edit control to the clipboard. The program contains traps for exceptions and displays an About.. box. Feel free to use this program for your own code; it is succinct and stable. The version displayed here is written for 32-bit Windows 95 and will not compile or run under earlier 16-bit Windows products.

```cpp
//─────────────────────────────────
//   Testbed Application
//─────────────────────────────────
//
//   Testbed.cpp
//
//   Main application module for C++ Components & Algorithms,
//   3rd Edition.
//
//─────────────────────────────────
//   Copyright 1995-1996 by Scott Robert Ladd. All rights reserved.
//─────────────────────────────────


#include "windows.h"   // Windows definitions
#include "limits.h"    // limits of types
#include "stdio.h"     // standard file I/O functions
#include "stdlib.h"    // misc. library functions
#include "string.h"    // C-style string functions
#include "strstrea.h"  // strstream definitions
#include "iomanip.h"   // stream manipulators

#include "DiagWin.h"   // diagnostic class for Windows
#include "FontUtil.h"  // font utilities and classes
#include "bool.h"      // boolean type

#include "resource.h"  // resource constants


//──────────
// type definitions
//──────────

enum ErrorType
    {
```

```
    ET_CRASH,
    ET_ERROR,
    ET_WARNING
    };


//——————————
// global data
//——————————


// constants
const char * TestbedClassName = "TestbedWindowClass";
const char * AppName       = "Testbed";
const char * AppVersion     = "3rd Edition, v1.0";
const LPCSTR MenuTestbed    = MAKEINTRESOURCE(MENU_TESTBED);
const LPCSTR IconTestbed    = MAKEINTRESOURCE(ICON_TESTBED);
const LPCSTR NameDlgAbout   = MAKEINTRESOURCE(DLG_ABOUT);
const int    DisplayID      = 1;
const DWORD  DisplayStyle = WS_CHILD |
                            WS_VSCROLL |
                            WS_HSCROLL |
                            ES_MULTILINE |
                            ES_READONLY |
                            ES_LEFT |
                            ES_AUTOHSCROLL |
                            ES_AUTOVSCROLL;


// variables
HANDLE      ThisInstance = NULL;
HWND        Display      = NULL;
HWND        MainWdw      = NULL;
DiagOutWin Diag(AppName);
Font        StdFont("Courier New",10,FALSE,FALSE);


//————————————--
// external function prototypes
//————————————--


int WINAPI WinMain
    (
    HINSTANCE instance,
    HINSTANCE prevInstance,
    LPSTR     commandLine,
    int       commandShow
    );
```

```
static BOOL InitApplication
    (
    HANDLE instance
    );

static BOOL InitInstance
    (
    HANDLE instance,
    int    commandShow
    );

LRESULT CALLBACK MainWindow
    (
    HWND    thisWindow,
    UINT    message,
    WPARAM wordParam,
    LPARAM longParam
    );

void RunTest
    (
    WPARAM testid
    );

void TestArray
    (
    strstream & buffer
    );

void TestStrings
    (
    strstream & buffer
    );

void TestHashFiles
    (
    strstream & buffer
    );

void TestBTreeFiles
    (
    strstream & buffer
    );

void TestRational
```

```
    (
    strstream & buffer
    );

void TestRandom
    (
    strstream & buffer
    );

void CopyBuffer
    (
    bool allFlag
    );

void ErrorMessage
    (
    const char * msg,
    ErrorType etype = ET_WARNING
    );

BOOL CALLBACK DlgAbout
    (
    HWND  dlg,
    WORD  message,
    WORD  wParam,
    DWORD lParam
    );


//—————————————————————
//  WinMain — program start and message loop
//—————————————————————

#ifdef __BORLANDC__
    #pragma argsused
#endif

int WINAPI WinMain
    (
    HINSTANCE instance,
    HINSTANCE prevInstance,
    LPSTR     commandLine,
    int       commandShow
    )
    {
    MSG msg;
```

```
    if (prevInstance)
        {
        ErrorMessage
            (
            "Testbed is already running!",
            ET_WARNING
            );

        return 0;
        }

    if (!InitApplication(instance))
        return 0;

    if (!InitInstance(instance, commandShow))
        return 0;

    try {
        while (GetMessage(&msg, NULL, NULL, NULL))
            {
            TranslateMessage(&msg);
            DispatchMessage(&msg);
            }
        }
    catch (ExceptionBase & ex)
        {
        ex.Explain(Diag);
        }

    return msg.wParam;
    }


//———————————
// initialize an application
//———————————

static BOOL InitApplication
    (
    HANDLE instance
    )
    {
    WNDCLASS wc;

    wc.style        = 0;
```

```
    wc.lpfnWndProc    = MainWindow;
    wc.cbClsExtra     = 0;
    wc.cbWndExtra     = 0;
    wc.hInstance      = instance;
    wc.hIcon          = LoadIcon(instance,IconTestbed);
    wc.hCursor        = LoadCursor(NULL, IDC_ARROW);
    wc.hbrBackground  = GetStockObject(BLACK_BRUSH);
    wc.lpszMenuName   = MenuTestbed;
    wc.lpszClassName  = TestbedClassName;

    return RegisterClass(&wc);
    }


//——————————
// initialize an instance
//——————————

static BOOL InitInstance
    (
    HANDLE instance,
    int commandShow
    )
    {
    HWND hWnd;

    // save the instance handle
    ThisInstance = instance;

    // create a window
    hWnd = CreateWindow
            (
            TestbedClassName,
            AppName,
            WS_OVERLAPPEDWINDOW,
            CW_USEDEFAULT,
            CW_USEDEFAULT,
            CW_USEDEFAULT,
            CW_USEDEFAULT,
            NULL,
            NULL,
            instance,
            0);

    if (!hWnd)
        {
```

```
            ErrorMessage
                (
                "Cannot create main window",
                ET_WARNING
                );

            return FALSE;
            }


    ShowWindow(hWnd, commandShow);
    UpdateWindow(hWnd);


    MainWdw = hWnd;


    // get size of client area
    RECT area;


    GetClientRect(hWnd,&area);


    // create edit control
    Display = CreateWindowEx
                    (
                    WS_EX_CLIENTEDGE,
                    "EDIT",
                    "",
                    DisplayStyle,
                    0, 0,
                    area.right,
                    area.bottom,
                    hWnd,
                    (HMENU)DisplayID,
                    instance,
                    0
                    );


    if (!Display)
        {
        ErrorMessage
            (
            "Cannot create output window",
            ET_WARNING
            );

        return FALSE;
        }
```

```
    ShowWindow(Display, SW_SHOW);
    UpdateWindow(Display);

    // set edit window font
    SendMessage
        (
        Display,
        WM_SETFONT,
        (WPARAM)StdFont.GetFont(),
        0L
        );

    // change edit window colors
    HDC dc = GetDC(Display);
    SetTextColor(dc,RGB(0,0,0));
    SetBkColor(dc,RGB(255,255,255));
    ReleaseDC(Display,dc);

    return TRUE;
    }


//——————————
// Main window function
//——————————

LRESULT CALLBACK MainWindow
    (
    HWND   thisWindow,
    UINT   message,
    WPARAM wordParam,
    LPARAM longParam
    )
    {
    switch (message)
        {
        case WM_COMMAND:
            switch (wordParam)
                {
                case IDM_TEST_RATIONAL:
                case IDM_TEST_RANDOM:
                case IDM_TEST_STRINGS:
                case IDM_TEST_ARRAYS:
                case IDM_TEST_HASHFILES:
                case IDM_TEST_BTREEFILES:
                    RunTest(wordParam);
                    break;
```

```
            case IDM_COPY:
                // copy edit selection to clipboard
                CopyBuffer(false);
                break;

            case IDM_COPYALL:
                // copy edit window to clipboard
                CopyBuffer(true);
                break;

            case IDM_ABOUT:
                DialogBox
                    (
                    ThisInstance,
                    NameDlgAbout,
                    thisWindow,
                    FARPROC(DlgAbout)
                    );
                break;

            case IDM_EXIT:
                // exit program
                DestroyWindow(thisWindow);
                break;

            default:
                return DefWindowProc
                        (
                        thisWindow,
                        message,
                        wordParam,
                        longParam
                        );
            }

        break;

    case WM_SETFOCUS:
        // set focus to edit control
        SetFocus(Display);
        break;

    case WM_SIZE:
        // resize edit control
        MoveWindow
```

```
                (
                Display,
                0,0,
                LOWORD(longParam),
                HIWORD(longParam),
                TRUE
                );

            break;

        case WM_DESTROY:
            PostQuitMessage(0);
            break;

        default:
            return DefWindowProc
                (
                thisWindow,
                message,
                wordParam,
                longParam
                );
        }

    return 0L;
    }


//————————————————
// framework for running test procedures
//————————————————

void RunTest
    (
    WPARAM testid
    )
    {
    const size_t strbufsz = 100000;

    char * strbuf = new char [strbufsz];

    if (strbuf == NULL)
        return;

    strstream buffer(strbuf,strbufsz,ios::out);
```

```
HCURSOR cursor = SetCursor(LoadCursor(NULL,IDC_WAIT));

try
    {
    switch (testid)
        {
        case IDM_TEST_RATIONAL:
            TestRational(buffer);
            break;

        case IDM_TEST_RANDOM:
            TestRandom(buffer);
            break;

        case IDM_TEST_STRINGS:
            TestStrings(buffer);
            break;

        case IDM_TEST_ARRAYS:
            TestArray(buffer);
            break;

        case IDM_TEST_HASHFILES:
            TestHashFiles(buffer);
            break;

        case IDM_TEST_BTREEFILES:
            TestBTreeFiles(buffer);
            break;

        default:
            buffer << "unknown test selection!";
        }
    }
catch (ExceptionBase & ex)
    {
    ex.Explain(Diag);
    buffer << "\r\nEXCEPTION! BUFFER IS INCOMPLETE!";
    }

// terminate buffer
buffer << ends;

// display buffer in edit control
```

```
SendMessage
    (
    Display,
    EM_SETSEL,
    0,
    -1L
    );

SendMessage
    (
    Display,
    EM_REPLACESEL,
    0,
    (LPARAM)(LPCTSTR)buffer.str()
    );

SendMessage
    (
    Display,
    EM_SETSEL,
    0,
    0
    );

SendMessage
    (
    Display,
    EM_SCROLLCARET,
    0,
    0
    );

// restore cursor and set focus to edit window
SetCursor(cursor);
SetFocus(Display);

// delete stream buffer
delete [] strbuf;
}


//——————————————
// Copy buffer to the clipboard
//——————————————


void CopyBuffer
```

```
    (
    bool allFlag
    )
    {
    if (allFlag)
        SendMessage
            (
            Display,
            EM_SETSEL,
            0,
            -1L);

    SendMessage
        (
        Display,
        WM_COPY,
        0,
        0L
        );

    SendMessage
        (
        Display,
        EM_SETSEL,
        0,
        0L
        );

    SendMessage
        (
        Display,
        EM_SCROLLCARET,
        0,
        0
        );
    }

//————————————————————
// Display an error message of given severity
//————————————————————

void ErrorMessage
    (
    const char * msg,
    ErrorType etype
```

```
)
{
UINT style;
UINT sound;
int response;
char text[128];

// copy message to output buffer
strcpy(text,msg);

// set values specific to error severity
switch (etype)
    {
    case ET_CRASH:
        sound = MB_ICONSTOP;
        style = MB_OK;
        strcat(text," PROGRAM WILL TERMINATE!");
        break;
    case ET_ERROR:
        sound = MB_ICONEXCLAMATION;
        style = MB_YESNO;
        strcat(text,"Click 'Yes' to terminate program,"
                    " or 'No' to continue");
        break;
    case ET_WARNING:
        sound = MB_ICONASTERISK;
        style = MB_OK;
    }

// match icon to sound
style |= sound;

// sound off and display message
MessageBeep(sound);
response = MessageBox(NULL,text,AppName,style);

// check for termination
switch (etype)
    {
    case ET_ERROR:
        if (response == IDNO)
            break;
    case ET_CRASH:
        PostQuitMessage(1); // boom-boom
        // program should never reach this point!
```

```
            }
        }


//————
// About... dialog box
//————

#ifdef __BORLANDC__
#pragma argsused
#endif

BOOL CALLBACK DlgAbout
    (
    HWND   dlg,
    WORD   message,
    WORD   wParam,
    DWORD  lParam
    )
    {
    switch (message)
        {
        case WM_INITDIALOG:
            SetDlgItemText
                (
                dlg,
                IDD_ABOUT_VERSION,
                AppVersion
                );
            break;

        case WM_COMMAND:
            EndDialog(dlg, TRUE);
            return TRUE;
        }

    return FALSE;
    }'
```

APPENDIX B

BIBLIOGRAPHY

Cormen, Thomas H., Charles E. Leiserson, and Ronald L. Rivest. *Introduction to Algorithms.* McGraw-Hill, 1990

Crandall, Richard E. *Projects in Scientific Computation.* Springer-Verlag, 1994.

Ellis, Margaret A. and Bjarne Stroustrup. *The Annotated C++ Reference Manual.* Addison-Wesley, 1990.

Folk, Michael J. and Bill Zoellick. *File Structures: A Conceptual Toolkit.* Addison-Wesley, 1987.

Knuth, Donald E. *The Art of Computer Programming, Volume 1: Fundamental Algorithms, 2nd Edition.* Addison-Wesley, 1973.

Knuth, Donald E. *The Art of Computer Programming, Volume 2: Seminumerical Algorithms, 2nd Edition.* Addison-Wesley, 1981.

Knuth, Donald E. *The Art of Computer Programming, Volume 3: Sorting and Searching.* Addison-Wesley, 1973.

Ladd, Scott Robert. *C++ Components & Algorithms, Second Edition.* M&T Books, 1990.

Ladd, Scott Robert. *C++ Templates & Tools.* M&T Books, 1995.

Press, William A., Brian P. Flannery, Saul A. Teukolsky, and William T. Vetterling. *Numerical Recipes in C: The Art of Scientific Computing, Second Edition.* Cambridge, 1992.

Sedgewick, Robert. *Algorithms in C.* Addison-Wesley, 1990.

Stroustrup, Bjarne. *The C++ Programming Language, 2nd Edition.* Addison-Wesley, 1991.

Zadeh, Lotfi and Janusz Kacprzyk. *Fuzzy Logic for the Management of Uncertainty.* Wiley, 1994.

INDEX